LIVES OF THE POETS
(WITH GUITARS)

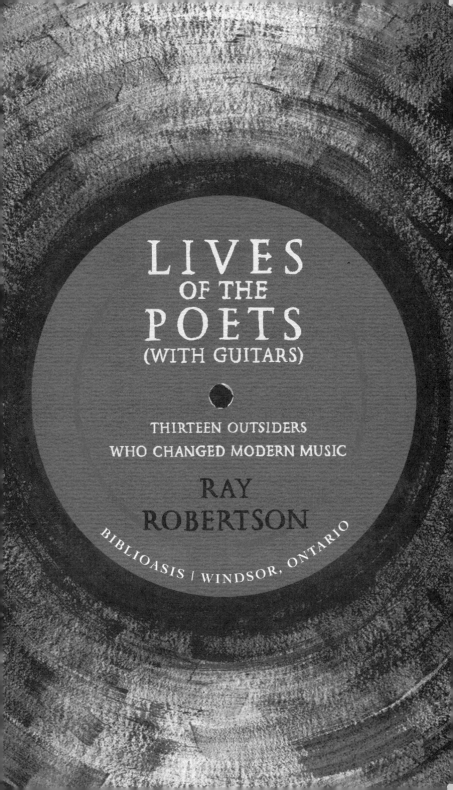

LIVES
OF THE
POETS
(WITH GUITARS)

THIRTEEN OUTSIDERS
WHO CHANGED MODERN MUSIC

RAY
ROBERTSON

BIBLIOASIS | WINDSOR, ONTARIO

FIRST EDITION

Library and Archives Canada Cataloguing in Publication

Robertson, Ray, 1966-, author
 Lives of the poets (with guitars) / Ray Robertson.

Issued in print and electronic formats.
ISBN 978-1-77196-072-4 (paperback).--ISBN 978-1-77196-073-1 (ebook)

1. Musicians--Biography. I. Title.

ML385.R652 2016 780.92 C2015-907386-3
 C2015-907387-1

Edited by Dan Wells
Copy-edited by Emily Donaldson
Typeset by Chris Andrechek
Illustrations and Cover Illustration by Chloe Cushman
Cover design by Gordon Robertson

Canada Council **Conseil des Arts**
for the Arts **du Canada**

ONTARIO ARTS COUNCIL
CONSEIL DES ARTS DE L'ONTARIO

Canadian Patrimoine
Heritage canadien

Published with the generous assistance of the Canada Council for the Arts and the Ontario Arts Council. Biblioasis also acknowledges the support of the Government of Canada through the Canada Book Fund and the Government of Ontario through the Ontario Book Publishing Tax Credit.

The author acknowledges the support of the Ontario Arts Council.

PRINTED AND BOUND IN CANADA

CONTENTS

A.F. Moritz
Poet, Teacher, Friend

And to everyone who listened — and listens —
Just one more . . .

"Is everything just sex and music?"
"No."
"You're awfully down."
"I need more sex and music."
—Barry Hannah, *Ray*

Brings me words that are not the strength of strings.
—Gene Clark, "Strength of Strings"

INTRODUCTION

The last sentence of Barry Hannah's delightfully riotous first novel, *Geronimo Rex*: "That *was* it. Good, good heavens. We're in the wrong field. Music!" Like many writers, I don't play an instrument, I can't sing, and I've never attempted to write a song, but none of that's ever stopped me from occasionally feeling as if what I do—the stringing together of words in the hope of delighting and inciting—is a middling impersonation of what musicians, *real* artists, are capable of. Musician envy: easy to acquire, even easier to understand.

"Music washes away from the soul the dust of everyday life" declared the novelist Berthold Auerbach, and who hasn't experienced the rejuvenating uplift of music at the end of the day, at the end of a relationship, when one feels quite simply at the end of the line? More than a convenient coping device, however—a pragmatic panacea for a too-stressful life—music can remind us that existence is about more than merely surviving; at its best, it offers us the chance for the sort of transcendence of the suffocatingly mundane that poets and theologians like to go on and on about but that musicians actually deliver. From Philip Larkin's poem "For

Sidney Bechet," an ode to the American jazz musician of the title: "On me your voice falls as they say love should/Like an enormous yes." Offering humanity its necessary dosage of Enormous Yesness: who wouldn't want that job?

Except that it's not mine—just as it isn't most people's—so one does the next best thing: listens, listens, and sometimes, if one is lucky, falls in love with a particular musician's entire body of work, coming to know their soul as expressed through the singular personality of their music as well as—or perhaps even better than—one's own. And like any love that's more than ephemeral infatuation, this love changes, deepens, becomes more complex over time. My youthful idolatry of Gram Parsons has ripened into middle-aged awe at his musical accomplishments mixed with occasional exasperation at his personal behaviour. When we become deeply immersed in an artist's work, we inevitably want to know as much as possible about his or her life. T.S. Eliot and a load of other over-orderly intellects would disagree, but an artist is inseparable from his or her life. More than that: because our favourite musicians are as close to real-life magicians as most of us will ever know (now you see your humdrum little world; hum along to my song and *abracadabra!* now you don't), it's understandable that we would want to know more about the source of that uncommon magic. In the process, we often become as fascinated by the life story as we are by the art that sprang from it. Occasionally we're as inspired by the life as much as by the art itself. Plato's dialogues are intellectually stimulating; his account of Socrates' last days in *The Apology* is wholly stirring.

I've certainly been inspired by both. It was the dazzling babble of Little Richard's lyrics and not Mallarme's poetry that provided me with an early lesson in the wonderfully malleable nature of words and what they can be pushed

and prodded into communicating. It was Gram Parsons'
voice, not Shakespeare's plays, that convinced me life is
essentially tragic. But I also learned from Ronnie Lane
that making the art you want to make—that you need to
make—more than compensates for the alternating opposi-
tion and indifference you'll likely encounter for living life
on your own terms. I learned from Townes Van Zandt
and Gene Clark that what can fire your imagination can
also extinguish it. And like any other itchy writer, it's not
enough to simply experience these truths—one wants
to convey in words what it is that makes for a musical-
ly-transformed, more-alive human being, to sing a hymn
in praise of a particular existence transformed by a lucky
lifetime blessed with enormous Yeses.

In one form or another, this desire has always been
there in my novels—what nature is to Jim Harrison's
books, I remember one day realizing, music is to mine—
but there's also always been a desire to one day drop the
fictional veil and directly espouse and explore, at length,
the lives of some of the musicians who have so deeply
enriched my own life. Which is what *Lives of the Poets (with
Guitars)* is about. I decided when I was twenty-six years
old that I wanted to write novels instead of pursuing philosophy because it seemed to me as if literature was the
more subtle tool for examining the maddening, miracu-
lous ambiguity of existence. In the following twelve essays
I employ much the same narrative approach as I do in
my day job, telling a life story while also investigating the
works of art that often gave that life its guiding purpose.

As my slightly tweaked title suggests, the biographical/
critical prefaces to the selected works of what were then
viewed as the greatest English poets that Dr. Johnson
agreed to undertake in 1777 at the urging of three British
booksellers—what we know today as his *Lives of the*

Poets—has been my loose model. (Johnson himself wasn't exactly a musical aficionado: "Of all noises," he said, "I think music is the least disagreeable." To a friend who praised a violinist because of the complexity of his performance, "Difficult do you call it, Sir? I wish it were impossible.") One of Johnson's biographers, the novelist John Wain, remarked that *"Lives of the Poets* is a work of memory, judgment and love, not a work of research." So is *Lives of the Poets (with Guitars)*. I've listened to everything each of my subjects has created (oftentimes incessantly) and read everything of interest that's been written about them (and when there hasn't been sufficiently illuminating material available, I've sought out and interviewed some of the people important to his or her story), but, as Johnson said, "If it rained knowledge I would hold out my hand. But I would not give myself the trouble to go in quest for it." Some truths are too important to embalm in facts.

Dr. Johnson was instructed by his employers who to write about in his *Lives of the Poets*; I've chosen my illustrious subjects. In this, I've made no effort to be exhaustive, inclusive, or representative. "Wide sympathies have their penalty," George Orwell warned, the worst being superficiality of understanding and feeling in exchange for appearing to be up to date in your enthusiasms. The thirteen poets with guitars gathered here do tend to fit a certain profile—their respective styles are grounded in American roots music (blues, country, raw rock and roll); most of them were underappreciated in their lifetimes (and frequently still), not only for their superlative songs and playing but also for their genre-obliterating iconoclasm; their life stories are as compelling as the best fiction and are infused, as all lives are, with enduring moral quandaries—but it's an entirely personal list. There *are* such things as good and bad art, but once one has made that necessary distinction, there's also something called taste. *Lives of the Poets (with Guitars)* is a taste of my taste.

As for the appended parentheses in my title, poetry isn't merely the vertical assemblage of words. It's not even exclusively manifest in words — or, if it is, not necessarily in purely representational terms. Dylan Thomas, of whom Gene Clark and Townes Van Zandt were both admirers, often used words as a painter employs colour: rhythm, sound, and strategic word placement conveying a poem's "meaning" as much as or more than any limp linguistic literalism. Most of the greatest popular music uses lyrics much as Thomas used words in his poems: to meld with the music and create something more than the mere sum of its lyrical/musical parts. (The poet Conrad Aiken on the best of Thomas' verse: "if at times his meanings are so nearly pure *aff*ect as to be practically nonsense, it doesn't matter: the thing is alive and beautiful, it hums, sings, whizzes, and in short it's poetry.") Karl Shapiro defined poetry simply as "greater or lesser heat," and that seems as satisfactory a definition as one is likely to get. And what could be hotter than the aural assault of Johnny Ramone's guitar, Little Richard's larynx-ripping voice, Gene Clark's brooding melodies?

"My purpose," Dr. Johnson wrote in the preface to *Lives of the Poets*, "was only to have allotted to every Poet an Advertisement, like those which we find in the French Miscellanies, containing a few dates and a general character" combined with "the honest intention of giving pleasure." Me, too. And my advertising, or — let's be honest at the outset — my proselytizing, is more that of an avid, if critical enthusiast than that of a detached historian. "For it is your hot love for your art," the novelist Ford Madox Ford advised, "not your dry delvings in the dry bones of ana and philologies that will enable you to convey to others your strong passion."

Hot love. What a great title for a song.

GENE CLARK

He was naturally learned: he needed not the spectacles
of books to read nature; he looked inwards, and found her there.
— John Dryden

G ene Clark was not an intellectual, and I mean that in the best possible way. Meaning, he didn't believe that having NPR on in the background while he drank his morning coffee made him any less bewildered about the shaky state of the world than the guy trying to tune in to last night's baseball scores on his car radio while en route to eight hours of minimum-wage servitude. Meaning, he didn't let it drop to reporters that, Oh, yes, he'd read Rimbaud (in translation, of course), late nineteenth-century French Symbolist poetry just one of the endlessly arcane literary influences detectable in his musical oeuvre if one just digs deeply enough. Gene Clark, if he could be bothered to read at all, stuck to comic books and the Bible. And whether with the Byrds, Dillard & Clark, or on his own, no one wrote grievy minor-key masterpiece melodies married to Rorschach-test tell-tale lyrics that even come close.

1

He was born Harold Eugene Clark in 1944 in Tipton, Missouri, the third of thirteen children, not quite a farm boy—his father graduated from fighting Hitler to working for the Swope Park, Missouri golf course—but certainly a country boy, the Clark family chopping the firewood that heated their home (a converted trolley barn) and milking the cows that gave them their milk and butter. Typically, the song most redolent of Gene's semi-rural childhood, "Something's Wrong," isn't a sentimental looking back, but an anguished update on a life bereft of the simple somatic joys of youth. Speaking of his primary source of inspiration, another poet Gene Clark probably never heard of, Philip Larkin, said, "Deprivation is for me what daffodils were for Wordsworth." Gene wouldn't have read the *Observer* interview where Larkin said this, but he would have known exactly what the prickly British poet was talking about.

He learned to play guitar from his father, and before he turned teenager could pull off respectable recreations of Hank Williams, Elvis, and the Everly Brothers, a pretty fair representation of what the best of his mature music has to offer: country soul, rock and roll desperation, superior melodicism. He joined the usual rock band—Joe Meyers and the Sharks—before forming the usual folk group, the sort of Kingston Trio knock-off that all ambitious early-60s greasers eventually gravitated toward (Dylan only being different in having the superior taste to choose Woody Guthrie and not the Limeliters as his musical model). Spotted performing in Kansas City by a member of the New Christy Minstrels, he joined the ten-member troupe and lent his voice to the group's successful emasculation of popular folk songs, learning, if nothing else, to hate traveling to eighteen cities in nineteen days and how giving people what they want is how you gain a steady paycheck but lose whatever integrity you ever had. Being a suit-and-tied singing puppet did take him to Winnipeg in February 1964, however. He would have heard the Beatles and had his life changed sooner or later anyway, but that was where he heard them first.

A couple of weeks later, while on tour in Virginia, he fed coin after coin into a coffee shop jukebox trying to figure out how "I Want to Hold Your Hand" and "She Loves You" could sound so fresh and so alive and so joyful. He quit the Minstrels the next day and decided to move to Los Angeles and do what the Beatles did. He got lucky, as most unusually ambitious people tend to get. Jim McGuinn, another dropout from the wholesome folk factory, had noticed what Gene noticed—how the Beatles were playing fifties American rock and roll and R&B with an energy and elation that hadn't been heard since Elvis started doing what the Colonel told him to and Little Richard found the Lord, but through the harmony-bending folky filter of British skiffle—and was playing a Beatles tune on his twelve-string acoustic on a slow night at the Troubadour when Gene asked if he could sit down and play with him. Later, when David Crosby, hanging out at the same club (never underestimate the value of determined idleness) added his soaring high-harmony tenor to the rich lead-vocal blend of the other two, they knew they had something. Something rock, something folk, something new.

"Mr. Tambourine Man"—a rough Dylan 1965 demo that the Byrds' co-manager Jim Dickson convinced them to cover—is the song that gave them their first hit and, in combining brains with a beat plus McGuinn's celestially chiming twelve-string electric Rickenbacker, helped give birth to the thing called "folk-rock." But it's Gene's originals that remain the most impressive items on the first two albums. Impressive because there's something compellingly different about them even now, fifty years later. This, in spite of the fact that all but a few are harmonically saturated in the sweetly sad minor-chord sounds of melancholy and self-doubt, Top-Forty gloom tunes. Not that anyone who ever acquired a unique way of doing anything ever achieved it by consciously setting out to be unique. As David Crosby noted, Gene "didn't know the rules about music so he ignored them blithely and that made for very good writing. He used chord formations and ways of doing things that other people just hadn't done because they were used to doing it by the common rules. He had no idea what they were so he just did what felt good."

But even as the Byrds soared in popularity and Gene Clark the songwriter took flight right alongside (songs like "Set You Free This Time" and "She Don't Care About Time" showing the lyric-liberating influence of Dylan, resulting in words almost as interesting as his melodies), Gene Clark the man was experiencing more earthbound troubles. Because he had more songs on the first album than anyone else and was therefore making exponentially more royalty money than the others, McGuinn and Crosby, the other two songwriters, began to blockade his new compositions in favour of their own generally inferior material, an understandably frustrating situation for someone for whom it wasn't unusual to write a half dozen new songs a week. Additionally, after already eroding his confidence as a rhythm guitar player to the point that Gene relinquished the instrument for a tambourine, Crosby, the archetypal entitled child of the Los Angeles well-off (every time naughty young David was expelled from private school his father, an Academy Award-winning cinematographer, would simply write a check and enroll him in another), began to openly mock Gene, on stage and off,

for not being—you know—*groovy* enough. That Gene, a
six-foot-two country boy who looked less like a rock and
roll star than a college linebacker, didn't simply punch the
butterball brat in the face is testament to Gene's well-man-
nered upbringing. As with the New Christy Minstrels,
he was also weary of living on airplanes and in hotels,
with the added aggravation of having to elude screaming
pubescent girls and teen-beat reporters wanting to know
what his favourite colour was.

So he had his reasons for flying the Byrds' nest. But,
as is often the case, external annoyances weren't nearly as
menacing as the mayhem swelling inside. Gene hated to
fly—more than once had gotten off a plane moments before
it was supposed to take off, sweat-soaked and ashen and
loudly adamant that it was going to crash—but his infamous fear of flying was only a symptom of either what
some of his brothers and sisters identified, in hindsight, as a
hereditary bi-polar disorder, or, at the very least, a propen-
sity for depression and attendant anxiety attacks (which
frequently manifested themselves as crippling stage fright).
Self-medicating his unacknowledged condition with alcohol and drugs (remembered band publicist Derek Taylor:
"as for Gene, he would do *anything*. He'd have a glass in one
hand and a pill in another") only exacerbated his moodiness
and excessive introspection. There were also rumours of a
go-go dancer and a disastrously bad acid trip. People who
can't drink milk are called lactose intolerant; people who
shouldn't dabble in consciousness-mining psychedelics are
called Gene Clark.

Still, his first solo album, *Gene Clark with the Gosdin
Brothers*, was recorded in 1967 and released the same week
his ex-bandmates' new album, *Younger Than Yesterday*,
appeared, guaranteeing diminished media attention for the
new guy and a divided listenership. The baffling release

5

date (both the Byrds and Gene were on the same record label) wasn't the only curveball the industry threw at him, nor would it be the last. The Gosdin Brothers added fine harmonies to Gene's new batch of songs, but that was the extent of it; they never even set foot in the studio while the album was being recorded, and clearly didn't deserve equal billing. (They and Gene shared the same manager who thought he could boost two sagging careers with one album title.) Gene wanted to call his first album—his declaration of independence from the Byrds—*Harold Eugene Clark*. Columbia Records told him no, that his real name simply wasn't catchy enough.

If Gene hadn't entirely shed his Beatles influences by the time of his inaugural solo record ("Elevator Operator" is not only transparently Beatles; it's transparently bad Beatles), and the string-swamped "Echoes" is baroque rock without the rock, there was enough good material on *Gene Clark with the Gosdin Brothers* to announce a major, many-sided talent. "Tried So Hard" and "Keep on Pushin'" are right there at the advent of country-rock, "Is Yours is Mine" is poppy hippy without being hippy dippy, and "So You Say You Lost Your Baby" picks up lyrically where Gene left off with "Eight Miles High," his last Byrds songwriting credit, casually throwing out images and associations worthy of anything Dylan was coming up with at the time. But when Crosby's noxious personality finally got him booted out of the Byrds and it became apparent that *Gene Clark with the Gosdin Brothers* wasn't going to sell, Gene's management (also the Byrds management) convinced him to re-join the band, at least temporarily, just in time for an impending concert tour. Gene lasted three shows before breaking down in Minnesota and taking the train alone back to L.A. while the rest of the band flew on to New York. Byrds roadie Jimmy Seiter remembered the next time he saw Gene, having been sent by management to pick him up at the train station after his long trip home:

> When I got there and met him at the train, he just walked past me at a fast pace, and he didn't say a word, got in a yellow cab and split to the office. Now, Gene was always afraid of small closed spaces. He never took elevators. We had this old fashioned elevator in the office building and Gene never took it. But for some reason he did that day. When I arrived at the office the police are there and the Fire Department—someone is stuck in the lift. Gene is stuck in the lift for two-and-a-half hours. When they finally opened it he ran out, soaking with sweat, and split. I didn't see him for six or eight months after that. The inside of the elevator was totally scratched up where he'd tried to get out. You should have heard him screaming. Unbelievable. He was going crazy in that elevator. He screamed at the top of his lungs for almost an hour.

Despite the commercial failure of his debut album, Gene managed to secure a contract with the recently formed A&M label, likely because of his Byrds pedigree. Regardless of how he got it, he got it, and had just set to work on a trunk full of new songs that weren't sounding in the studio like he heard them in his head when he stumbled upon an old friend. Doug Dillard was exactly the right person for Gene Clark to run into at this moment in his life. A former member of the legendary bluegrass group the Dillards, Doug's Beachwood Canyon home was a nightly magnet for every progressive picker in town, and Gene soon joined in on the fun, the number one requirement if whatever you're doing is going to have any lasting value. Doug Dillard was a brilliant banjo player and a flesh-and-blood reminder of Gene's country music roots, but, best of all, he was a skinny hillbilly Buddha, an always-grinning good ol' boy from Gene's own Missouri who never worried about much of anything except keeping his instrument in tune and his pot stash full. Older than him by a full seven years, there was a lot Gene could learn from Doug.

Unfortunately, Doug Dillard was also exactly the wrong person for Gene Clark to run into at this moment in his life. Jim Dickson:

> When Gene got with Douglas Dillard, things changed. Douglas was amazing. He came into town on a vodka drunk, then discovered grass, and kept drinking and doing grass. Then he discovered acid and you would find Douglas drinking, smoking dope, and doing LSD at the same time. How he survived it, I have no idea. But he's fine now. Sweetheart of a guy, but he had an influence on Gene. While it didn't hurt Douglas because he didn't care, Gene was way too high-strung and too complex to deal with that.

There's no record of Friedrich Nietzsche espousing a love of banjos and fiddles alongside his touting of the Will to Power, but when he wrote that "one must still have chaos in oneself to be able to give birth to a dancing star," he might have been talking about Gene and Doug, because the music that these two wild boys from the Show Me State put together on 1968's *The Fantastic Expedition of Dillard & Clark* more than justified whatever hangovers and burgeoning bad habits either had acquired. Gram Parsons died younger, and with a lot more flair, so he gets better press, but regardless of who inched the country and rock worlds closer together first, it's who did it best that matters most. And as a songwriter in a musical genre he helped create, Gene Clark has no equal.

The original vinyl version of the pair's first effort runs less than thirty minutes, but every original tune is a Gene Clark gem. "She Darked the Sun" is bluegrass slowed down and made to grow up; "Don't Come Rollin'" is 1867 back-porch picking meets 1967 Summer of Love wishful thinking; "With Care From Someone" is packed full of quintessential linguistic Clarkisms wed to some beguiling descending chord changes and marvelous three-part harmonizing; and when the whole thing wraps up nine songs later with the aforementioned "Something's Wrong," you'd like to cry but are too busy singing along. Even the album's sole cover — Lester Flatt's "Git in Line Brother" — is transformed from a fundamentalist's cautionary tale into a joyous ode to jay-smoking bliss by the clever changing of one simple preposition in the song's title ("in" to "on") and the delightful subversion of the traditional banjo picking and acoustic guitar strumming by a honky tonk harpsichord run. Get it on, indeed.

Their album a pioneering masterpiece (the Flying Burrito Brothers' equally brilliant, albeit very different, *The Gilded Palace of Sin*, wouldn't appear until four months later), it was time to promote it live. For the band's debut at the Troubadour, Gene and Doug thought it a good idea to head to Dan Tanna's, the Italian restaurant next door, after the afternoon soundcheck and begin steadily drinking martinis until show time five hours later. At some point it was also decided that this would be an excellent time to drop acid. The show began with Gene sitting on his amplifier facing the wall and went downhill from there, Doug merrily jumping up and down on his fiddle at the conclusion of the group's second song. Chastened by club management, the remainder of their weeklong residency was greeted with enthusiastic reviews — as was their just-released album — but no one had a chance to hear them outside of the L.A. area because Gene refused to tour. Not surprisingly, band members began to desert, and without tour support the album didn't sell except to the already converted.

This time the record company wasn't the bad guy—pre-music videos and the internet, how else but hitting the road could a band spread the word, particularly a strange new compound word like country-rock? A&M still believed in the boys enough to let them record a stand-alone single, Gene's gorgeously grief-struck "Why Not Your Baby?" The single fared as poorly as the album did on the charts, and when Doug Dillard invited his girlfriend, Donna Washburn, to join the band, and the original songs Gene brought to the sessions for the next album were bypassed in favour of banal bluegrass covers (one of which the warbling Washburn butchered so badly it sounds like a corn pone parody; another of which even the vocally inept Dillard attempts to sing), Gene knew it was time to be going. (Although not before managing to place three instant standards on what came to be the *Through the Morning, Through the Night* album: the dirge-like, faintly ominous title track; the archetypal country-rocking "Kansas City Southern"; and "Polly," another Clark classic of sorrow, longing, and unconventional chord changes.) He left the city and some of his more self-injurious behavior behind and moved near the ocean and got married, and when he was ready to make music again, it was to record the greatest singer-songwriter album of the seventies.

It's as utterly clichéd as it is undeniably true: genuine artists don't choose their subjects, their subjects choose them. Whether it was the nearby sea or the centuries-old redwoods or the morning ocean breezes—or new love, a clear head, a clean start—1971's *White Light* is the warm sound of wood and wire and human hands careful to coax out just the right note to wed to just the right word. Primarily acoustic and sympathetically produced by Jesse Ed Davis, former Taj Mahal lead guitarist and session player superstar, *White Light* is a perfect Mendocino day made aurally even more perfect: gently rising golden morning ("Because of You"; "The Virgin"); bright afternoon sunlight magnificence (the title track; "One in a Hundred"); full, goodnight yellow moon mirrored by a midnight Northern California ocean ("While My Love Lies Asleep"; "1975").

Then there's "Spanish Guitar," another plane of aural splendor altogether, Gene Clark at both his best and his most characteristic. A delicate but assured acoustic guitar opening; lyrics more impressionistic than literal, yet always marvelously evocative (how many songs can get away with employing the word "dissonant" in the first verse?); an achingly melancholic melody with a chorus even more irresistible: "Spanish Guitar" is a four-minute-and-fifty-seven-second mini-masterpiece that isn't marred by Gene's not untypical misuse of "whom" for "who" when singing of the beggar who thinks nowhere is far, but, rather, is only more indelibly stamped by the one thing that distinguishes all great art: the creator's undeniably stained but intrepidly singular soul.

Naturally, even though those who had the ears to hear it were astounded (the always-hip Dutch rock critics voted it album of the year), it didn't sell any better than any of his other records, and as a capping indignity, the record company somehow forgot to print the title of the album on the cover, leading confused listeners to refer to it, even today, as alternately *White Light* and "The Gene Clark" album. If a person wasn't already inclined toward self-stupefaction with drink and drugs . . .

A&M was, however, willing to finance the sessions for another album—a captivating hybrid of Dillard & Clark twang with *White Light*-style woodsmoke mysticism—but not only ended up shutting things down before all of the songs were recorded, but refused to release what was completed, a crime against civilization that in a better world would be punishable by death from long-term exposure to Pablo Cruise records. Tunes like the existentially anthemic "Full Circle" and the intoxicatingly hazy "I Remember the Railroad" are, remarkably, matched in their brilliance by the covers, such as the elegiac reconstruction of Flatt and Scrugg's "Rough and Rocky" and his own Byrds-era "She Don't Care About Time," which gets slowed down and made even more stunningly yearning. Great players always want to play with great songwriters, and Sneaky Pete Kleinow's innovative steel guitar and Byron Berline's forlorn fiddle and Clarence White's always tasteful guitar only further enrich several remarkable compositions. Several remarkable compositions released, eventually, only in the Netherlands (where Gene was revered, Dylan his only peer), leading to the perfect absurdity—typical, unfortunately, of so much of Gene's career—of North American fans having to buy expensive imported copies of what became the *Roadmaster* album, an album recorded in North America by a North American recording artist.

After contributing the only two good original songs to the Byrds' limp reunion album ("Remarkably, the best stuff was Gene Clark's," contended Byrds road-crew member Al Hersh. "For a guy that couldn't string a sentence together, he could write some incredible lyrics"), David Geffen temporarily rescued Gene from label-less limbo by signing him to his own Asylum Records—named as such because Geffen maintained he wanted to provide a sanctuary for ambitious recording artists from cold commercial storms. Utter bullshit, of course — Geffen soon revealed his true turncoat colours by asking the justifiably proud producer of Gene's next LP, Thomas Jefferson Kaye, what the hell Asylum was supposed to do with an album with only eight long songs on it and no obvious single? — but this is what the majority of businessmen do — lie in order to make themselves feel better for wasting their lives. Artists, in turn, are advised to cease being surprised and disillusioned by such money-dictated mendacity, and, instead, steal as much cash from the ignorant sonofabitches as possible before the till gets slammed shut. To their credit, Gene and Tommy Kaye managed to steal a lot — the reported budget for their album was $100,000, a tremendous amount of money in 1973 for a musician with Gene's poor commercial track record — and not a penny of it was wasted on what was to be Gene's most elaborately produced (but never slick) album.

Grounded in solitude, but not ground down by isolation; enjoying a smoke or a shared bottle or two with friends and not having to apologize the next morning for what went down the blurry night before; attentive to nature's quiet lessons without turning into a back-to-the-earth ninny; a family man, finally — finally being a part of a family of one's own choosing — but never forgetting that we're all, all of us, all alone together: the stars aligned, his yin shook hands with his yang, maybe he just got lucky. Anyway, Gene was ready to make his masterwork. He called it *No Other*, and he was right.

"Life's Greatest Fool" starts things off, and might (and maybe even was intended to) mislead: a jaunty country-rocking opener with a very catchy chorus, it's not until the words fall away from the melody that it becomes apparent this is no ordinary twang tune. Life's winners and losers, and whether freedom or fate decides who's who, and what's the best seat in the stadium for watching the whole silly competition take place: Gene and his usual collection of stirring sidemen (Jesse Ed Davis's stinging electric guitar work and the wailing, choral-like contribution of the assembled background singers being particularly impressive) manage to keep your feet tapping while setting your soul sailing, a rare rock and roll double play. By the time the next cut, "Silver Raven," is even a minute old, however, the veil is lifted, and you know why you were danced from there to here. *No Other* will think you by crooning you and calm you if confound you and eventually send you singing back to yourself only to discover that you were right there all along. "Strength of Strings," meanwhile, is the best song ever written about the transformative, dwarfing power of music, "Some Misunderstanding" isn't just about a relationship gone wrong and just might be about how feeling truly alive means flirting with dying, and "Lady of the North" is the only song on the entire album that directly addresses romantic love—in this case, a love that's too real, too intense, too exquisite to continue for very long. Not incidentally, Gene never sang better (not only instrumentally, but vocally, *No Other* is his densest LP), or more ambitiously. In places, his reaching, soaring voice is the record's most distinctive and compelling instrument. It was the same voice, but it was a long, long way from what he'd been doing with it in the New Christy Minstrels.

This is where things begin to get ugly. His album another artistic success and commercial catastrophe, Gene didn't improve relations with his record label any by threatening to kick David Geffen's ass at Dan Tanna's one night for undervaluing and under-promoting *No Other*, the trickle of support Asylum had been supplying to the album immediately turned off at the tap. Gene was drinking more than ever, and had added cocaine to his arsenal of self-obliteration, an ill-advised pharmaceutical decision for someone already perpetually anxious and agitated. But just as ruinous as what he was putting up his nose was what he was putting himself through because of *No Other*'s lack of commercial success.

Gene grew up in a music business that operated by two very simple rules. One, a big-money major label was the only place for a legitimate artist. Two, the way that you stayed signed to a big-money major label was to have a hit record. This is what happened to The Byrds, after all, and was why Gene became increasingly confused, angry, and bitter as, stunning album after stunning album, his diminishing commercial worth failed to keep pace with his mounting critical reputation. Today, he'd be making records for an artist-friendly independent company, or perhaps even for his own label, and using the internet and other social media to connect with the kind of open-minded, non-mainstream audience that every authentic artist needs in order to survive. Instead, he played the game—at the time, the only game in town—knowing, at least at some level, that the race was rigged and that he'd never rate anything more than an honourable mention. Which made him confused about his place in the music industry, angry at whichever label he was with at the time for not doing enough to promote his work, and bitter with the public for not listening closely enough to what he was doing and for not supporting his vision. All of which made him a fairly miserable human being.

Miserable enough, in fact—and desperate enough to do what he could to change—to actively tour for the first time since he went solo nearly a decade earlier. This created its own set of problems—domestic problems, for example. Gene's wife, Carlie:

> Pretty soon he started to change. When he started going on tour he would come back and it was like his eyebrows were just sticking up and his eyes were rolling around in his head. It was just insane and I got to absolutely dread it when he was coming home . . . The real manic stuff was always when he had been drinking. He was the kindest, gentlest, most loving soul in the world as long as he wasn't drinking.

The Silverados, the three-piece band Gene assembled with himself on acoustic guitar and harmonica, Duke Bardwell on bass and banjo, and Roger White on electric guitar, was predicated on economy more than on any new minimalist aesthetic, but the result was high-lonesome wonderful—as can be heard on the posthumous *Silverado 1975* release—at least on the nights when Gene wasn't too drunk or stoned. Bardwell: "I think if someone is looking for a reason for him to get as fucked up as much as he did, then panic disorder's as good as any . . . I don't think he was comfortable with performing, but it was like a part of it that he really had to do. What else was he going to do? Sell cars?"

Adding to his growing sense of professional failure was the decidedly cut-rate nature of his touring. Label-less again (and with a growing reputation within the industry as a money-losing loose cannon) and without any tour support—this while several of his far less-talented former colleagues travelled by Lear jet to their sold-out concerts at hockey rinks and baseball stadiums—the Silverados took turns driving a used Dodge van to their modest club dates, unloaded and loaded out their own equipment, and were frequently confronted with small audiences disappointed not to hear a Byrds greatest hits show. But on a good night in front of a good audience—as thankfully captured on *Silverado 1975*—it was worth it, goosebumps and a humming head several decades on, as close to immortality as any of us is ever going to get.

And he kept writing—even at the otherwise miserable end, he was still writing new songs—and what he was coming up with was frequently first-rate material. So productive was he, in fact, that several of the best songs from this period, like "Daylight Line" and "What is Meant Will Be" and "Wheel of Time," were never recorded and released, testament as much to Gene's resilience and his deep need to keep making music as to his sizeable talent. Brother Rick Clark: "Gene was one of those people who couldn't sit down and discuss what he felt inside with most people. His pain came out through his art, his writing. And even though it was heartbreaking and emotional, he created some of his most beautiful songs and work through expressing those feelings."

If emotional pain and suffering were a large part of what was necessary to cook up good art, then Gene had all of the main ingredients to whip up one hell of a new album. Compounding his career troubles, Gene's wife had finally had enough, packed up the couple's two young boys and sued him for divorce. Abandoned by his family and without a record contract once again, he took the Silverados into the studio and got to work on spec, paying for the sessions himself. Soon, however, Thomas Jefferson Kaye, back in the producer's chair, dismissed Roger and Duke and brought in various session musicians. On a purely musical level it wasn't a damning decision—old friend Doug Dillard's rollicking banjo powers "Home Run King" just fine, and Jerry McGee and Jeff "Skunk" Baxter were highly in-demand guitar players for a reason—but it did hint at what plagues both what became *Two Sides of Every Story* and every project Gene subsequently involved himself in, feel and instinct being nudged aside in favour of professionalism and calculated commercial ambition. It's easy to be a self-righteous snob about this, but, then, it is helpful to remember that he was thirty-three years old and the radio had begun to sound like a foreign language and mortgage payments don't particularly care about feel and instinct.

Not that *Two Sides of Every Story*, which was eventually picked up by RSO after every other record label passed on it, doesn't contain some wonderful songs. "Home Run King" makes for a sprightly sing-a-long opener, and the doleful quartet of original songs on side two exploring the breakdown of his marriage are all quintessential, melodically beguiling, brooding Gene. But the remake of Dillard & Clark's "Kansas City Southern," which is meant to sound contemporary circa 1977, sounds instead like a bored bar band circa anytime, and the cover of "Marylou" dresses up an already weak song in an unfortunate, faux-fifties arrangement. (NB: If you're going to sell out, be sure to sell.) Even the four core ballads on side two are string-sweetened to the point of borderline syrupy, and the album's most effective cover, James Talley's "Give My Love to Marie," is nearly smothered in violins. Gene's voice—particularly when wedded to a song as sadly powerful as Talley's—never needed a string section to make its point.

The next time Gene recorded was as a third of McGuinn, Clark and Hillman, a not-so-super group assembled because Capitol Records had a hunch that three ex-Byrds could replicate a portion of the success of one of their many imitators, the Eagles. All three members were professionally stalled, and the upfront money from the label was too tempting to pass up, and if by the time they entered Miami's Criteria Studios to record their first album Gene and McGuinn were so estranged they were using roadies to communicate, and Hillman was still sulking because Gene's name was going to come before his on the album cover, it was at least a relief for everyone involved to be making music again. As for the music itself, Capitol Records had a substantial investment to make back, so they did the only sensible corporate thing: put the band in the studio with a pair of producer brothers who would give the album the hip and happening disco sound that had recently rescued the Bee Gees from commercial irrelevancy. It's unnecessary to individually examine Gene's four contributions to the album for the same reason that four turds in a toilet bowl are, whether considered separately or cumulatively, just a bowlful of shit.

If the songs Gene recorded during this time are, to anyone who loves Gene Clark's music, quite literally unlistenable, what he was up to personally is noteworthy, if for all the gone-wrong reasons. Road manager Al Hersch recalled how during this period

> Gene was into [heroin] big time. Terri [Gene's new drug-dealing girlfriend] had this little metal strong box. I never got to look at it firsthand, but there was a famous incident one night. They got into a horrendous fight, they were always fighting, and my recollection of it was the two of them running down the street stark naked with this strong box in this incredibly wealthy neighborhood in Miami and Gene tackling her right in the street.

"Near the end Gene was barely able to finish a sentence, he was such a mess," Hillman remembered.

For Gene, the eighties were mostly a decade of demos, debauchery, and increasing disillusion. The majority of the songs he recorded during this time (as can be heard on a seven-CD bootleg and on 1984's *Firebyrd*, recorded for the lightweight Takoma label) are lyrically thin and musically mediocre and made worse by being marred by archetypal eighties production values, all three being sad signs of Gene aspiring toward contemporary relevancy but only managing to sound like what he most feared: a has-been willing to do anything for a hit. There were periodic attempts to get clean, some more successful than others, and an unfortunate, debasing decision to front something called the Twentieth Anniversary Tribute to the Byrds. If clubs were unwilling to pay Gene Clark the solo artist properly, they were happy to book what was essentially a Byrds tribute band for the growing Baby Boomer nostalgia crowd. For someone who'd been attempting to escape the shadow of his former group's enormous wingspan for nearly two decades, it must have been artistically humiliating, if financially rewarding.

No matter how messed up he got on drugs or alcohol during this time, though, or how frequently he compromised his enormous musical gift, he still had his supporters, some of whom were admirers of not only his considerable backlog of wonderful songs, but of him as a human being. Michael Hardwick, a talented guitar and pedal steel player who was part of the Firebyrds' touring band, recalled how Gene

> barely had management . . . barely had bookings. I got paid a lot of money with Jerry Jeff [Walker, his previous employer] and I just walked away to play with Gene . . . I had already worn out two copies of *No Other*. I know I was present during certain problems, he had his problems and I was there when some unpleasant things went on and

everybody has lots of stories about Gene, but I was also there and I saw a real goodness in Gene . . . He had a good heart. I remember we were loading out in Santa Fe, the very first show, and he grabbed my amplifier and he's carrying it out behind the club and he almost slipped in the snow. And I said to him, "Oh, you don't need to do that, I'll carry it," and he goes, "Ah, I don't mind." And I'm thinking, 'Here's Gene Clark of the Byrds carrying my amp out, loading out after the club's closed, stomping around in the snow.' The other guys were all inside having drinks.

Despite suffering from an ulcer so severe it would eventually result in Gene having the majority of his stomach lining removed, when he decided to record a duet album with Textones front woman Carla Olson toward the end of the eighties he was clearly moving in the right direction, musically and otherwise. Abetted by being simply too broke to score hard drugs or indulge in weeklong binges, he was sober enough to begin putting his neglected finances and health in order, filing his taxes for the first time in years and even going so far as to start working out. While *So Rebellious a Lover* can't be called classic Gene, it was the best music he'd been a part of in a decade. Only "Gypsy Rider" rouses vintage-Gene Clark goosebumps (and there are far too many covers, even when they're wonderful, as with "Fair and Tender Ladies"), but the singing is committed and passionate, the harmonies Olson lends to Gene's lead vocals are superb, and, best of all, the production is as uncluttered and unprocessed as music could be during the eighties. Released today, with a name roots producer like T-Bone Burnett attached to it, it would have been the honest segue back into public consciousness that Gene so craved. As it was, it appeared and disappeared faster than you could say *I want my MTV*.

What killed him before he could make the follow-up LP that Olson and he were planning is cruelly ironic to a degree that rarely exists outside of bad movies and maudlin novels. Justifiably concerned that the Twentieth Anniversary Tribute to the Byrds was cheapening their former band's image, McGuinn, Crosby, and Hillman briefly reassembled for a few concerts in an attempt to bolster their lawsuit intended to keep the bogus Byrds off the road. At one of these, long-time Byrds fan Tom Petty was in attendance and was inspired enough to record a song from the group's rich catalogue for his next album, a sure-fire royalty bonanza for whomever the lucky writer turned out to be. Unfortunately, it wasn't one of the three ex-Byrds performing that night at the Ventura Theatre, but Gene, whose "I'll Feel a Whole Lot Better" was included on Petty's massive-selling *Full Moon Fever* album. The Byrds helped give him his start, the Byrds would help finish him off.

With the promise of regular royalty cheques that would eventually amount to well over $100,000, Gene wasted little time in getting to work spending his windfall, no one more gluttonous than a starving man. He bought a Cadillac and a motorcycle, but mostly he bought drugs — crack cocaine in particular. When it was discovered he had throat cancer, the fun turned ugly, Gene frequently disappearing with just his pipe and the sort of Hollywood hangers-on who always manage to attach themselves to someone determined to enjoy himself to death. At the end he was down to 130 pounds and the Petty money was almost gone and quart bottles of vodka were where he spent the majority of his remaining days.

The coroner ruled the cause of death to be heart failure, which really means he wore himself out. Gene had wanted to be buried in St. Andrew's cemetery, just outside

Tipton, Missouri, and his family made sure that his wishes were respected. What's engraved on his headstone is simple and honest and undeniably moving, just like the man underneath it. It reads:

HAROLD EUGENE CLARK
Nov.17 1944 May 24 1991
NO OTHER

RONNIE LANE

I will be conquered; I will not capitulate.

—Samuel Johnson

You knew he was a handful just by looking at him. A half-in-the-bag, naughty little woodchuck in filthy white overalls with a sparkling secret in his dancing brown eyes he somehow managed to smuggle into every one of his songs, it was good trouble, though—the kind that may make for an upset stomach and throbbing temples the inescapable morning after, but also abundant memories when those same temples are one day defaced with grey. He made plenty of mistakes because he always did the right thing, and in the end it was his body that betrayed him, not his principles.

For someone who sang that he wanted his church to be the open road, he didn't do too badly, a London East End WW II baby who ended up being buried in Trinidad, Colorado in one of his beloved cowboy outfits. His father was an affable lorry driver, his mother a multiple sclerosis sufferer. Ronnie and his brother used to wonder why their mum always seemed to be in a bad mood. After Ronnie, as an adult, was diagnosed with the same fatal disease that attacked his mother, he finally understood.

His father told Ronnie when he was a boy that if he learned to play an instrument he'd never have any trouble finding friends, and he took his old man's advice early on. Ronnie's brother Stan:

> Outside our house the buses used to change drivers and conductors and Ronnie would go down and play to them, strumming a little toy ukulele. He was only about five or six. He'd wear a cowboy hat like Roy Rogers and they used to give him pennies and halfpennies and he'd come back in with a big pocket of money.

Thirty years later he made his living doing pretty much the same thing, the money being slightly better.

A technical college (naturally) dropout (not surprisingly), what else but a plumber's mate, an amusement-park lackey, a men's outfitter's sales assistant, and, for a girlfriend, an aspiring hairdresser, with fish and chips on Friday night at the local and a few pints of lager and a few laughs and a quick cuddle and before you don't know it, Monday morning, six a.m., here we go oh no all over again. But as the song says, his life was saved by rock and roll—initially, the home-grown variety, skiffle and the Shadows and the Beatles, of course; later, American R&B and Fats Domino and Bo Diddley boom chicka boom, et cetera—Ronnie's Dad not only supplying the down payment for his first electric guitar but his first bass once on-the-ball Ronnie discovered that bass players were always in demand. A chance meeting—are there really such things?—with another working-class East-Ender named Steve Marriott who had a great record collection (plenty of Tamla Motown and Stax and American soul) and just as much cheek as Ronnie, led to an invitation to join Ronnie's band, the Muleskinners, on stage that night for a number or two. Drummer Kenney Jones:

> We had a residency at a pub over in Bermondsey. Ronnie and Steve ended up getting paralytic. Steve got up with us, sang a song and then he brought the house down with his Jerry Lee Lewis routine on the upright piano they had. He was jumping up and down on top of it and breaking all the keys on the keyboard. We got thrown out of the pub, lost the gig there, the other guys [in the band] had gone off, they weren't speaking to Ronnie and I because we'd brought Steve along. We were sitting on my drum kit outside on the curb. The three of us just looked at each other and burst out laughing and that's when we decided to form a band together.

The band they formed in 1965 with keyboardist Ian McLagan was the Small Faces ("faces" because they were all mod wannabes, "small" because three-quarters of the group were short). Soon signed to a management deal with Don Arden (who, in spite of virtually no experience inside the studio, appointed himself as their producer), the group had a hit with their first single, "Whatcha Gonna Do About It," a tune typical of their early material: clearly derivative (compare, for example, "Whatcha Gonna Do About It" with Solomon Burke's "Everybody Needs Somebody to Love") and crafted straight for the charts, but energetically performed and undeniably exuberant, Marriott's cockneyfied James Brown/Otis Redding/Wilson Pickett-copped screeching and screaming the group's most distinctive sound. Quickly tiring of performing covers and R&B rip-offs, Lane and Marriott discovered they made a promising songwriting team; the group also discovered that someone other than them—Arden—was pocketing the majority of their concert and record-sales cash. When they heard what was supposed to be only the demo of "My Mind's Eye" playing on the radio and announced as their new single, they made their move, getting out from underneath their management deal with Arden and signing a recording contract in 1967 with former Rolling Stones manager Andrew Loog Oldham's new hippie-hip Immediate label (the company's credo was "Happy to Be a Part of the Industry of Human Happiness"). They wouldn't end up any better off financially than they did while on Decca, but Oldham promised—and delivered—unlimited studio time to craft the increasingly more original music they wanted to make and the chance to produce their own records.

Twenty-five years after the fact, when an interviewer asked Ronnie why the Small Faces' music became more thoughtful and psychedelic around the time of their shift to Immediate, Ronnie sensibly replied that by that point they *were* more psychedelic and thoughtful. To working-class boys used to chasing pep pills with Scotch and Cokes, daily hash holidays with the occasional round-the-world acid trip didn't open new creative doors, it kicked them off their hinges and used the shattered timber to make a smoldering sonic Technicolor bonfire. The band's first Immediate single, for instance, was "Here Comes the Nice," an ode to your friendly neighbourhood drug dealer, exceptional not just for its then-scandalous subject matter but for Ronnie's witty wordplay and apt employment of lyrical shades of light and dark (and without sacrificing any of the band's rollicking R&B-earned grit, either; engineer Glyn Johns described working with them in the studio as like "being up against the English rugby team"). Music is, foremost, *music*, however, not stand-alone poems put to guitar, bass, organ, and drums, and the real breakthrough once they moved to

Immediate was in the sound of the Small Faces now that harpsichord, horns, bells, acoustic guitar, and mellotron were routinely added to the mix, with the added bonus of utilizing eight recording tracks instead of four. Plus, the band was simply better, as both musicians and songwriters. If you can't translate it into words and sounds that others can appreciate and enjoy, no experience—no matter how personally revelatory—is artistically useful. All of those underpaid one-nighters and rushed recording sessions had at least paid off in terms of helping the band develop the necessary skills to transfer what was in their pleasantly hazy heads onto hard black plastic.

Pro-dopers, yes, but not professional dopes: the band, and Ronnie in particular, knew that any insights gained from drugs were for better understanding and appreciating everyday life, and not for isolating oneself in a hermetically-sealed, hippified world of Tolkien and incense and kaftans. Ronnie's increasingly meditative lyrics made it clear that you didn't have to go to San Francisco with flowers in your hair to find inner peace; smoking a spliff and feeding the ducks in an East End park on a nice spring day can do the sartorial trick just fine. Similarly—and fairly uniquely among their peers—the Small Faces indulged in no annoyingly excessive soloing, their belief in the transformative power of the classic two- and three-minute pop song one of the reasons their music remains refreshingly alive today, while so many of their contemporaries' once-esteemed records, crammed full of boringly proficient guitar (and—even worse—drum) solos, are justifiably forgotten. The Small Faces—and, again, Ronnie in particular—had a sense of humour, and the fortifyingly leveling perspective that comes with it.

The band's second Immediate album, *Ogdens' Nut Gone Flake*, despite containing several fine songs (including

Ronnie's thoughtful "Song for a Baker"), suffers from both too little and too much of an infusion of this same humour. Routinely hailed as their best work and a bona-fide sixties classic, the "concept" that fills up side two—in which a witless character named Happiness Stan searches for the missing half of the moon—comes across as equally pretentious and silly, while the between-song spoken-word narration (delivered by elderly actor Stanley Unwin at his Jabberwanking worst) has never failed to give me a headache, what was presumably intended to be droll emerging as merely irritatingly dull (as opposed to the majority of Marriott's vocals, which sound as if they were performed by a speed-spiked Leprechaun and are only irritating). But for a few more good songs released post-breakup, the rest is the usual rock-business soap opera—the band was in debt to their new label, their newest work (the single "The Universal") was a frustrating flop, and Marriott and Lane began to snipe over whose songs were to be recorded and how (Marriott wanted to move the group into a much heavier, less textured direction, a foretaste of his slow descent into boogie-rock purgatory with Humble Pie). After Marriott walked off stage during a 1968 New Years Eve gig, it was all over but for some contractually obligatory shows.

After the remaining three Small Faces decided to regroup and recommence, adding journeyman singer Rod Stewart and Jeff Beck-sideman Ronnie Wood (neither of whom was vertically challenged), the band became the Faces, the dropped adjective not the group's only major change. Out went the hallucinogenics and in came the hootch. Lots and lots of hootch. Chemistry colours everything, and the band's newly developed, well-soused sound was as endearingly ramshackle (on both the predominant knees-up numbers and the gentler, more meditative material, the majority of which was written by Ronnie) as its makers.

The Faces played rock and roll the way it's supposed to be played: loud, rude, and horny. They also celebrated—rather than, as was the custom of the time, concealed—their working-class roots, their preference for the old-fashioned joys of drink, and their rawer-is-better, soul-over-virtuosity musical aesthetic. When the Faces were in the room, you knew they were there. And sometimes even in the room next door. Songwriter Graham Lyle: "I remember this commotion going on in the next dressing room. It sounded like a fight had started. And it was the Faces had arrived." As an antidote to a period (musical and otherwise) crowded with over-cultivated sensibilities and overblown musical egos, the Faces provided a much-needed reminder that art—like life—is best when it's simple, sincere, and not too worried about getting its clothes dirty. Future members of the Sex Pistols and the Replacements are just some of those who've testified to the band's iconoclastic early-seventies influence. (Pistols' bassist Glen Matlock: "They didn't seem to give a toss about anything . . . If there were no Faces, there would have been no Sex Pistols"; Replacements main man Paul Westerberg: "Faces—that's my band. They had fun. Humour . . . No Bogus mojo hokum. London's loud, lean, laughin' louts.") Although the Faces had their detractors (Ronnie recalled being dismissed early on by another band as "East End Tarts" who "don't know where it's at"), disc jockey John Peel was among the band's early converts. He remembered:

> I was a very serious hippy when I met the Faces for the first time backstage during one of their concerts. I felt absolutely shocked—sober and precious as I was—when they stumbled

out of their dressing room, loud, vulgar and very cockney. "Ahm, no thanks. No, really," I mumbled nervously when they called after me, something that sounded like "Come on, John—old sod, we'll have a drink!" While they stormed down the hall and disappeared, I realized that the Faces were having a lot more fun in life than I had. Next time they invited me I went along. And the other times, too. The Faces ... changed my life. During one of their gigs I'm supposed to have danced with a bottle of Blue Nun in my arm. And I'm a person who never ever dances. Never, never, never.

Around the same time that the Faces were establishing their reputation as the premier high-energy, high-times rock and roll band on the concert circuit (and becoming, in the process, the first band to install their very own bar right on stage), Ronnie woke up to wooden music—US dusty high-lonesome twang gussied up just right with blood-pudding British dancehall stomp—and could hence-forth always be counted on to place a couple of unfail-ingly melancholy, yet always powerfully consoling beau-ties on every Faces album to balance out the predominant raunch and roll. On the band's first album the standout is "Stone," a reincarnation narrative born out of Ronnie's interest in the philosophy of the Indian religious leader Meher Baba, and which is made most musically tasty by a spry Cajun swagger that's all the more delicious for a tart Limey twist. (The song was obviously important to him, as he recut it on Pete Townshend's—a fellow Meher Baba devotee—first solo album, and then again once he himself went solo.) As cosmology, it's nonsense, but as personal philosophy it's just short of profound—and a lot more fun to dance to than anything St. Thomas Aquinas ever wrote.

"Richmond" is Ronnie's quiet killer contribution to the Faces' second album, *Long Player*, Wood on slide and

Ronnie on acoustic guitar all that's necessary to help evoke a bad bout of good old homesickness experienced while on tour for too long in the US of A. It's easily the standout track on an LP long on agreeable party rock but short on soulful songs, and the fact that the band wouldn't allow him to sing it on stage because it would slow down the crank-it-to-ten good times was both a musical mistake and the first warning of the artistic suffocation that would eventually send Ronnie gasping for air and running for a resuscitating solo career. The Faces' second release of 1971, *A Nod's is as Good as a Wink . . . To a Blind Horse*, contains the band's only American hit, the rollicking "Stay With Me" (Rod Stewart never sounded so convincingly crass again), but the best track was again a Ronnie number, the aching "Debris," a paean to both his father and an East Ender's long ago black and white London.

More extremely lucrative Stateside touring; more of Rod Stewart prancing around the stage like a cross-dressing showgirl (and becoming such a solo success with his monster single "Maggie May" that the band was more than once greeted with a marquee that read APPEARING TONIGHT: ROD STEWART and the FACES); more hotels and more hangovers and four a.m. awake in Wichita, Kansas, wondering what the fuck, what was the point — was *this* what he was put here for, was *this* what he was supposed to be doing with his life? He kept writing songs, though — songs that the other Faces treated like a family dog who's a good boy, he really is, but who's not allowed on the furniture and please don't feed him from the table, you'll only encourage him. (Drummer Kenney Jones' wife Jan remembered how "They always used to take the mickey out of Ronnie's songs. Kenney used to laugh about it. He'd come in from Olympic [recording studio] and I'd say, 'How'd it go?' and he'd say, 'We've got the statutory Ronnie Lane song, rinky-dinky-dink.'")

Then one weekend back in England he and the wife of one of his friends informed her husband and Ronnie's wife that they were taking the Land Rover and going to Ireland and don't wait up, they weren't sure when they'd be back. They took along the woman's infant daughter and Ronnie's acoustic guitar and a mutual friend, Billy Nicholls, and Ronnie and Billy played the Irish pubs for drinks and suddenly music was fun again, playing songs he wanted to play for people whose appreciative smiles he could actually see.

The woman was Kate McInnerney, the daughter of a wealthy London solicitor, who either saw through the shallowness of Western materialism and perceived a way out through a hyper-hippie lifestyle or else was trying real hard to piss off her well-heeled proper parents. Chicken or egg, it made no difference—what mattered was that Ronnie was in love. With Kate's body and face—she was tomboy-elegant with long brown hair and a successful criminal's smile—and with Kate's wannabe gypsy soul, a soul he was immediately sold on as a solution to his problems, those as much existential as aesthetic.

Not that everyone was as thrilled with Ronnie's abrupt change of face. Band roadie Russ Schlagbaum, who was later to work as road manager for Ronnie when he went solo:

> Ronnie Lane always used to dress so impeccably with his three-piece suits—"three-piece," that was his nickname. We knew he had run off and left Sue [his wife] so all of us were, like, "What the fuck is Ronnie thinking?" In he walks with Kate in tow and baby Alana in a wicker basket. His ears were pierced, he's got all these bangles, he's turned into a

gypsy. And he's walking around, miles away from everybody. He's not joining in the frolics like they would do, falling over each other and all that shit. He was completely aloof
and everybody was wondering, "What the fuck's happened
to Ronnie Lane?"

His fellow Faces weren't impressed with the suddenly
gypsyfied Ronnie, either. Ian McLagan: "When The Faces
toured England [in December 1972], we saw plenty of
Kate. We'd been five guys touring, and now suddenly we
were four guys and a shabby, grubby guy with his shabby,
grubby girlfriend. It didn't gibe well with us."

The four guys and the shabby, grubby guy managed
to make one more album together, but it wasn't easy, the
tension between the increasingly reticent Ronnie and the
others only exacerbated by Stewart's reluctance to do
anything that might impede his flourishing solo career,
which meant that he rarely found the time to show up
in the studio. Derided upon its release because it lacked
enough Stewart-sung rave-ups (no more than by Stewart
himself, who, soon after it came out, said, "It was a
bloody mess . . . It was a disgrace, but I'm not going
to say anything more about it"), *Ooh La La* is the Faces'
finest moment precisely because, in Stewart's absence,
Ronnie took creative control, writing or co-writing six
of the album's ten numbers. Ronnie didn't just stand
out quantitatively, however: "Flags and Banners" is an
American-Civil-War déjà vu dream-cum-nightmare set
sprightly country-rocking (how's *that* for a musical amalgam?); "Glad and Sorry" is an aching mix of folk, country, stinging electric guitar, and unadorned but arrest-
ingly reflective lyrics, the sort of song he'd soon perfect
during his solo career; and the title song is a bouncing
folk-rock number powered by crunchy acoustic guitars,

harmonium, and music-hall piano, and with an irresistible chorus, a song that perfectly captures Oscar Wilde's
assertion that youth is wasted on the young. (Compare
these with the album's lead-off track, a hook-less Stewart-
Wood rocker whose title, "Silicone Grown," tells you all
you need to know about it. Lest we forget: carnal doesn't
mean juvenile; simple doesn't mean stupid.)

The only sign that Ronnie wasn't ready to pull a complete about-face and make an entire album's worth of
what, after warming up on the four Faces albums, was
becoming undeniably "Ronnie Lane" music, was his reluctance to sing all of his own material, "Glad and Sorry"
being a duet with Wood and "Ooh La La" sung by Wood
alone. Inevitably, though (probably not long after Ronnie
reportedly said to Stewart, after the latter wondered what
Ronnie thought he was up to dressing like a boho hobo,
that he'd rather look like that than like an old tart who's
going through the change—if the story isn't true, it should
be), even if everyone's bank account was getting fatter and
the band traveled by jet now and stayed in only the best
hotels while on the road, Ronnie took his bass and went
home, used the money he'd saved up not buying Cadillacs
and rhinestone jumpsuits and vacation homes in Bermuda
to purchase a farm on the English/Welsh border to raise
his new family (he'd married Kate by this point) and to
make his own music. He also set up a mobile recording
studio to record his new songs and to rent out to other
bands to help pay the bills. Because the guy was no dim
dreamer—it was 1973, he knew what he heard in his head
wasn't what the kids watching Top of the Pops wanted to
hear. He knew what he was up against. For Chrissake, he
called his new band Slim Chance.

It takes time to become yourself; sometimes even an
entire lifetime isn't long enough. But by the time Ronnie

and his new family were installed at the shabby Shropshire farm they dubbed Fishpool (visitors knew it was Ronnie's place because of the Faces' gold record nailed to the front door), everything that had gone into who he was up to that point, plus all of the things he wanted to be but hadn't known he'd wanted until he met Kate, came together to make up who he happily now was. When it came time to assemble the players to help him record his new old-sounding music, there was to be none of the usual networking through the stale rock-star grapevine that went into the formation of most new veteran bands. Feel and fate were to determine who was asked to join Slim Chance, as fiddle player Steve Simpson learned:

> So, there I was, sitting in on fiddle with a bunch of friends who were playing a gig at The Barmy Arms, opposite Eel Pie Island, Twickenham, when a little guy in a green velvet drape jacket stepped up for a chat. He said he was making a record and asked whether I'd like to play on it. This guy turned out to be Ronnie Lane, who then loaded up his pockets with several bottles of barley wine and led me off to Wick Cottage, where he played me a rough of "How Come" and introduced me to Kate and one-week-old Luke.

Benny Gallagher and Graham Lyle, who were to add so much to Slim Chance in its first incarnation, were roped in when, the night after Ronnie and Kate's son Luke was born, Ronnie staggered drunkenly into a Gallagher and Lyle recording session after having crashed his car driving back from the hospital. Seizing the opportunity, he played the duo some of his new material, and before too long they were in the studio backing *him*.

When he finally settled on the right mix of musicians and was ready to record, he did it his way, making the musicians come to the farm. The bass player on Ronnie's first solo album, *Anymore for Anymore*, Steve Bingham:

> It was in 1974 that I received a call from former Joe Cocker [and subsequent Slim Chance drummer] drummer Bruce Rowland who invited me to meet Ronnie Lane at his farm in the Welsh borders with a view to joining the band Slim Chance. I was amazed to arrive in the middle of nowhere to find Ronnie and his family happily living amongst dogs, cats, chickens and ducks, in a small cottage surrounded by old barns with a fantastic mobile recording studio parked outside! After a good session at the local pub we piled into his barn and began playing along to some of Ronnie's songs which went on to become the classic *Anymore for Anymore* album. I asked Ronnie where I could stay and he showed me to an old caravan with no heating, no facilities whatsoever and a leaking roof! That was the start of my stay at Fishpool Farm.

The first fruit of the original version of Slim Chance (the cast constantly shifted, as the musicians who played with Ronnie often left him, reluctantly, for less musically interesting, but far more financially rewarding work) was the single "How Come?" backed with a remake of one of Ronnie's typically tender Faces songs originally sung not nearly as movingly by Stewart, "Tell Everyone," and another new tune, "Done This One Before." The two recently written numbers typified the poles of human experience Ronnie was to mine over the course of his solo career. "How Come" is a spry ode to Kate's bewitching (in the song, literally) beauty, anchored by an extremely catchy mandolin line, a song that is as much a love song to frequently bewildering but always beguiling life as it is to any one person. "Done This One Before" is the

180-degrees downer opposite in both music and meaning (as if the two things are ever divisible), a deeply melancholic organ- and harmonica-drenched lament to bleary morning-afters and the sad futility of wishing it could all have somehow been otherwise. On the cover of the 45's colourful sleeve there's a picture of Ronnie and Kate and his now-adopted daughter walking through the woods on a sunny afternoon. On the back, after the musician and song-writing and production credits, it simply reads: DEDICATED TO KATE. A labour of love for real.

The frisky-folky music-hall-rock of "How Come?" did better than anyone could have expected (reaching number eleven on the British singles charts, the first and last time any of Ronnie's solo material ever sold in significant quantities), and next up was the completion of the album *Anymore for Anymore* for the small GM label. The front of the album jacket is a rare case of justifiably judging a record by its cover: entirely text-less, there's a murky shot of a couple of horse-drawn rag-and-bone men heading off into the sunset amidst what looks like smoggy London motorway traffic. If you're going to go against the grain, it seems to say, do it with vigour, do it with dignity, do it with style. Which is precisely what the music contained inside the cardboard sleeve does.

Anymore for Anymore's highlights are numerous — the title track (a gentle hymn to freedom from onerous acquisitiveness); "The Poacher" (a soaring, oboe- and strings-abetted statement of spiritual independence); "Roll On Babe" (a *carpe ∂iem* strumming sing-along) — but the strongest impact is made by the sound of the album as a whole. Shades of folk, country, Dixie, rock, blues, Cajun, and much else fade and flicker in and out of one another, resulting in a trad-rich musical mix not quite of its time, yet never sterilely revivalist. This is music inspired by the sounds of the past, but which is very much of the pulsating present, its makers audibly revelling in—rather than slavishly revering—their seasoned musical sources. So much was the emphasis on feel over professional formality, when Ronnie went outside one morning with just a cup of tea and his guitar, and one by one the other musicians woke up to join him in working on a recent song he was besotted with, the proceedings were taped, the sounds of the wind on the hillside and the children playing atop it included, the end result being the actual take of "Anymore for Anymore" that appears on the L.P. On the back of the album, "Any rumble on 'Anymore for Anymore' is wind in the microphone," it counsels, "please do not adjust your set."

But the iconoclasm of his mission wasn't complete, the deck wasn't stacked against him quite enough, not yet. To promote his first album with Slim Chance, Ronnie decided he wasn't going to gig the usual big city concert halls; rather, he decided to bring something he called The Passing Show (an expression of life's ephemerality borrowed from Meher Baba, but which had existed for as long as there have been philosophically humble human beings) to every provincial outpost in England that would have failed a cost/benefit touring analysis, a rock-and-roll circus with clowns and jugglers and fire eaters and, most of all, the rocket-fuel mandolin music he wanted to tell everyone about. And naturally it was the wettest British summer in thirty years and the antique gypsy coaches he'd bought to haul around the musicians and their families and all of the equipment broke down every fifty miles and local firemen wanted to see permits and the sanitation officials wanted to know where exactly the portable toilets were going to be located and by the end of it they were pawning equipment just to buy enough diesel to get to the next show, which was just about the same time that musicians started to jump off the sinking ship ("One morning we woke up to find [sax player] Jimmy Jewell had left a note on Ronnie's trailer saying 'Goodbye Cruel Circus, I'm Off To Join The World,'" recounted Russ Schlagbaum). Ronnie lost a small fortune and a year after *Anymore for Anymore* came out you could buy it in a discount bin for a buck (although it now goes for close to a hundred on eBay), but the handful of ecstatic people who saw the show never purchased another Rod Stewart LP again.

While many were charmed, if initially flummoxed, by the dilapidated splendour of control-centre Fishpool (Lyle: "Kate would be washing the clothes in a tub and putting them through a mangle. An enormous cauldron of soup sat on the fire from day to day") as well as by Ronnie's militant anti-materialism (Billy Nichols: "[W]e were driving along the motorway and he opened his wallet and the wind caught all this money and blew it out everywhere. I said, 'Ronnie, aren't you going to go back and get it?' He wasn't even fazed. 'No, must keep going'"), others wondered whether Ronnie's priorities—and simple common sense—weren't being compromised in the process.

"I hated to see Ronnie and Kate playing at being farmers," Schlagbaum admitted, listing a litany of what were to his mind bad business decisions that might have easily been avoided if the couple had been less interested in acting like bucolic sages and more like responsible rock and rollers:

We got pawned off to the wrong people. Ronnie first went to Chipperfield's but they couldn't take it on. Then he asked Gerry Connell who said, "I can't do it but I know a fellow who has all this gear in storage. He's been off the road for awhile." What he didn't say is that he'd been off the road for twenty fuckin' years! So he put Ronnie on to Wally Luckins and of course, right away, Wally charms Kate and she says, "Ooh he's lovely, Wally's lovely" so Ronnie falls for it. He was following what Kate wanted and Kate was in his ear all the time . . . We were resorting to the old circus ways. When I met the circus blokes I thought, "These guys are criminals" but I had no idea how criminal they were. Luckins . . . must have thought, "Here comes this gullible pop star with a lot of dough" . . . The trucks he supplied belonged in the London Transport Museum. I got the dubious pleasure of driving this 1947 Bedford flatbed truck from Marlow to Bath overloaded to the gills with canvas, with my living van behind it, a little four-cylinder gas job. I never even got down the motorway. I pulled in to the first service area and went into the garage and told the mechanic, "I don't know what's wrong but start by changing the points and plugs." The guy pulled out a spark plug and said, "I've been a mechanic for 25 years and I've never seen one like this." I finally managed to coax the fucker to the Bath site. I was fuming because I'd spent all fuckin' night just to travel 100 miles . . . I was pissed off, tired, and I thought, "Christ, this is not the way to do it."

True, true, no doubt true. But. But the flip side of idealistic is impractical, and if Ronnie and Kate had been less of the latter they might also have been less of the former. Better a flawed vision than a competent compromise. The Passing Show was a fiasco, okay, and what do you know? We're still talking about it forty years later.

Poorer, pissed off, but unrepentant, Ronnie recorded another album (*Ronnie Lane's Slim Chance*) for another label (Island) with another version of Slim Chance (among the new recruits, string man deluxe Charlie Hart, who would stick and pick with Ronnie until the end). More catchy, contemplative songs passionately performed ("Little Piece of Nothing," "Anniversary," "Tim and Tambourine"— the latter recycling the melody of an old Faces song, "Devotion") more touring (of the more traditional sort), more general indifference. The British version of the LP ends with an old cowboy song, "Single Saddle," which the Dillards also recorded on their 1968 country-rock classic *Wheatstraw Suite* (and where Ronnie may have heard it for the first time), but the brief version that concludes *Ronnie Lane's Slim Chance* is pure Ronnie. Beginning with the sounds of everyday life at Fishpool—birds, ducks, a single tractor—we hear a mandolin, some handclapping, Kate softly calling Ronnie's name, an accordion, then Ronnie (with Kate helping out on background) singing a simple song of a simple love for wide open spaces and the wisdom of open endings. Simply beautiful.

One year later, one more time, this one called *One More for the Road*. The songs were Ronnie's best collection yet, the playing was focused and fiery, there was more determined touring, and the second to last song on the second side, "Nobody's Listenin'," could have been the album's commercial epitaph. But a piece of art exists even if no one in the forest hears it fail, and *One for the Road* is a piece of art to be proud of. "Steppin' An' Reelin' (The Wedding)" is a roaring love song to Kate, "Harvest Home" is a throbbingly melancholic instrumental co-written with Charlie Hart that says all there is to say about the life cycle without saying a word, and as for the title track, I've left instructions for it to be played when it's time for my ashes to be scattered. The number-one selling song of that year, "Dancing Queen" by Abba, will not be played.

The belated release of the soundtrack to the Canadian movie *Mahoney's Last Stand* that Ronnie and Ron Wood had recorded four years earlier as members of the Faces provided a few much needed dollars and the chance to hear, along with some spirited incidental music, "Just for a Moment," a song underrated by even Ronnie's most ardent admirers, likely because of its obscure source.

43

In some ways it's the quintessential Ronnie Lane song, at once gorgeously sorrowful, shamelessly affirmative, and impossible to get out of your head long after you've heard it. (Never one to waste a good melody, parts of an otherwise unremarkable song off the Faces' first album, "Nobody Knows," are lovingly salvaged to great effect.) It was another collaboration that same year, however, that got him back in the recording studio. And it was also there that Ronnie's collaborator—his old friend Pete Townshend—realized that Ronnie was suffering from the disease that was to eventually kill him.

The idea for the album that became *Rough Mix* came about when Ronnie recognized that, without a substantial cash infusion, he was likely to go bankrupt and lose his farm. The Who were then one of the world's biggest bands, so working with one of its members would likely bring in a healthy advance. For his part, Townshend was growing restless with his day job supplying power-chord rockers for Roger Daltry to over-sing, so the fit was right on both sides. Sometime during the sessions that ran from late 1976 to early 1977, Townshend remembered how

> Ronnie was often right in my case, ready to tell me the truth as he saw it . . . but the thought [Ronnie had upbraided Townshend for cheating on his wife] made me explode. I lashed out at him, pushing him hard squarely on both shoulders. Ronnie flew like a man made of paper and came very close to smashing his head on a concrete step at the foot of the stairway. I could have killed him. At first I thought I didn't know my own strength, but later learned that Ronnie was exhibiting the first symptoms of multiple sclerosis.

Ronnie, though, wasn't ready to accept what was becoming obvious to everyone else. "Ronnie would wake up in the morning and his hand would be numb and he couldn't hold a pen, couldn't write," Russ Schlagbaum remembered. "He put it down to drink and drugs and everything else. His mother had MS but Ronnie never for a moment would admit that perhaps that's what it was." Slim Chance drummer Bruce Rowland claims that Ronnie had been running from the inevitable for years, purposefully omitting telling hospital officials about his family's history of multiple sclerosis, for instance, when a doctor a couple of years previous was treating what in retrospect were obviously early MS-related symptoms.

Veteran producer Glyn Johns (the Faces, the Who, Ronnie's first solo single) was excited to work with the pair, but wanted a guarantee that they were doing it for the right (that is, not merely monetary) reasons. He needn't have worried—no less than two bonafide beauties resulted on Ronnie's end: "Annie" (Ronnie up to his old tricks, borrowing the melody from his own "Give Me a Penny" and adding new and exquisitely improved lyrics) and "April Fool," a stirring piece of self-examination featuring Eric Clapton's emotive dobro work. Clapton, one of the album's all-star contributors, was someone who Ronnie, in spite of his failing health, managed to develop a close friendship with. Typical of Ronnie, though, it wasn't through rock-star hobnobbing that they first made contact. Schlagbaum:

Ian Stewart called Ronnie one day and mentioned, "Oh, by the way I ran into Eric the other day and he asked how you were." And Ronnie was mystified. He said to me, "What the fuck does Eric Clapton want? I don't even know him that well." Stu kept saying Eric's been asking after you so Ronnie asked Stu for his number. I was there when he made the call. "Eric? This is Ronnie Lane, just what the fuck do you want?"

Clapton fully bought into Ronnie's gypsy lifestyle—even writing his lovely song "Wonderful Tonight" around a late-night bonfire at Fishpool—and attempted to return the favour by inviting Ronnie to open several shows on Clapton's upcoming European tour. Playing icebreaker for rowdy crowds wanting to hear long guitar solos wasn't the ideal Slim Chance gig, however. Schlagbaum: "Ronnie was still drinking heavily and the MS had started. He would get so drunk and obnoxious. He hated being a support act." On returning home, he officially received the medical diagnosis he'd been dreading for years.

Ronnie broke up Slim Chance—again—and decided to circle his broken-down wagons and raise chickens and sheep until the coldest British winter in thirty years (and the diseases that blew in with it) killed most of his animals, at which point Townshend convinced him to sell his farm and move back to London and commit himself to treating his MS. Even as the life he'd so carefully constructed out of the firmest ethical and spiritual foundations collapsed underneath him (Ronnie complained to a friend that, because of the destabilizing nature of his illness, he couldn't even drink himself to death), he continued to write songs, songs that needed to be recorded, whether anyone was paying attention or not. They weren't.

The album, though, 1979's *See Me* (which Ronnie, understandably, contributed to instrumentally only perfunctorily), brims with small wonders like "Kutchty Rye" (if Charlie Hart's joyful accordion was eccentric in 1976, it was utterly suspect at the dawn of the synthesizer age), the earthy yet elegant Lane-Clapton co-write "Barcelona," and the delightfully filthy "Good Ol' Boys

Boogie." Regardless of his worsening physical condition, Ronnie, as Charlie Hart pointed out, always "had a brilliant innate sense of composition and wrote great melodies." As music, *See Me* is first-rate; as testament to a little man encountering a big obstacle and coming out bigger because of it, it's enough to make you feel proud, however briefly, to belong to the human race.

The rest is the kindness of strangers and Ronnie doing his best not to hurt too much. He left Kate (as Ronnie so movingly sang in "April Fool," the wheels of the gypsy caravans were rusting in the backyard and their dreamy roaming days were done), he left the woman he left Kate for, he left Britain to seek medical help in Florida, in Houston, in Austin. In the latter, although condemned to a wheelchair and his voice sometimes not much more than a husky dribble, he made music with friends and tried to laugh as he grew smaller and feebler. His last wife, whom he met in Austin, moved him to Colorado in the mid-nineties, and that's where he died July 4, 1997.

For most of his solo career, at the end each of show, Ronnie would enjoin God to bless us all.

What a lovely idea.

THE RAMONES

Any fool may write a most valuable book by chance, if he will only tell us what he heard and saw with veracity.

—Thomas Gray

I always liked loud music—the Stooges; Hendrix; early, crunchy Crazy Horse—but it wasn't until I hit thirty that loud and fast and catchy—that alluringly cacophonous combination of sound that the Ramones virtually invented—began to make sense. Young and resolute and oozing adolescent energy I didn't know what to do with, why would I want an accompanying soundtrack of driving frenzy blaring in my ears? But older and slower and every year wearier than the last, an aural pick-me-up began to have its appeal. Take two minutes of this and Hey-Ho-Let's-Go call me in the morning.

Reducing the powerful attraction of the Ramones' peerless music to its motivational utility, however, is as crude a critical diminishment as claiming to enjoy sex because it's good for your cardiovascular system. Energy can be intoxicating; energy as an end in itself is empty and ultimately unfulfilling, an open tab at an abandoned bar with all of the lights left on. The music of the Ramones makes you move and makes you laugh and makes you sing and makes you remember what's so wonderful about real rock and roll: it's a ferocious reminder that we're alive. The Ramones are also an example of the alchemical (and frequently inflammatory) constitution of all significant art and a lesson in the limits of limitation.

Before any of that, though, they were just four bored guys from the Queens, New York, suburb of Forest Hills, whose greatest ambition in life was to avoid having to get a real job. Before he became himself, Joey Ramone was Jeffrey Hyman, another kid from another broken home with the added burden of being too tall and too skinny and with bad eyesight and burgeoning obsessive-compulsive disorder, and whose lifeline was a transistor radio and a shitty stereo in the basement rec room. The Who and the Kinks and the Beach Boys and the Stooges weren't entertainment—they were medicine.

John Cummings couldn't have been any different from his future fellow Ramone—Johnny liked baseball and to steal things and to beat people up who wouldn't do what he wanted. His musical epiphany was seeing Elvis on the Ed Sullivan Show in 1957, but more than anything else he wanted to be a New York Yankee. He liked the British Invasion bands enough to get a guitar, but couldn't figure out how to play it sufficiently well, so he decided to quit when it got too hard.

Like Joey's, Doug Colvin's parents divorced when he was young, but the boy who would grow up to become boy-man Dee Dee Ramone never did anything in half-measures, not even family dysfunction. His alcoholic master-sergeant father was thirty-eight years old when he married Dee Dee's seventeen-year old mother; Dee Dee was born in Virginia but grew up on a series of German army bases for the first fourteen years of his life; his favourite childhood occupation was searching old battle sites for Nazi artifacts to sell to American soldiers. (Occasionally—as when he discovered several tubes of morphine—he kept the loot for himself.) It was while his father was briefly stationed back in the US that Dee Dee heard rock and roll loud and clear for the first time, while buying potato chips at the PX Snack Bar in Atlanta.

The oldest of the original Ramones, Tommy Erdelyi, aka Tommy Ramone, was born in 1949 and moved to America with his family from Hungary when he was seven. He was also the (relatively) normal one—worked in a recording studio in New York after high school and liked to watch foreign films at the MoMA during lunch breaks and played in a handful of third-rate glam and hard-rock bands. In such a relatively insular suburban community, it's not surprising that the four knew each other. (Who else would want to know them?) All in all, four Forest Hill fuck-ups who helped save rock and roll. It's really that simple; it's really that confounding.

Obviously, there were influences. The Stooges' bass, drums, and guitar greaseball assault and disarmingly honest lyrics (about being bored, being apathetic, being bugged by other people); the MC5's full-on metallic ferocity; the Beatles' masterful melodicism; sixties girl group sha-la-la's; the sunny pop pleasures of early, surfboarding Beach Boys; the local live example of the decked-out, drugged-out New York Dolls, clearly having—gasp!—a ball up on stage, something the oh-so-serious music industry of 1973 frowned upon as puerile and unprofessional; an unapologetic love of popular culture, from comic books to horror movies to the shlockiest television programs to the most disposable of bubblegum music. But other people, other bands, had similar enthusiasms and inspirations, yet none of them ended up making the music that the Ramones did. The short version is that the Ramones were more than the sum of their parts. Without the inimitable, intensely personal contribution of even one of the four, the group's pioneering music wouldn't exist as we know it.

The Beatles were one of Johnny's favourite bands, which would account for why he went to see them perform live when they came to New York. Johnny's teenage friend Richard Adler explains—or, rather, *describes*—what happened after that: "Once we all went to see the Beatles at Shea Stadium and John brought a bag of rocks and threw them at the Beatles all night. It's amazing nobody got hurt. These were rocks as big as baseballs." Without Johnny's unrelenting annoyance—at life? himself? both?—the Ramones wouldn't have played at such a wonderfully ridiculous speed or with such bracing aggression right from their inaugural rehearsal (well, not the *first* rehearsal, when they couldn't play their instruments well enough to do much more than try to stay in tune). Because of Joey and Dee Dee and Tommy, though, who wrote the lyrics and arranged the tunes, the songs never soured into emptily angry diatribes. Instead, they were suffused with twisted humour and affirmative vitality and married to enriching melodies. Rage can be cleansing and even (briefly) constructive; indulged in exclusively, however, it can also be a gateway emotion to a purposeless pit of self-pity. The Ramones meant it, man, but unlike, say, welfare-state whiners like the Sex Pistols, their music *still* means it; cozily ensconced in California cupidity, John Lydon isn't thinking about anarchy in the UK when he drives down the freeway on the way to his favourite sushi restaurant. Joey, on the other hand, lived for beating boredom and having fun and making the best out of the worst that life can come up with right until the end.

(What was the title of his posthumous solo album, which he worked on throughout his long struggle with cancer? *Don't Worry About Me*. What was its most affecting song? A cover of "What a Wonderful World.")

Even the Ramones' respective members' individual strengths and (mostly) weaknesses as neophyte musicians contributed to the band's immensely inventive sound. Yes, you can hear the brutally repetitious attack of Led Zeppelin's "Communication Breakdown" and Black Sabbath's "Paranoid" in Johnny's signature buzz-saw guitar style. And, yes, Johnny was on record as saying he hated the turn rock and roll had taken toward instrumental virtuosity and prolonged, self-indulgent soloing, though the fact that he played downstroke barre chords almost exclusively suggests necessity more than conscious innovation. (The Ramones always got outside musicians to play whatever short guitar solos were necessary on their records simply because Johnny wasn't capable of doing them as well.) And this was no chic faux-primitivism, either. Flamin' Groovies front man Chris Wilson remembered a telling hotel-room encounter: "I passed my guitar to John and said, 'Have a go,' and he went, 'I'm sorry, man. I only know how to play bar-chords.'" Also, Johnny—who was the band's central image maker and the one who insisted that they all wear the black-leather-jacket-and-torn-blue-jeans uniform (although it was Dee Dee who took the surname "Ramone" for himself after learning that "Paul Ramon" was Paul McCartney's pseudonym, and who convinced the other band members to adopt it as a sign of unity)— admitted he simply liked the way he looked in the mirror with the guitar slung low over his shoulder, like a gunslinger, which made any technique *but* the downstroke nearly impossible to pull off.

Perhaps because he was the least intriguingly scandalous of the original four Ramones (meaning: he wasn't a drug addict, mentally ill, or psychotic), Tommy tends to get short shrifted for his enormous contribution to the band's sound, not least by the other band members themselves (in the excellent documentary, *End of the Century*, for example). Even more than Johnny, who had at least played a guitar before beginning to practice in earnest when the Ramones formed in 1974, Tommy approached his instrument with few preconceptions, never having even played the drums before, and only took over behind the kit because none of the drummers that the novice band auditioned was right for the group, most being heavy-metal bashers in the manner of the day. In the end, the anti-style he developed—essential to the group's musical aesthetic, yet minimal to the point of being utterly subservient to the song; metronome-steady yet neck-and-neck fast with Johnny's furious downstroking—became an estimable, much-imitated style. Thoroughly utilitarian *and* instantly identifiable: a hard trick to pull off, but one made easier, ironically, by Tommy's inexperience. As *Rolling Stone* writer and Ramones fan David Fricke pointed out, "Tommy was able to unite the others over his backbeat, which you'd think anybody could have done . . . [But] Tommy play[ed] at the same speed, the same beat, the same patterns all the way through. Most drummers are genetically incapable of doing that. He knew that simplicity was king." He also didn't know any other way to do it, which meant simplicity was also a necessity.

Rock-and-roll songs usually have words as well as music, though, and the Ramones' lyrics were no less forged from their ostensible shortcomings as their sound. Unless you count comic books or *Mad* magazine, none of the Ramones were what you'd call big readers. Which means that entire songs sometimes consist of only a few lines of words, resulting in repetition to a compulsively hypnotic, almost rhythmic degree. Which also means that while the band wasn't capable of something in the lyrical league of "Suzanne" or "Like a Rolling Stone," they also weren't going to concoct a piece of pseudo-profundity like "Celebration of the Lizard" or "Stairway to Heaven." A little bit of education can go a long way toward a lot of bad art. More than just safeguarding them against avant-garbage tendencies, however, the Ramones' genius lay in honestly embracing what they really did know and care about, rather than feigning interest in what they were supposed to find important. Fellow musician Richard Hell was among the first to recognize this:

> All their songs were two minutes long, and I asked them the names of all their songs. They had maybe five or six at the time: "I Don't Wanna Go Down to the Basement," "I Don't Wanna Walk Around with You," "I Don't Wanna Be Learned, I Don't Wanna Be Tamed," and "I Don't Wanna" something else. And Dee Dee said, "We didn't write a positive song until "Now I Wanna Sniff Some Glue." They were just perfect, you know?

Perfect because they played short songs because they found long songs boring; perfect because they preferred *Night of the Living Dead* to *Long Day's Journey Into Night* and didn't need a French literary theorist to say it was okay; perfect not just because they were honest—after all, Jim Morrison honestly believed he was a poet—but because, by celebrating their sincerest passions in song, they consecrated those passions, art's highest function.

Joey, the one who sang the words to the songs, was the human embodiment of wringing eventual victory from seeming failure, the ultimate DIY success story. Contra Mick Jagger, the archetypal cock-strutting lead singer of the era, Joey was (at least early on) clearly emotionally insecure and physically awkward up on stage, a black-clad praying mantis with self-esteem issues (he'd been kicked out of his previous band not for his singing ability, but because he wasn't good looking). He was also the sum of his LPs, his record collection's collective unconscious, and his accent when singing was part New York, part British, part entirely unpersuasive bravado, a self-fabricated verbal mishmash of whoever he wanted to be—and, in time, he was, at least come show time. He was, in other words, any one of the band's audience members, the daydreaming outcast who somehow ended up with the microphone in his hand.

Eyewitness accounts of the band's first shows are illuminating. There's virtually no ambivalence: it was either instant adoration or incredulous dismissal. Performing at CBGB—the now-legendary spawning ground of American Punk, then-Bowery cesspool with a liquor license—the audiences were sparse and the reaction intense. *Punk* magazine co-founder Legs McNeil: "It looked like the SS had just walked in, they [the Ramones] looked so striking. I mean, these guys were *not* hippies, this was something completely new. And the noise of it was . . . it just hit you." Blondie bassist Gary Valentine:

Until I saw the Ramones play, I thought the Dolls were the loudest band ever. They were fantastic, 20 songs in 15 minutes, one after the other, one minute, two minute songs. There was this tacit, pent-up notion of violence in the background, but on stage they were a lot of fun, in a Saturday morning cartoon, "Hey hey we're the Ramones" way. Even though the songs were different they all sounded the same—it was like Beethoven over one-and-a-half minutes, with Joey Ramone mumbling over the top.

Legendary scene-maker and music journalist Danny Fields, whom Tommy, the group's de facto leader, had been pleading with over the phone to come and see their show, reluctantly attended one of the band's gigs at CBGB and came away so impressed he immediately offered to be the band's manager:

> The Ramones had everything I liked. The songs were short. You knew what was happening within five seconds. You didn't have to analyze and/or determine what it was you were hearing or seeing. It was all there, and every aspect of what they were doing was excellent, from the clothes to the posture to the lyrics. Everything. It was excellent. It was the sound that got me. I thought the music of the Ramones was pretty much dealing with everything that the world needed then. You know, fill up that syringe and here's my arm. Give it to me! Shoot it!

On the other hand, Mark Bell, later Marky Ramone when he took over from Tommy behind the drums, had a different initial impression: "When I first saw them at CBs I thought they sucked because there were no fills, no drum rolls because that's what I'd been doing all my life." Monte Melnick, who would go on to be the Ramones road manager for over twenty years, couldn't quite believe what he was seeing: "I watched them and it was like I was laughing, you know? Because I was more a serious musician, you know? And watching the Ramones was like a joke, really."

Danish physicist Niels Bohr famously stated that, "When the great innovation appears, it will almost certainly be in a muddled, incomplete, and confusing form. To the discoverer himself it will be only half-understood; to everybody else it will be a mystery. For any speculation which does not at first glance look crazy, there is no hope." When Alan Vega of the band Suicide told Johnny he thought the Ramones were fantastic, that they were just what rock and roll needed, Johnny's first thought was, *This guy's crazy*. He later told Dee Dee that if they could fool Vega, maybe they could fool more people.

After hearing enough people say the same thing, though, and after enough gigging and seeing the audiences at CBGB grow from twenty or so friends and fanatics to three-hundred-and-fifty people a night, the band's confidence grew to the point that they saw their mission as nothing less than messianic. Craig Leon, who produced their first record with Tommy's assistance after the band had signed to Sire Records, remembered:

> Hell, I thought they were going to be massive off their first record and so did they. They were thinking they were in like the Beatles, Herman's Hermits territory, not any kind of underground Stooges/performance-art damage. The Ramones thought they were going to revitalize pop music.

As impossibly naive as this sounds now—the Ramones, the quintessential cult band, aspiring toward mass acceptance—it's one of the key reasons why the band's eponymous 1976 debut remains so novel, so dynamic, so resounding: like all true eccentrics or creators of genuine "outsider" art, the Ramones sincerely believed that they were normal and that what they were doing was what everyone should be doing.

Ramones' most famous song, for example, lead-off track "Blitzkrieg Bop," was written partly because Dee

Dee was an irony-free Bay City Rollers fanatic. Play them one after the other and it's obvious that "Blitzkrieg Bop"'s signature "Hey Ho Let's Go" chant is simply the Ramones' version of the Rollers' "S-A-T-U-R-D-A-Y Night" chant. Of course, as peppy and catchy as, say "Saturday Night" is, because it was intended exclusively to sell in large numbers to homogenous hordes of sub-urban teenage girls, there's not much beyond that pep-piness and catchiness to recommended it. "Blitzkrieg Bop," on the other hand, is informed not only by a belief in bubblegum music's pure pop appeal, but generous dol-lops of raw energy, humour, and danger born of the band members' other delightfully disparate loves/obsessions. Bubblegum tastes good and is fun to chew — until the fla-vour's all gone and you get tired of chewing. "Blitzkrieg Bop" is as resilient as a rock and roll song gets because in 2:12 seconds it's a nice fresh piece of Dubble Bubble dosed with a snort of cocaine, a whiff of laughing gas, and a bracing smack in the face.

Sire Records got thirteen more songs for the prepos-terously paltry $6,200 that the album cost to make (*cf.* the Sex Pistols lone album, the budget of which was well over $100,000 dollars — not bad for impoverished anarchists). "Beat on the Brat" is about exactly what it sounds like, immediately raising the question of just how much these guys were joking around. Beating up obnoxious neighbourhood rich kids with a baseball bat — sure, we've all secretly wanted to do it, but Joey isn't really singing that we *should*, is he? *Is* he? Ditto for "Loudmouth," as pre- a PC-relationship song as there is. "I Don't Want to Go Down to the Basement" feeds off phobias directly inspired by slasher films, while "Chain Saw" is an ear-splitting tribute to a very specific film, *The Texas Chain Saw Massacre*. "I Don't Wanna Walk

Around With You" and "Now I Wanna Sniff Some Glue" perfectly encapsulate yin and yang as they exist in the Ramones' universe. "Today Your Love/Tomorrow the World" uses—gulp—a Nazi metaphor for conquering true love, while in "53rd & 3rd" a male street hustler who feels bad when he doesn't get picked by the assembled johns and then repulsed by himself once he does, decides that the only way he can maintain his dignity is by stabbing his trick to death. Proving that life isn't all aggravation and bewilderment occasionally punctuated by a sniff of airplane glue, there's "I Wanna be Your Boyfriend," a sweet, almost chiming reminder that's there's unrequited love to look forward to as well. And the album's sole cover—an amped-up, sped-up, Ramones-ized version of the early sixties Chris Montez hit "Let's Dance"—serves to remind everyone what the whole thing (the Ramones, the album, existence) is really all about. Fourteen songs in twenty-eight minutes, fifty-three seconds, and if at the end of side two you're as emotionally and intellectually off balance as if you'd been physically and psychologically pummeled, that's all right. That's what art is supposed to do.

After being welcomed as conquering heroes in England, it was back to playing for fifty people in the US, unless the venue was on home turf Manhattan. It didn't help that radio wouldn't have much to do with them either. Sessionman Andy Paley, who worked with the Ramones on the *Rock 'N' Roll High School* movie:

> The Ramones didn't stand a chance. It wasn't so much their image as their sound—as much as I thought they were fun, the radio people didn't. Radio hasn't been very good in America for a long, long time. Originally, in the Fifties and early Sixties, you'd have great regional DJs in different

towns, but it got worse and worse, and then . . . FM radio took over, and it got turned into a . . .corporate thing.

Any successful corporation eschews controversy — why risk offending a potential customer? — and by the time the band began recording their second album, *Ramones Leave Home*, the group had been lumped in with the nascent "punk rock" movement. In mainstream media terms, this meant safety pins stuck through filthy, unemployed people's noses, the kind of people who spit at their favourite performers on stage and who, in general, acted like murderous lunatics. That the media image of the proto-punker was taken primarily from the British scene, where fashion and violence seemed to be some sort of dual statement against an unjust society (or something) and that the Ramones basically considered themselves just a plain old contemporary rock and roll band didn't much matter. Add to the mix four very . . . unique individuals traveling in a small van several hundred miles every day to play before less than a hundred people (if they were lucky), and you've got a recipe for incipient disillusionment, infighting, and mental strain.

Even if the Ramones had been flying first class to sold-out stadiums full of adoring fans there would have been trouble. Here's Chris Frantz, the Talking Heads drummer, whose band opened up for the Ramones in Europe:

The first indication to me that Johnny Ramone was weird was on that first European tour. We flew to Switzerland and we went right to the sound check. After that we went to a little café, and the services promoter ordered us a beautiful *caprese* — a really nice salad, with mozzarella cheese, tomato, and delicious, high quality lettuce. Johnny said, "What's this?! You call this lettuce?!" Johnny was actually upset that the lettuce wasn't iceberg lettuce . . . [Later on] we went to Stonehenge and Johnny stayed in the van. [And insisted that his girlfriend also stay, even though she wanted to join the others.] He'd snarl, "I DON'T WANT TO STOP HERE. IT'S JUST A BUNCH OF ROCKS!"

Mickey Leigh, Joey Ramones' brother, who briefly road-ied for the band before quitting to pursue his own musical career, recalled having to list his occupation on an immi-gration form at the airport:

as a gesture of good luck and omen for the future, I wrote "musician." When Johnny saw it, he freaked. "Whaddaya puttin' that in there for?" he screamed at me. "You're not a musician! You're not a professional!" . . . It was John getting his jollies humiliating someone. What else was new?

Tommy remembered how

[w]e got known as the group who would punch each other out on stage, but there were only a couple of instances where that actually occurred. Mostly John would just give people *very* dirty looks. He perfected that as one of his psychological weapons. It was effective because you knew what was behind it. John always prided himself on his control, but he had a very short temper. You could see it in his eyes. Johnny was *scary*.

Monte Melnick, who travelled with the band for twen-ty-two years, was more succinct: "He was Mr. Negative. He was a very controlling person who radiated fear and anxiety."

Dee Dee wasn't interested in dominating anyone—he just wanted to do the opposite of everything Johnny, the band's self-appointed overseer, demanded. ("We used to call them the Marones because Johnny was such a drill sergeant," Dead Boys' guitarist Cheetah Chrome remembered. "They're not the Marines—they're the Marones.") Melnick: Dee Dee's "first wife Vera Davie said that he was diagnosed as being bipolar. It didn't help that he did drugs constantly. He started doing drugs when he was young, so who knows if it was chemical or not. I'm sure he definitely had a split personality and who knows what that does to your internal chemistry." Vera Davie: "I had no idea what each day would be like and would be cautious to even speak in the morning when he got up. You never knew which Dee Dee you were getting . . . I walked on eggshells every morning until he decided the mood of the day and who would be his victim." Photographer Bob Gruen: "He used to walk around without a shirt on in the middle of the night carrying a baseball bat."

Joey came by his instability naturally—it wasn't enough to be freakishly tall, skinny, and myopic (his childhood nickname was "Geoffrey Giraffe"), he also suffered from obsessive compulsive disorder to a frequently debilitating degree. Melnick: "We had a central meeting place when we'd leave on a van trip, in front of Joey's apartment house on East 9th Street in the East Village. Whatever time I told Joey we had to leave, I'd tell the band an hour later because that's how long it would take him to get ready and touch everything. It was hell getting him in the van." Booking agent John Giddings: "He'd get in and out of the elevator ten times before he'd actually go anywhere. There was a weird moment in Spain where Joey couldn't decide when to cross the road. He got off the curb, got back on the curb, got off the curb and so on, until this car was so bored waiting, it hit him."

Tommy was suffering from plenty of weird moments himself, mostly because he was often stuck inside a van with Johnny, Dee Dee, and Joey. He'd been the one with the original vision to encourage Dee Dee and Johnny to start a band because he thought they were such compelling personalities; to move Joey from behind the drum kit to centre stage because he recognized Joey's potential as both a singer and an arresting, unorthodox front man; who'd been instrumental in helping to transfer the band's live sound and ideas onto tape in the studio—being a touring drummer playing one-nighters across America was never his ambition. Several members of the Ramones' circle remember him relying on valium when they toured and being so consistently anxious his hands shook.

Still, *Ramones Leave Home* was recorded and released a mere six months after the band's debut, mainly because they'd written approximately thirty songs before they even had a recording contract and then decided to record them all in the order they were written. Just like in the song, second verse same as the first: more songs about mental illness ("Gimme Gimme Shock Treatment"); chemical self-abuse ("Carbona Not Glue"); anti-love songs ("Glad to See You Go" and "You're Gonna Kill Girl"); tender love songs ("I Remember You" and "And I Love Her So"); Nazi piss-takes ("Commado"); horror-movie homage ("You Should Never Have Opened That Door"); outsider anthem ("Pinhead"); and another perfect (i.e., fun, fast, and sincerely frivolous) cover song ("California Sun"). Because they had more time and money the second go around, *Ramones Leave Home* sounds more obviously produced than the first album, but only in that the snarl and bite of the songs is more pronounced, the slightly higher production values only accenting the lyrical sleaze and musical sparkle. Tommy co-produced the album with Tony Bongiovi, who couldn't help wondering if it was going to be one "of the biggest things ever done or one of the greatest flops." As with all seminal art, ambivalence wasn't an option.

Then it was back in the van, back on the road, back to sometimes being heroes (future Dead Kennedy's singer Jello Biafra: "[T]he Ramones mowed down everybody in the room. It totally blew me away, in part because I kept turning around and seeing the looks of shock and horror on people's faces, them going, 'No, no! Make them stop!' and I'm going, 'Yes, yes! More, more'"); sometimes being villains (opening for Black Sabbath for example; Arturo Vega, the band's graphic designer and artistic director: "The metal fans were by far the majority of the crowd, so they came ready to kill—and they tried, aiming at the band with cans full of beer. After six songs, the amps and the stage were all covered with garbage. That was scary, but it got worse"). Through it all—the commercial indifference, the sometimes-uncomprehending and often hostile audiences, the strain of living in each other's smelly pockets—the Ramones pushed on, secure in their mission, at least, and fortified by their street-rat resilience. Arturo remembers the band playing "in Manchester, in some school, and Dee Dee must have been doing drugs that day—or maybe he did them right before they went on stage. So Dee Dee's playing and he's getting sick. So he goes to the side of the stage and vomits. And he never stops playing!" Even Johnny, who would fine band members for being late for soundcheck or for drinking before the show, had to have been impressed.

By now, as Joey's brother recounted,

the Ramones didn't socialize with each other anymore. Johnny rarely left his house if they weren't playing. Dee Dee spent more time with Johnny Thunders, or anyone else with dope or pills. Tommy was more than happy to be in the studio . . . [And] Joey still needed a lot of care . . . [His girl-friend] Robin tried to keep him clean and healthy.

None of which stopped them from writing a new batch of songs and recording their third classic LP in a row, 1977's *Rocket to Russia*. Although there were some Ramones firsts—"Here Today, Gone Tomorrow" is downright tender; there are two cover songs this time ("Do You Wanna Dance?" and "Surfin' Bird," both of which are so respectively infectiously joyful and goofy that they sound as if they could have been written for the band); there's even a (short) guitar solo—*Rocket to Russia* is almost a duplicate of the first two albums, which makes its aesthetic success more than a little surprising. More songs about mental illness, personal dysfunction, and rock and roll as liberation? How many times can these guys go to the well and come up with a brimming bucketful? At least once more, anyway. And all because the songs were great, the production polished but punchy, and Joey never sang better. "Teenage Lobotomy" would be terrifying if it weren't hilarious; ditto for "We're a Happy Family," the one where everybody in the clan is on Thorazine and daddy secretly likes men; "Sheena is a Punk Rocker" is feminism for everyone; and "Rockaway Beach" is pure Ramones, celebrating something lousy until it becomes something sacred (if only in your mind). Live, the Ramones played so loud and fast it was almost impossible for Joey to shout out the words quickly enough; on record, though (at least on the first five albums), you heard what an increasingly effective instrument his voice had become, capable of adolescent yearning, ironic hilarity, and pissed-off nihilism from one song to the next.

Although "Sheena" garnered the band their first serious airplay (getting as high as number thirty-six in the UK,

where the Ramones were initially a much bigger deal—
the 1979 live album *It's Alive* was recorded in Britain and,
for many years, released there only), the band still wasn't
selling enough records to lift them out of the exhausting
club circuit. It was at this time that Tommy told the others
he was quitting the band, but would stay on to help write
songs and produce the albums. First they tried to talk him
out of it; later on they dismissed him as not being a "real
Ramone," someone who couldn't hack life on the road. All
of the original Ramones died relatively young, but Tommy
outlasted the other three by many years, so draw your own
conclusions. In the end, when Marc Bell, late of Richard
Hell's the Voidoids, became Marky Ramone, the band definitely got a "real" Ramone. Arturo:

> Marky is the character that goes out in the backyard, plays,
> gets itself all muddy and dirty, comes into the living room
> and shakes itself out and gets everybody in the family and
> the furniture dirty. You wanna kill him but you don't—he's
> your pet, that's what pets do.

Tommy could teach Marky, already a fine musician, his
signature Ramones drum style, but he couldn't instruct
him in how to be a human buffer zone between feuding
bandmates or how to be a calming presence in the van or
in the hotel or sometimes even on stage.

Road to Ruin, the initial album recorded with Marky
behind the drums, was the first indication that the band
was in trouble artistically. Whereas the first three albums
were released within a sixteen-month period, *Road to Ruin*
didn't appear until nine months after *Rocket to Russia* hit
the shops. The Ramones weren't the kind of band that
benefited from a long gestation period and a protracted
recording schedule. Instinct eschews prudence.

Ironically, it wasn't the band's attempt to make a more commercial record that was *Road to Ruin's* major flaw. Engineer Ed Stasium admitted that "We [the band] came to a decision that Tommy and I would try different bass and guitar parts—keep what the Ramones were, but appeal to a broader audience," and for the most part the tinkering was creatively rewarding. The introduction of acoustic guitars into the band's sound works surprisingly well, particularly on the album's first single, "Don't Come Close." For some reason, both Legs McNeil in his notes to the expanded CD reissue of *Road to Ruin* and Everett True in his normally reliable and highly informative biography of the band, *Hey Ho Let's Go*, dismiss "Don't Come Close" as a "country and western tune," a bizarre categorization. The Ramones never disguised their love of bubblegum and other atypical "punk rock" influences, and "Don't Come Close" is an admirably catchy power-pop confection that wouldn't have sounded out of place on an early Todd Rundgren album. Maybe Johnny reportedly hated it so much because there was no way he could have played the cascading acoustic guitar runs that anchor the song. On the album's sole cover, a version of the Searchers' 1964 hit "Needles and Pins," and on the unabashedly vulnerable ballad "Questioningly," Joey's voice—and not Johnny's guitar—is the lead instrument, variations of intonation subtly enriching the band's trademark sound. The album's one undisputable classic is the chugging "I Wanna be Sedated," another tale of mental illness made palatable by the usual laugh-aloud lyrics and winning melody, but also by an uncharacteristically bouncy rhythm, happy happy hand claps, and some refreshing light/shade guitar interplay.

And that's about it. For the first time on a Ramones record, the majority of the songs sounded . . . stale. Trying to sound primitive never sounds authentically primitive.

No matter how much Tommy and Stasium augmented the group's playing, the riffs and melodies were becoming predictable, the lyrics barely concealed rewrites of previous songs. If titles like "I Just Want to Have Something to Do," "I Don't Want You," "I'm Against It," "Go Mental," and "Bad Brain" sound disappointingly familiar, that's because they are. You can—as the Ramones did—reenergize rock and roll and even create an entirely new subgenre, but popular music is still all about the songs, and *Road to Ruin* simply doesn't have nearly enough good ones. The last tune on the album is "It's a Long Way Back." The title doesn't refer to the band's increasing loss of inspiration and inability to recapture their initial primality—it's just one more number about Dee Dee and Germany—but it might as well have.

Because, once more, an album of theirs didn't sell—an album that was *constructed* to sell—the band became even more fixated on commercial success. Which is why they agreed to appear and perform in schlock-auteur Roger Corman's *Rock 'N' Roll High School*. Why the Ramones thought appearing in a cheesy B-film would give them mainstream credibility is hard to comprehend. But desperate people do desperate things. The pay for their participation in the movie was so poor that they had to play gigs around Los Angeles on off-days to remain solvent. Performing regularly in LA clubs did have one significant impact on the band's career: bowing to record company pressure to let an experienced producer oversee their next album in a bid for commercial pay dirt, they agreed, after getting to know him better, to Sire's desire to have Phil Spector produce what became *End of the Century*. Spector had been a fan of theirs for a couple of years. ("Phil just loved their music," veteran Spector session-man David Kessel recalled. "It was like, 'God, you mean there's a rock-and-roll band around?' The simplicity of the chords; the lack of improvisation. He thought that it was right back to Buddy Holly.") The album's title was apt. *End of the Century* is the Ramones' last essential record, it was the last meaningful work Spector ever did, and what little genuine band dynamic was left evaporated when, around this same time, Joey's girlfriend left him for Johnny.

In 1979 Phil Spector was, yes, still a legend in the recording industry, but he was living on not just past royalties but past successes, was an increasingly forgotten, bitter little man with a toupee on his head, lifts in his shoes, and an unearned sense of artistic entitlement. His behaviour during the recording of the album is much more interesting than the actual work he did on it. Vera Davie:

> Phil never came to greet us at the entrance [of his baronial house]. Instead, as we entered the main living quarters, we saw and were greeted by Grandpa Munster himself, Al Lewis, sitting in a big chair with a high back ... Lewis was very friendly, but it was obvious he had been sitting there for quite a while, because he was pretty much intoxicated by the time we arrived. We waited with Lewis for at least an hour before Phil made his grand entrance and bestowed us with his presence. Soon after we were led into his private recording studio where he blasted all of his hits for us over and over again ... After listening attentively to Phil's albums, he decided we should all watch his new favorite movie, *Magic*, starring Anthony Hopkins. We watched as Phil rewound his favorite parts and showed the movie again and again, just like he did with his songs. By this time it was six o'clock in the morning, and Dee and I were exhausted. Johnny had somehow managed to leave around midnight, but Dee and I had to beg and plead with Phil to

let us go home . . . We couldn't just leave and walk out the door because we had to be electronically buzzed out; it was up to Phil to let us leave.

It's not surprising that Johnny didn't wait for Spector's permission to go home—Johnny gave orders, he didn't take them—just as it wasn't surprising that he chafed under Spector's dictatorial production technique. Stasium:

> The sessions were grueling, especially for Johnny, who hated Phil. Joey loved Phil [and vice versa]. We were there for hours and Johnny got fed up doing take after take after take. I have a little diary and he played "This Ain't Havana" back like 353 times. Over and over at absurd volumes. Of course, we'd start at 10 p.m. for these sessions, which was ridiculous. The final blow was the infamous "Rock 'N' Roll High School" intro. Johnny made it sound like eight hours we were there, but it was probably more like two hours. But it was a helluva long time playing one chord.

After Johnny threatened to quit the sessions and Spector promised to tone things down a bit (which really meant drinking less in the studio), the album was completed and the mixes were given the legendary Spector production treatment and the result was . . . okay. (And ended up selling just okay as well; it was certainly the band's best-selling album, but nothing like the top-ten monster they thought they'd created. At $200,000, it was by far the costliest Ramones LP to make.) It would have helped if it hadn't contained such formulaic fluff as "Let's Go" and "All the Way" and the embarrassingly self-referential "The Return of Jackie and Judy." Still, opening track "Do You Remember Rock 'N' Roll Radio?" was a rousing success, the characteristic Spector production touches (organ, saxophones, a booming drum sound) expertly complementing the Ramones' raging tribute to the redemptive power of rock and roll. "Rock 'N' Roll High School" was an ideal tune for Spector to work on — beefed up, Doo-Wop-influenced fifties rock and roll — that's as furiously fun as it is enjoyably idiotic. Spector was used to working with singers, not bands, and part of Johnny's resentment toward the producer was undoubtedly born of jealousy over the disproportionate amount of attention Joey received in the studio (Spector had originally wanted to record a Joey solo album). Whatever discord this created within the band, however, was justified by the wonderful vocal performances Spector got out of the Ramones' singer. "I Can't Make it on Time" is Joey at his power-pop belting best, the string-drenched cover of "Baby I Love You" isn't really a Ramones song (none of them play on it), but Joey, the rock-history worshipper, is plainly glorying in being a vocal stylist for once *à la* one of his heroes, Ronnie Spector, and "Danny Says" is simply a lovely love song.

"Danny Says" is about Linda Danielle, who was Joey's girlfriend at the time it was recorded, and by the time *End of the Century* was completed Joey wasn't the only one in love with her. People fall in love with people they shouldn't fall in love with every day, so attempting to discern who was right and who was wrong in matters of the omnipotent, unreasonable heart is pointless. The bottom line is that Johnny and Linda fell in love with each other, Joey felt doubly betrayed, and the two band members were never friends again. It probably didn't help that neither Johnny nor Linda ever talked to Joey about it. Joey's brother Mickey:

Too many people around the Ramones would become

noticeably quiet if Joey suddenly appeared. Were people laughing at him? Some probably were. That would have been consistent with Johnny and the Ramones' philosophy: no sympathy, no apologies, and no display of sentiment or concern. For Johnny, any form of empathy was for hippies and wimps.

In fact, except for absolutely unavoidable Yes's and No's, Joey and Johnny didn't speak to each other for the next sixteen years, including in the increasingly claustrophobic van (roadie George Tabb: "Monte [Melnick] was a translator between Johnny and Joey, which was kinda funny because they were next to each other. They would literally talk through him"). They forced themselves into that van for sixteen more years because, as Melnick pointed out, "The friendship died after the Linda incident, yet they carried on for the sake of the band like a couple staying together for the children."

Except that sometimes a clean break is better for all concerned. To Johnny's credit, he later admitted that if he'd been able to financially afford it, he would have retired his guitar after *End of the Century*, by which time he knew that the band was never going to have any substantial impact on mainstream culture and that they'd clearly peaked creatively (and that what were once close comrades were now barely tolerated workmates). For nine more decreasingly relevant studio albums released over the next decade and a half, however, Joey kept the faith, hoping, each time out, for the elusive hit that would elevate them to the commercial heights achieved by some of their one-time opening acts such as Blondie and the Talking Heads. (Not because of the money, but because he thought the Ramones were the greatest rock and roll band in the world and justifiably wanted the greatest number of people to know it. It's easy to retrospectively counsel the dead on how they should have acted tranquilly and untroubled while alive, but the idea of hearing "Blitzkrieg Bop" routinely played at hockey games was unfathomable when the band was still around, and very few real artists get to live as legends, confident in their lasting creative worth.)

Live, the Ramones never let their fans down, not even when Dee Dee quit the band in 1988 because he was tired of being a middle-aged juvenile delinquent, and they hired a Dee Dee clone to yell "1-2-3-4!" before every song. But between Johnny's emotional resignation, Joey's continuing disappointment, and Dee Dee's desertion, the individual Ramones grew to be not very happy people. And these were never particularly well-adjusted individuals to begin with.

By the time Joey died of lymphoma in 2001—abetted by an OCD-related broken hip, the treatment for which fatally impaired his cancer fight—the only Ramone to visit him in the hospital was Marky, despite the fact they'd been feuding on the Howard Stern show not long before. When Dee Dee died a little more than year later of a sadly inevitable heroin overdose, he hadn't been an official Ramone for over a decade (even if he'd never managed to escape being Dee Dee Ramone). Typically, Johnny outlasted the other two, but only by a few years, the colon cancer that claimed the life of the non-smoking, virtually non-drinking guitar player probably caused as much by his searing, never-abated anger and aggression as it was by genetics. We tend to die the way we live.

Although all rational people can agree that such an institution should not exist, when the Ramones were inducted into the Rock and Roll Hall of Fame in 2002, it was worthwhile if only for this: Dee Dee wouldn't sit with Johnny; Johnny wouldn't sit with the deceased

Joey's brother and sister; Marky told Joey's brother about a rumour going around that Johnny wanted the rest of the band to turn their backs on him and his mother when they came up to accept Joey's award. True or not, it didn't matter—because of mismanagement on the part of the presenters, Joey's trophy got left behind on stage. When someone finally handed his mother the award, she was understandably, if belatedly, pleased—until she discovered it had Dee Dee's name on it. Elsewhere in the ballroom, Dee Dee realized he had Johnny's award, while Johnny learned he had Joey's. Ramones whether they wanted to be or not. Forever.

SISTER ROSETTA THARPE

Music alone with sudden charms can bind
The wand'ring sense, and calm the troubled mind
— William Congreve

Sometimes it's not so much what someone has done as much as how they did it. A shimmering discography isn't the only way to innovate and inspire. Though the best of the pioneering rock and roll of Elvis Presley and Little Richard and Jerry Lee Lewis isn't strictly gospel music, without bump-and-grind gospel singer Sister Rosetta Tharpe, rock and roll as we know it likely wouldn't sound the way it does or even have been born when it was. Gospel music is theodicy in song, the world made better, or made to go away, or made into another, kinder, happier, more-just place where, winged or not, we come to know for certain all of the things we ordinarily only merely—flimsily—believe. By adding the beat of boogie-woogie, the relentless rhythm of the blues, the irresistible energy of any number of other musical sources, Rosetta was only adding to the theological argument. Ask any empiricist or soul singer (any singer, that is, who sings with soul): if you want to sell the song, the listener can't just understand it—they need to *feel* it. And feminist role models don't come much better than an African-American woman in early twentieth-century America standing alone in the spotlight while squeezing incendiary sounds from her blisteringly loud electric guitar. You don't have to believe in God to shout Hallelujah.

Born in Cotton Plant, Arkansas—guess what her parents did for a living?—in 1915, Rosetta Nubin moved to Chicago when she was six years old so that her mother, Katie (who left her husband behind), could better pursue her dream of being an evangelist for the Church of God in Christ (COGIC), a relatively new Pentecostal denomination. There also wasn't any cotton to pick in Chicago, as good a reason to leave town as any. Katie supported herself and her daughter by hiring herself out as domestic help until she felt confident she could provide for her and her daughter preaching full-time. COGIC emphasized a strict moral code (no alcohol, dancing, or tobacco; no make-up or jewelry for women) as well as the sacredness of speaking in tongues, an example of direct human interaction with God. Unlike most other Christian churches, COGIC allowed for the use of non-traditional church instruments when singing God's praises (guitars, trumpets, and even drums and tambourines) and encouraged its members to shout, stomp, and clap along to the deeply rhythmic music made up from fragments of hymns, slave spirituals, work songs, and even elements of the blues that seeped in off Chicago's streets. Keeping the beat and rolling with the rhythm might not have been as clear an indication of God's presence as speaking in tongues, but it was better than being a humming Presbyterian sitting on his hands.

Already a competent guitar player by the age of six, Rosetta began accompanying her mother while she preached, Katie herself distinguished on mandolin and piano. The novelty of a child peering over an adult-sized guitar might have been what initially got people's attention—that, and the fact it was a girl and not, as was the norm, a boy, playing—but it was the music she made with that guitar and her voice that kept their interest. Childhood friend Musette Hubbard:

> It was just her singing and her picking that guitar that just drew. You just got attached to it. She could really hit that, now. You can sing, and it's a beautiful voice and everything, but if you sing with an *understanding* and the feeling of what you're singing it's altogether different. And that is what she did, more like to me. Even though she was young. It was a gift. Yes.

Although Rosetta's performances were limited to Sunday services because COGIC members considered themselves "sanctified"—set and saw themselves apart from not only non-Christians, but from other, less worldly-exclusionary denominations—word began to spread of the little girl with the big guitar and the even bigger voice to the degree that non-Pentecostals began to attend the Fortieth-Street church just to hear her perform.

By age twelve Rosetta had left school to work with her mother saving souls full-time, eventually playing not just Chicago churches but the "gospel circuit" of revivals, tent meetings, and out-of-town churches. Aside from the satisfaction of doing the Lord's will and being able to pay one's way in the world being self-employed at something one enjoyed doing, playing noisy revival meetings had aesthetic implications for Rosetta's art as well. All genuine artistic innovation is born out of necessity, not clever ostentation, and the distinctive way Rosetta picked individual notes on her guitar to accent certain lines of lyrics—as opposed to strumming along to all of the words—was initially done only so as to make herself heard over the frenzied attendees. (Coincidentally, honky-tonk was born out of the same sort of conundrum. How could a country-and-western band manage to make themselves heard in a tavern full of drunken rowdies? By playing electric guitars and by doing more picking than strumming.) Eventually, the stinging licks Rosetta coaxed out of her guitar infused her performances with an electric bite not heard in any other gospel performer and became one of her performing trademarks.

Nineteen-year-old Rosetta Nubin became Rosetta Tharpe when she married a nomadic COGIC preacher named Thomas J. Tharpe. Doubly sanctified as a COGIC member *and* a minister, he was, nonetheless, a bit of a scumbag. Spousal beatings, a girlfriend on the side, and a marital inclination that turned out to have less to do with romantic love than it did a smart career move (Rosetta was an up-and-comer in the gospel world; Thomas an unknown itinerant preacher) were the sheltered Rosetta's first lessons in how talking the righteous talk isn't the same as walking the righteous walk. Nor would it be her last.

But the Lord not only taketh, He also giveth—at least it seems that way on the more-good-than-bad days—and working hard touring the country as a preaching/performing tandem with her husband allowed Rosetta to further develop her singular style while bringing her even greater exposure. So much so, that it wasn't long before record companies and concert promoters came calling. And while many people within her Miami church (where she and her husband had relocated—you might as well be warm while doing God's will) were astonished and aghast when Rosetta decided to embark upon a secular career, it made sense spiritually, aesthetically, and in purely worldly terms.

Singing to the converted the majority of the time means you're not spreading the Word to those who most need to hear it (like people in New York nightclubs). "Sanctified" can turn into "smug" if taken to hermetic extremes.

Artistically speaking, by age twenty-three Rosetta had simply outgrown the church, even a musically adventurous one like the Pentecostals. "She would sing a line, and she would put a little *hmmmm* into the end of it," recalled friend Camille Roberts, "and it just look like you could just feast off that little *hmmmm*. I think that's why she moved out into the world, because she couldn't [help but] put a little oompf into the song." Once you've got the *oompf* in you, it's near impossible to pluck it out. Leaving the church also meant leaving behind her wife-beating, two-timing, parasitic husband (there's no room in the Cotton Club for preachers unless they're willing to pay to see the floor show). And no one thinks more about money than those who've never had it—and why shouldn't Rosetta and her mother have a clean house to live in and nice clothes to wear and a new car to drive? If you're black and poor and a single woman living with your mother, the Kingdom of Heaven includes the American Dream.

Rosetta made an immediate impression. Between her resonating, steel-bodied National guitar and her commanding voice, New York club patrons and newspaper reporters were captivated, even if they weren't quite sure what it was they were so enthralled with. Most were familiar with hymn singing, but not hymns that *swung*; a hot, loud guitar player wasn't uncommon, but a *woman* doing the picking was. The record-buying public had much the same reaction. Rosetta's first recordings for the Decca label—whose only other excursion into the gospel field were tracks by singer Mahalia Jackson, a lovely voiced, if much more traditional performer—featuring just her and her guitar, just like back on the gospel-circuit, are among her best. "Rock Me," for instance, is nimble picking and bluesy intonation, a sexy song of worship (God is love; love is God). Enough people were intrigued by the sound of this Pentecostal Pop to buy her first few records in sufficient quantities to warrant further sessions. The records also helped land her a spot on the From Spirituals to Swing 1938 Christmas concert organized by John Hammond at Carnegie Hall. On her biggest stage yet Rosetta was the unexpected star, even among choice company like Count Basie, who remembered, "She sang some gospel songs that brought the house down. She sang down-home church numbers and had those old cool New Yorkers almost shouting in the aisles." A spoonful of rhythm-and-swing makes the blessed medicine go down.

In spite of her growing success, however, wherever she played Rosetta would inevitably be attacked in the press by religious conservatives for, at best, demeaning, and, at worst, desecrating, her religion. (She also suffered the passive censure of her own mother, who, according to friend Roxie Moore, while certainly enjoying the material fruits of her daughter's worldly labours, "would never say [that she was proud of her.] She followed her, she would go where Rosetta went if it was local and if she could go she would go, and be backstage with me. She would sit there and wait until Rosetta was finished performing.") Regardless, Rosetta kept recording and performing (including extended periods with Cab Calloway's travelling show and a shorter stretch opposite Louis Armstrong at the Cotton Club). Ironically, to modern ears, it isn't the all-out secular songs that she came to record (like the strutting "I Want a Tall Skinny Papa") that offend, but the religious material that she recorded under the influence of bandleader Lucky Millinder, big-band arrangements of songs like "Rock Me" losing in lean, soulful intensity what they gained in instrumentally fattened accessibility. "There is no such thing as a moral or immoral book," maintained Oscar Wilde. "Books are either well-written or badly written. That is all."

Although she maintained her God-given right to sing non-religious songs, Rosetta didn't abandon the gospel market; in fact, it was in 1944 that she began billing herself as "Sister Rosetta Tharpe." Not that labels like "gospel" and "secular" really matter when dealing with an artist of Rosetta's depth and passion: her secular songs were informed by her gospel roots, while the gospel material was infused with good-time rhythms and earthy emotions. In fact, the hardest-hitting songs she ever gathered together were recorded for the 1944 album *Gospel Hymns*, which included "Strange Things Happening Every Day." The entire album is instrumentally scaled back from the Millinder sessions — Rosetta's guitar and voice at the forefront, but with plenty of pounding piano courtesy of Sammy Price — but "Strange Things Happening Every Day" benefits, in particular, from the pared-down approach. It's as good a place as any to date, if not quite the birth of rock and roll, then at least its cacophonous conception. Jerry Lee Lewis (who played the song, among others, at his audition for Sun Records) certainly thought so: "I said, 'Say, man, there's a woman that can sing some rock and roll.' I mean, she's singing religious music, but she is singing rock and roll. She's . . . shakin', man . . . She jumps it. She's hitting that guitar, playing that guitar and she is *singing*. I said, 'Whoooo.' Sister Rosetta Tharpe."

Someone else at the rock-and-roll vanguard, Little Richard, was also a huge Sister Rosetta fan ("[M]y favorite singer, Sister Rosetta Tharpe"). But not only did she inspire the teenage Richard Penniman with her music, she also provided an act of kindness not common among entertainers and artists who are usually — if necessarily — egoistically incapable, or unwilling, to help those on the way up (for fear of being passed on the way down). Richard:

One day when Sister Rosetta was coming to play the [Macon, Georgia] auditorium [where Richard had a part-time job selling refreshments as a teenager] I hung around the theatre while they were unloading the cars and setting up the equipment. When I saw her come in I started singing one of her songs. She had a hit record out at that time on Decca called "Strange Things Happening Every Day" . . . She came over and talked to me. She asked me if I wanted to come up on stage that night and sing a song with her. During the show, in front of everybody, she invited me up to sing. Everybody applauded and cheered and it was the best thing that had ever happened to me. Sister Rosetta gave me a handful of money after the show, about thirty-five or forty dollars, and I'd never had so much money in my life before.

Strange things happening every day, indeed.

And kept on happening. Just before the release of *Gospel Hymns*, Rosetta married for the second time, and this one was even less successful than the last. Not just because it was over in less than three years; if Thomas Tharpe used Rosetta's celebrity status to boost his own fame and fortune as a preacher, Foch Allen wasn't even that ambitious, being content to simply spend his wife's money when, that is, he wasn't complaining that there wasn't enough of it. By now Rosetta had begun performing and recording with a younger gospel singer named Marie Knight, and although the music the two of them made together, such as the jaunty "Didn't it Rain," is top-shelf if slightly less trailblazing than some of Rosetta's solo material (it's still a tasty amalgam of gospel and rhythm and blues), it might well have been Marie's friendship that was most important to Rosetta, who wasn't yet thirty but already zero-for-two in the matrimonial department. When Rosetta eventually bought a house — her first — in a middle-class African-American suburb near Richmond, Virginia, Marie joined Rosetta and her mother living there. It was around this time that rumours began to circulate in the close-knit gospel world that Rosetta and Marie were more than just colleagues and friends. Marie, who outlived Rosetta by decades, claimed that that was just what they were—ugly rumours—although there were others who were happy to offer anecdotal evidence to the contrary. Whatever the truth, openly bisexual gospel singers were professionally unfeasible in mid-twentieth century America. Lord knows, still are.

Anyway, there was a bigger threat to Rosetta's career than sexual innuendo: Mahalia Jackson. Whatever goes down easiest will always be what most people prefer, and Jackson's music (traditional gospel) and image (e.g., steadfastly refusing to play non-church engagements) were silkier and safer than Rosetta's. As Rosetta's popularity began to taper off in the early fifties, Decca did what any corporation would have done if the competition pulled ahead: forced her to copy Jackson's lusher arrangements and less controversially rhythmic material. After Marie's two young children died in a fire, it wasn't long before she left Rosetta and attempted (with middling results) to embark upon a solo career. As she had always done, though, Rosetta kept moving, recruiting a local Virginia vocal group called the Twilights to accompany her on tour. Decca may have called the shots in the studio, but on the road it was all Rosetta's show, so even if an increasingly large number of gospel fans preferred their daily dose of divine musical inspiration in the form of warm milk instead of fortified wine, Rosetta continued to sock it to them in their bodies because that's where the soul resides.

Rosetta kept moving on the love front as well, marrying Russell Morrison in 1951. And if, by all accounts, Morrison was just another in a distressingly long line of user-husbands, Rosetta never gave up on the idea of having a partner to share with and to find support in and to love—and be loved by—unconditionally. She had faith. Might not have had much reason to and it might not have ever paid off practically, but she continued to have faith that such a love existed until the day she died. (She also continued to be a clever business woman, turning her wedding into a 20,000 person spectacle at Griffith Stadium in Washington, complete with an after-service gospel show and souvenir stands full of reasonably priced mementos that did very good business, thank you very much. To many, of course, this only confirmed their contempt for Rosetta's worldly ways—her marriage as unseemly as her mongrel music.)

To be fair, there *was* something uncomfortably tacky in the way Rosetta took so readily to the worst of middle-class comforts like the big lawn, the three-car garage, wall-to-wall shag carpeting, and gaudy fox furs. When she toured Britain in the mid-sixties as part of the American Folk, Blues, and Gospel Caravan along with out-and-out bluesmen like Muddy Waters and "Blind" Gary Davis, an unpleasant whiff of *nouveau riche* condescension was in evidence. Tour manager Joe Boyd:

> The first morning in the hotel, Sister Rosetta and her manager/ husband—she had a fur coat and he had a camel hair—she found herself sitting across the table from Reverend Gary. I thought, "Well these two will get along because they're from this deep south gospel tradition." Gary, he orders two friend eggs and he kind of feels the plate—he's blind—picks up one of the friend eggs and has yolk spilling down his front and drops it in his mouth. Sister Rosseta went, "Puhlease!" She said, "I don't ever want to sit at the same table as that man again."

Another boy from the country, bluegrass master Lester Flatt, wrote a song that it's unfortunate Rosetta likely never heard: "Don't Get Above Your Raising."

Besides cultivating, through dedicated touring, an entirely new audience in Britain and Europe, where she was as much a revelation of electrified spiritual jingle-jangling as she had been in America three decades before, the remainder of Rosetta's life was filled with well-meaning but artistically mediocre musical experiments (a duet with country star Red Foley; a brief reunion with Marie; even some outright R&B) and continued personal strife (her house was repossessed because of lapsed mortgage payments and she and her wastrel husband were forced to move into a hotel—although, in typical style, she eventually made enough money to buy another home; her omnipresent mother died; she developed diabetes that she was too busy touring to treat properly, leading to the eventual amputation of one of her legs).

But, again characteristic of Rosetta, even with only one leg she was soon back on the road, now performing most of her shows while sitting down, but, when the spirit moved her sufficiently, hopping around on one foot while continuing to blast away on her guitar. She died of a stroke on October 9, 1973, the day before she was supposed to go into the studio to record an album, her first in four years, for the Savoy label. Her death was as difficult as her life. Disc jockey Walter Stewart:

> When I saw Rosetta lying in that hospital rolling about there in her coma, right there in a hospital ward, one of our *greatest* stars, leaving the world like that . . . all I could think of was that old spiritual line . . . 'I want to die easy when I die.' God knows Rosetta didn't.

Although obviously not in the best of health, Rosetta had been excited about her upcoming session date. There were plans for her to record a song called "I've Got a Secret Between Me and My Lord." It was gospel, all right; just like it was also a twelve-bar blues.

TOWNES VAN ZANDT

Thus I live in the world rather as a spectator of mankind than as one of the species.

—Joseph Addison

The foolish things we do even when we believe we're being wise. Knowing that I was all about what was then—the mid-nineties—going by the name "alt-country," a graduate-school friend (and native Texan) told me that I should come with him to an Austin club the following week when Townes Van Zandt would be playing.

"Who?" I said.

"Townes Van Zandt. He's great. You'll really like him."

"What kind of music does he play?"

My friend thought about this for a moment. "It's hard to say. It's just him and a guitar. He's a great songwriter."

A folksinger, I thought. A strummer. A wimpy, simpering folksinger.

"I don't know," I said. "Things are pretty tight time-wise right now. I should probably get caught up on a bunch of stuff." Besides, it wasn't as if I was actually going to be missing out on something by not going.

I did miss out, obviously—I wouldn't be writing this essay if I hadn't—but I didn't, too. I didn't get to see in person a songwriter better than Bob Dylan and a performer as potentially mesmerizing as Hank Williams, but I also didn't have to witness (as my friend afterward told me he did) not just a botched performance brought on by too much alcohol, but an act of intentional self-abasement so painful to witness that many in the audience had no option but to leave before show's end. Shakespeare wrote, "For sweetest things turn sourest by their deeds:/Lilies that fester smell far worse than weeds," and if Shakespeare said it, you know it has to be true.

Townes Van Zandt was a beautiful human being from the year 1968, the year of his first album, until 1978, the year of his last really good one. He was like everybody—had advantages like being born rich, and disadvantages like being born rich and suffering from depression and undergoing electroshock therapy that left him with virtually no memory of the first ten years of his life—but when he played his guitar and sang his songs he was beautiful, he was perfect. The music he made came from what Texas does best, glopping together all of the good stuff from folk and country and blues and rock and roll and with a generous peppery dash of good old old America weirdness. I said once in a novel I wrote that when so-and-so sang, he made a broken heart seem like an attractive option. I say it again now, about Townes.

But he hurt himself. With booze, mostly, although it's not just what you put inside yourself that can wound you. And for someone who believed that a good song was rarer and more important than anything else in the world, the worst part was that he ended up hurting his music, went from being a deft finger-picker with hands like delicate spiders to a lackluster plunker, and his voice, which was once fragile but forceful, became whispery and croaky weak. I know that the songs he wrote and the shows he played during those ten teeming years are better and will last longer than anything I'll ever do, and what right have I got to flick pebbles at the sun, but it's sad to watch beautiful things turn ugly, is all, it's just really sad.

There was nothing sad about the arrival of John Townes Van Zandt on March 7, 1944, the second child of Dorothy Townes and Harris Williams Van Zandt. You can't get much more Lone Star than the Van Zandts' pedigree: Townes' great-great-grandfather served in the congress of the Republic of Texas before its annexation by the United States, and Van Zandt County was named in his honour; the main building of the University of Texas at Austin School of Law is named after Townes' great-grandfather, the school's first dean of law; Townes' father's father was a prominent Houston lawyer with ties to the oil industry; his own father followed in the family tradition and was a successful enough corporate lawyer for Pure Oil to eventually be appointed the company's vice president. Even when Townes finally broke away from his family and the upstanding kind of existence they'd always proudly led, he was still an upper middle-class Texan who always addressed older men and women as *Sir* and *Ma'am* and who never forgot *noblesse oblige*, even when, as was frequently the case, he could have used as much assistance as those he invariably helped.

Townes isn't the only musician in this book whose life was changed on September 9, 1956, when Elvis Presley performed "Don't Be Cruel" on *The Ed Sullivan Show*. Country music had come first, mournful magic on the family car radio, but even Hank Williams couldn't compete with the energy and exhilaration and sexual excitement of early Elvis. Soon, a first guitar for Christmas, just like he

asked for, and further fascination with other first-generation rockers like Jerry Lee Lewis, The Everly Brothers,
and Ricky Nelson (and honourary rocker Johnny Cash).
The blues came next—Lightnin' Hopkins and Mance
Lipscomb and Mississippi John Hurt—guitar stylists as
much as distinctive vocalists and songwriters.

Few were immune to the folk revival of the early sixties,
and Townes wasn't one of them, scrupulous story-telling
added to his developing musical DNA (we're born with
our bodies; our souls we create). A good student when
he was interested in the subject, Townes was enough of a
reader (Robert Frost and Dylan Thomas being especially
influential, the former for his deceptively simple disquisitions on life and death, the latter because he used words
like a musician uses notes) that when Bob Dylan brought
it all back home, Townes gratefully stepped inside and
stayed, sense joining sound as the new songwriting standard, popular music come of age.

Townes came of age, too—an average high-school student and okay athlete whose parents moved a lot and who
ended up graduating from Shattuck Military Academy,
twenty-two in a class of seventy-six, with an uncredited
major in guitar playing and a minor in glue sniffing—and
enrolled as a freshman at the University of Colorado, where
his older sister had just matriculated. Because Townes'
father had been a member of the Sigma Nu fraternity back
in Texas, Townes was automatically a member of Sigma Nu
too, although, as college friend Bob Myrick remembered,
Townes wasn't ideal fraternity material:

> We had been drinkin' all afternoon and were drunker than
> skunks until we finally ran out of booze. They were having a
> formal dance next door at the Sigma Nu house. They always
> gave Townes shit for being their worst pledge. They didn't

hate him, but they didn't think he was a very good pledge. And he wasn't. Townes *never* wore his pledge pin. So we strolled over to the Sigma Nu house to say hi to everybody and hit the punch bowl. Townes didn't even have his shirt on. No shoes, no socks, just a pair of jeans. They started givin' him plenty of shit right away. So he pulled his pledge pin out of his pocket and damn if he didn't pin it right through his skin. There was this little dribble of blood runnin' down his chest. He said, "Okay, look you guys, I'm wearin' it." Then he walked over to the punch bowl and started drinkin'. Those goddamn actives were *horrified*.

Despite spending the majority of his time alone drinking cheap wine and listening obsessively to Lightnin' Hopkins and Hank Williams and Bob Dylan albums and practicing the guitar for entire days, to anyone who asked (including himself), Townes was a pre-law student. We are what we do, though, not what we say. And Townes was doing exactly what he was supposed to be doing — studying music as hard as the most dedicated scholar on campus — even if he didn't know he was doing it.

After Townes and a friend unsuccessfully forged a letter from his parents granting their son permission to withdraw from university, Mr. and Mrs. Van Zandt paid a visit to said son and decided — because Van Zandts simply didn't do things like lie to the dean of the university and have empty wine bottles lying all over their bedroom floor — that the best thing for him was to check into the University of Texas Medical Branch Hospital. There, he was diagnosed as manic depressive and administered three months of electric shock- and insulin-therapy. Although he had to be re-introduced to his fiancée and mother upon his release (and claimed, afterward, he didn't remember much of the first decade of this life, although he heard from others that it was real nice), he eventually got married, moved back to Texas, enrolled at the University of Houston, and tried his best to be normal. Then Townes discovered the Jester Lounge and normal didn't stand a chance.

If it was a good night—if you were opening up for a well-known performer, say, on his way out of town after playing somewhere else larger and more lucrative first—maybe you made ten bucks; other nights, five; others, a passed hat nearly as empty upon its return as when it was turned upside down and sent around the room. But a chance to try out songs you actually wrote on an actual audience and to learn what it takes to force a crowd to shut up and really listen and an opportunity to play on the same small stage on the same night as people who'd previously been just pictures on record album covers and who'd made you want to be up there in the first place, people like Mickey Newbury and Lightnin' Hopkins and Mance Lipscomb. The Jester was also where Townes met fellow songwriting neophyte Guy Clark, who would become a lifelong best friend, as well as Jerry Jeff Walker, who helped point the way toward to where Townes was travelling all along anyway. Walker:

> None of us were doing full sets of original material yet. We were still gaining confidence in our own songs. Townes had written a couple things, but he still had one foot in the academic world. He said to me, "Man, you're travelin' on the road, livin' the songs, and then playing them." We both agreed that's what you *had* to do. You had to make a total commitment.

The "manic part" of manic depression isn't a bad character trait to have if you're an aspiring anything—encourages single-mindedness and accesses outsized energy resources, essential attributes if you're going to slave your way past dilettantism. Towne's first wife, Fran, remembered how

> [i]n the first apartment we lived in there were two walk-in closets. The little one off the bathroom he decorated with posters, music posters, and made into his own little studio. There was just enough room to have a chair and a little amplifier and a little tape recorder, and a little table. You had to step in sideways to be able to sit down. That is where he started writing his first songs. He loved going in there; he would shut the door and stay there for hours.

By now Townes was also regularly appearing at The Sands Mountain Café, another Houston folk club that featured established acts but also allowed songwriting apprentices like Townes to learn on the job. Unlike The Jester, however, the Sands had a no-alcohol policy, which is how Townes met guitar player Mickey White. "In the back room Mrs. Carrick [The Sands' owner] introduced me to Townes," White recalled. "As soon as she left, Townes asked me, 'Do you drink?' I said, 'Sure.' And he opened up the window, and there was a gallon of wine hangin' on a rope. We took a couple of shots, and we were friends ever since."

At this point, and for a long while longer, booze was still spirit-fuel—helped him go places and see things and do things that tend not to happen when you're sensibly sober. Barelycorn nerve medicine, yes: take a shot, take a chance, take a blurry but brilliant memory home with you to rave aloud about or silently regret, but either way remember and, later, write about, what was before just something that happened magically magicked into something—a song—that always will be. Energetic excess, then. And if a man or a woman knowingly and willingly

sacrifices a few hospital years at the inevitably messy end
for the sake of several wine-primed years made even more
prime, that's called principled devotion and sacred servitude and call that life a life well lived.

Townes' father died unexpectedly at age fifty-two and
Townes dropped the pretense of caring about school and
left university for the last time and kept gigging anywhere
that would have him (although still mostly around Texas)
and wrote and wrote and wrote and ran the tap until the
tap ran hot and some of the songs that came out didn't
sound like Delta blues rip-offs or talking blues knock-offs
or half-baked Bob Dylan dittos but sounded, instead, like
him. Songwriter, novelist, painter, person: a voice, a style,
a singular way of being in the world is the single most difficult thing to achieve and the most enjoyable and enriching thing to hear or read or see or know.

After hearing a demo of "Tecumseh Valley" that Mickey
Newbury had pushed on Jack Clement, Kevin Eggers
instantly decided that Townes had to be recorded properly because everyone in the world needed to know his
songs. On the downside, Eggers' fledgling Poppy Records
was micro-small and underfunded and understaffed and
unknown to radio stations and record buyers; on the plus
side, Eggers believed that Townes was a genius. Many of
Townes' friends, then and later, thought he could have
made a better business decision. Poppy would go bankrupt five years later after not being to sell more than a piti-
ful number of astounding albums, and much of Townes'
back catalogue went and stayed out of print, making it all
but impossible for his few but fervent followers to hear all
of his music. But between 1968 and 1972 six albums were
recorded and released because Kevin Eggers believed
Townes was a genius. They're all in print today, and every
year they sell more than the last.

Townes' debut album with Poppy was *For the Sake of the Song*, as apt a first album title summation of an artist's entire career as you can get. There's undeniable filler—"The Velvet Voices" and "Sad Cinderella" are pretentiously sophomoric (too many of the songs trying too hard to be poetic, instantly invalidating them as poetry) while "Talkin' Karate Blues" is borderline moronic, even for a supposedly humorous talking blues—but several of the selections are out-of-the-gate stunners, songs that Townes would perform live for the rest of his life. "Waitin' Around to Die" (which was melodically recycled from "Big Country Blues," a demo unreleased in Townes' lifetime) is as darkly desperate as it sounds, but avoids pathos because of the churning melody and the scrubbed absence of self-pity. "Tecumseh Valley," another reclamation project (evolving from the similarly unrecorded "Colorado Bound") possesses an instantly captivating melody and lyrics that somehow manage to capture the tragedy of a single life in seven short stanzas. The title song may be about the complex, crumbling relationship between a man and a woman, but its title encapsulates Townes' near-immaterialism, his belief in the transcendent worth of a piece of art regardless of its material manifestation.

Immaterialism is an admittedly handy doctrine to subscribe to when you're forced to live in a world where Engelbert Humperdinck is a millionaire with hundreds of thousands of devoted listeners and you have to eat ketchup sandwiches and never know if the bar staff at your next gig will outnumber the clientele in the audience, but sustaining, otherworldly indifference can sometimes degenerate into slothful worldly apathy. The production on *For the Sake of the Song* is distracting at best, ruinous at worst. Townes' consistently moving melodies are ethereal enough—they don't require harpsichords and recorders and overly busy percussion to prop them up. Likewise, his seductively sincere but never-solemn voice shouldn't have been buried in reverb or buttressed by over-the-top backing vocals (here sci-fi shrieky, there Lawrence Welk smaltzy) to lend it extra "significance." Unfortunately, that's precisely what producers Jack Clement and Jim Malloy ended up doing. With Townes' consent, explicit or otherwise. Guy Clark:

> It breaks my heart to hear the way they overproduced some of his stuff. He was not unaware of it. Townes is really the one who's responsible. It's nobody's fault but his. You can't let him off the hook. He didn't have time to mix the fuckin' records 'cause he was too busy drinkin' and shootin' dice. The way Townes looked at it, his job was writin' songs and playin' 'em for people, not puttin' 'em on tape and makin' records out of 'em. Unfortunately, he wound up workin' with people that didn't know shit about that. It was a travesty. His attitude was, "I wrote these songs; you *can't* fuck 'em up."

It's actually not that difficult to imagine what Clement and Malloy were thinking while busily applying the baroque touches that tarnish Townes' first album. Because the best of his lyrics were infinitely richer and more rewarding than anything else in the country field they were both most familiar working with, it's obvious that they decided to present Townes in the literate-singer-song-writer mold of someone like Leonard Cohen, whose first album of songs producer John Simon tastefully comple-mented with instrumentation more likely to be heard in a symphony than on a pop record. But while Cohen's songs and sensibility were essentially European, making the vio-lins and female choruses entirely appropriate to his gypsy folk music, Townes was, in spite of his considerable way with words, Texan to the marrow, and, musically speaking, country or country-folk at core. What he was was Hank Williams blown back hip, and the sparse but sympathetic production his songs required was still a few records away. Technology comes first, but it's always a step behind.

Townes and his wife, Fran, separated because when he wasn't in the closet playing his guitar or out getting drunk or high he was on the road, if only gigging in nearby states like Oklahoma, but eventually they reconciled and Fran soon became pregnant. Once again, Townes tried to do the Van Zandt thing and be a grown-up, but was too far gone along the road of who he was to turn back and be who he should be. Although Fran was always a supporter (emotionally and financially) of Townes' burgeoning songwriting,

> [a]fter J.T. [their son] was born, the one thing that made me not able to tolerate his lifestyle was that I just didn't want it around our baby. I would come home and he would have drugs in the house with the baby right there. At that point I started to have a different focus. I told him I would not tolerate it. I couldn't live that way. That really started the final split . . . I never actually saw anything but pot at first, but I started finding out that he was going way off the deep end [i.e., taking heroin]. I would get phone calls late at night to come get him, and I would have to go get somebody to take care of the baby and then go find Townes. He would be in some just God-awful places. Then I knew.

Just because you can write beautiful love songs doesn't mean you know how to love—or, even if you do, that you're willing to put in the necessary time and work to keep the love alive. We need beautiful songs, but we also need parents and partners and friends to love us, so should be thankful if our lives are filled with enduring art and our parents or partners or friends don't leave their dope lying on the baby's changing table.

1969's *Our Mother the Mountain* continued the mis-employment of strings and flute and other inappropriate instrumentation, but Clement and Malloy, with an assist from Eggers, were getting closer to figuring out the best way to sonically represent Townes' songs, which was essentially to leave them alone. The filler this time isn't as cringeworthy as on his debut, but simply undistinguished, songs like "My Proud Mountains" and "Snake Mountain Blues" evidence that Townes, too, was finding his way. This time there were four indisputable Townes classics, including a re-done "Tecumseh Valley," take number two containing unexpurgated lyrics (the version on the debut had deleted the word "whorin'") and cleaner, less distracting production. The title track is minor-key spooky sultry, "She Came and She Touched Me" an Elizabethan hurtin' song, and "Kathleen" might be about a woman or it might be about heroin but either way what it's really about is being willing to give up anything to wake up from day-to-day nightmare nothingness. Among the sidemen were Nashville stalwarts James Burton on guitar and dobro and Charlie McCoy on harmonica, further proof that Townes' country and folk roots were closer to being effectively realized on record.

To promote the new album Poppy sent Townes out on the road for real, including shows in New York and along the East Coast. As would be the case throughout his career, sometimes the gigs were transfixing ("[We] were stunned; we couldn't move," remembered the Cowboy Junkies' Michael Timmins of an Atlanta gig in the eighties. "It was one of those performances that reaffirms one's belief in the power of music to uplift, redeem, and heal"), sometimes they were shambolic ("[O]ut comes this guy that I had been raving [to his friends and family] about," recalls songwriter Darden Smith, "this king of all song- writers, who was smashed out of his mind. He sang two songs, almost fell off his chair, and proceeded to tell bad jokes for the next ten minutes"). In later years, the ter- rible shows would outweigh the brilliant ones as alcohol abuse and life on the road began to take back what they had given, but the hit-or-miss quality of Townes' perfor- mances was part of his psyche from the beginning. Booze was *how* he sabotaged gigs, not *why*. Anyone whose job is to transport himself and others to a higher, more enlight- ened plane knows it can't happen every night, no matter how much everyone wants it to. Anyone whose job is to transport himself and others to a higher, more enlightened plane got that job in the first place because they're nec- essarily spiritually greedy, have little or no tolerance for the ordinary, the just okay, the everyday. Better a debacle, then, than boredom. Nothing comes without a price, not even heaven.

Townes' perpetual need to gamble was rooted in this same psychic restlessness. Like many gambling addicts, he chose losing over stopping if stopping meant monotony settling in over his soul. Occasionally he'd even give away his winnings once he'd gotten what he really wanted: the rush of risk. His games of choice were cards or dice, but anything was preferable to nothing. Fellow Texas song- writer Ray Wylie Hubbard tells the story of attending a Jerry Jeff Walker show with Townes: "Townes bet me $100 that he'd go onstage and stand on his head for the whole song while Jerry did 'Mr. Bojangles.' I bet Townes the $100. Jerry started playing 'Bojangles,' and Townes went out there and stood on his head the whole time. That was the last time I gambled with him."

Townes' third album in three years (the simply titled *Townes Van Zandt*) was short on gamble and long on getting down on record something closer to the spare sound of his live shows. Not only did a handful of new songs like the tender "Don't Take it So Bad" and the harrowing "Lungs" benefit from the pared-down recording aesthetic, but the decision to re-record four numbers from the instrumentally flawed first two albums was a wise one, "For the Sake of the Song," "Waiting 'Round to Die," "I'll Be Here in the Morning," and "(Quicksilver Dreams of) Marie" all featuring Townes' subtle finger-picking—a consistently underrated aspect of his music—at the forefront of the mix. The album's overall sound is essentially augmented folk (hand drum, wailing harp, et cetera), which is at least preferable to baroque folk. *Townes Van Zandt* didn't sell much better than the first couple of albums, but in Texas, at least, his reputation was growing. Mickey White, who would sometimes join Townes live on second guitar:

> Townes would call up and say, "Hey Dale, or Rex, [co-owners of Houston club The Old Quarter], I'm leaving Montgomery, West Virginia, or wherever, and I'll be there in two nights. Can I book a gig?" So Dale would immediately put the word out, *Townes is Coming*, like the Messiah or something. And whoever was booked that night—and it might well have been me—was immediately fired.

The zealotry Townes was starting to inspire was due in part to his live shows (usually sublime, occasionally chaotic, never dull), but mostly because of the body of songs he was assembling. Songs of profound desolation, predominantly. (When an interviewer once asked him why all of his songs were sad, Townes replied that they weren't all sad, some were downright hopeless.) To call compositions like

"Waiting 'Round to Die" or "Flyin' Shoes" or "Snow Don't Fall" "sad," however, is an act of adjectival attenuation of the coarsest degree. "Sad" is what you feel when experiencing or learning of an action or idea that is unfortunate, even fatally so. The best of Townes' songs, on the other hand, transcend personal or pragmatic grief. (He rarely, for example, wrote anything even resembling that staple of the country music canon, the "she/he-done-me-wrong" song.) A Townes tune uses the particulars of existence as a segue to something much more profound in the same way that a Philip Larkin poem utilizes the mundane minutiae of the poet's own life to shed light on universal concerns like loneliness, existential uncertainty, and mortality. In both cases, instead of a simple sob story, we participate in cosmic sorrow; in place of enfeebling self-pity, we experience absorption in absolutes (conveying joy *and* despair) and attain (however fleetingly) purifying perspective. Edith Wharton's assertion that "The years are tragic but the days are jubilant" could stand as Townes' songwriting credo.

Townes the human being knew as much as Townes the artist that shade without light is uninhabitable, impenetrable darkness, and just as he pierced his personal tendency toward depression with practical jokes and willful goofiness (Billy Joe Shaver remembers the time that "Townes had somehow acquired these leather pants, and he had his face all painted up with tears like a clown"), so he peppered his live act of darkly gorgeous disquisitions with corny jokes and stories and light musical relief. The title track to 1971's *Delta Momma Blues* is such a song, a genial ode to Robitussin DM cough syrup and the sticky codeine high it provides if drunk in sufficient quantities (which Townes liked to do). "Brand New Companion" is a Lightnin' Hopkins-indebted twelve-bar blues played with lusty conviction and, being a Townes tune, full of fresh imagery and witty wordplay, as when he celebrates his new lover's ability to cool him off with her warm breathing and how she keeps him safe from howling bottles of wine. Production-wise, *Delta Momma Blues* is a twin of the previous year's album, Townes' guitar the dominating sound and the songs rarely enhanced, or at least not significantly undermined, by extraneous instrumentation.

Every Townes album except the last couple contains a minimum of three certifiable gems, and *Delta Momma Blues* is no exception. "Nothin'" is an updated Mississippi Delta blues, all of the unnerving wisdom of Soren Kierkegaard reduced down to eight compact verses and carried along by some insistent minor-chord picking. "Where I Lead Me" is a stomping exploration of oblivion's undeniable pull and the corresponding compulsion—and need—to resist. Melodically, "Rake" is—one loathes to use the thread-bare term, but in this case there really is no other that suffices—haunting, befitting a song that is a swelling soundtrack to the battle between instinct and idealism, madness and sanity. And "Tower Song" is a prototypical Townes love song: not really about his or her hurt feelings or who was right or wrong, but about the paradise of authentic connection between two human beings and the impossibility of existing there for as long as one would like.

Life may be mostly wasting time, and Townes wasted his share of his—he began to more than dabble with heroin; he met a woman, Leslie Jo Richards, whom he actually wanted there the next morning; he spent plenty of time with Guy Clark and his future wife Susanna, who were living near LA, where his next record was to be recorded—but sometimes we aren't just living, sometimes we're doing the thing that gives the living its meaning. Although he'd recorded four albums in four years, he hadn't come close to emptying the well, the bucket was still coming back up full of fresh and unforgettable songs. *High, Low and In Between* (1971) was not only faultlessly produced this time, it offered a whopping seven Townes standards. As testament to how good the album is, even the filler isn't really filler, the original gospel tunes "Two Hands" and "When He Offers His Hand" lyrically slight but convincingly sung and feelingly performed, and "No Deal," the record's token "funny song," is not only actually funny (as opposed to being simply a respite from the darker material), but a droll slice of slapstick wisdom.

"You Are Not Needed Now" was purportedly inspired by the death of Janis Joplin (whom Townes knew slightly back in Houston), but is really about the danger of contentment and the rewards of unrest. As on the remainder of the album, the mix here is pristine and the production crisp and uncluttered, twang-tinged electric folk. "Greensboro Woman" and "Standin'" are confused declarations to a new lover, appropriate to that exhilarating, bewildering state. "Mr. Mudd and Mr. Gold" is a metaphysical mindfuck disguised as an account of a poker game, "Highway Kind" is a consoling sigh of nihilism, and the title track is a tender plea for cosmic forgiveness and acceptance. "To Live Is to Fly" is as good as Townes gets, an avowal of his tragic-yet-inspiring core personal philosophy and the song I always play when attempting to turn someone onto his music.

As easy and productive as the recording of *High, Low and in Between* was unfolding, everything was shattered when Leslie Jo Richards was murdered while hitchhiking, stabbed fifteen times and left beside the highway to bleed to death. Townes was devastated, composing a song for her, "Snow Don't Fall," that would appear on his next album and which he vowed to never perform again (he didn't). After the sessions limped to an end, he headed back to Texas and immediately got strung out, overdosing and almost dying in hospital. The day he OD'd he was supposed to be visiting his almost three-year-old son, J.T., whom he rarely saw. (J.T's mother, Townes' now-ex-wife Fran, recalled: "When J.T. would swing he would sit on the side of the swing and say he was saving room for his father to sit with him.") Townes' solution to the pain he was causing his ex-wife and son and his own mother (it was in her house that he'd overdosed) was to distance himself even further, literally and figuratively.

The grief he caused his friends was of a different kind, and far from inadvertent. Guy Clark: "[H]e would fuck with people just to watch them squirm. It's not what I'd call a nice trait, but he did it. He fucked with everybody all the time." Rodney Crowell: "Townes was fond of me, but he picked on me, man. He was smarter and faster and quicker than me, and I was always on guard." A very young Steve Earle, who idolized Townes, remembered a particularly upsetting instance of emotional torture:

> I don't even remember how it started because we were both pretty drunk, but he started loading one chamber [of his revolver] with a shell, spinning it, and putting it to his head and pulling the trigger. And every time I'd reach for him to try and get it, he pulled the hammer back and I was afraid that I'd cause the gun to go off if I grabbed it. I watched him do it about three times.

Like many of Townes' friends, Guy Clark could only wonder, "Goddamn you, you motherfucker! I adore you, and you treat me like this?" Probably for the same reason he gambled so recklessly, Townes tormented his friends to relieve boredom. That's a pathetic reason for hurting the people who care for you and it contradicts everything his songs are about. This is why, as if we needed reminding, you don't listen to the artist, you listen to his or her art. Overly busy brains rarely make for soothing souls.

Not that he was a needling prick all of the time — more than once he emptied his pockets for a stranger who needed the money (albeit barely) more than he did; to friends like songwriter Nanci Griffith he could be memorably compassionate, as when he patiently guided her through a long and disorientating acid trip. And even to those — usually those he was closest to — who he did occasionally provoke for perverse pleasure, he was still *Townes*. Rodney Crowell:

> Whenever Townes would show up the whole scene would revolve round him. He had an unspoken magnetism . . . Whenever he walked in the room, the water in the toilet would start runnin' in a different direction. Like Miles Davis, Townes could be one intimidating motherfucker. I mean, look how smart and connected to his art he was. With that comes a swagger.

Anyone can be a moody, manipulative, self-involved substance abuser and tell themself (and anyone else who will listen) that they're complicated and enigmatic; it takes a Townes, with an uncommon gift for living and generating joy in others, for other people to say that about *you*, even long after you're gone.

Swagger's stripes need to be earned every day, and when it came time to record his next album, Townes proved he still had his strut. *The Late Great Townes Van Zandt* (the title was an in-joke concocted by Kevin Eggers to reflect both Townes' near-anonymity as far as the record-buying public was concerned and his fear that Townes wouldn't secure a deservedly wide audience until he was dead) may be Townes' weakest album overall (of the eleven songs, three are pleasant but inconsequential covers, two are trivial co-writes, and one, "Sad Cinderella," is a remake from *Our Mother the Mountain* that didn't warrant its reprise, it still being an overly precious précis of Dylan's "Queen Jane Approximately"), but of the remaining five tunes, three are tours de force.

The aforementioned "Snow Don't Fall" is an understated eulogy for the recently deceased Leslie Jo Richards, managing the rare feat of being touching without being sentimental, even if it is marred by the unwelcome reappearance of a string section (the "less is more" aesthetic having somehow been temporarily forgotten). "If I Needed You" is probably Townes' second most well-known song, Doc Watson's and the Dillards' almost immediate cover versions giving Townes his first real mass(ish) exposure. A pretty melody married to a gentle plea for/pledge of unconditional devotion, it's a lie of love you want to believe in. "Pancho and Lefty" would also be given the cover treatment (Emmylou Harris, Hoyt Axton), but it was only when Willie Nelson and Merle Haggard recorded their tarted-up, number-one-hit version ten years later that Townes made some real money from his music for the first time. Over a gently mesmerizing melody, Townes tells an enticingly opaque tale of two outlaws, a betrayal, and the life that was left over for both of them. It's a song people will be singing as long as they're still singing songs.

Just as Townes was beginning to experience some slightly increased exposure—albeit through others' versions of his songs—Poppy went bankrupt, putting his immediate recording future in doubt and making his earlier albums that much more difficult to locate. He headed back to Texas and continued to gig—he never stopped, even when, later, the songs did—and, as friend Peggy Underwood recalled, he

> pretty much drank all the time and shot heroin as much as he could. He'd shoot up cocaine too. This was the first time I ever saw anybody shoot up drugs. He and a friend were shooting up bourbon and Coca Cola. Bourbon and Coca Cola. Somebody said they'd seen him shoot up vodka before. He would talk to his mother, he would get on the phone and call his mother and cry and cry and cry. He'd talk for an hour or two. His mother told him he had to be the man of the family and he wasn't capable of being the man of any family.

Alcohol (and to a far lesser degree, drugs) still had a job to do—helped numb the numbness of the road, for one thing, the one place where he knew he could always get his songs across, insolvent record companies and indifferent radio stations go to hell. As Matthew Arnold wrote, however: "—such a price/The Gods exact for song: to become what we sing." As a young man Townes decided to be an old bluesman, sacrificing everything—health, family, conventional happiness—for the sake of the song. The song made it, Townes didn't, and to his considerable credit he never lamented the terms of the deal he'd cut; occasionally lamented that he couldn't do what he should do as well as what he had to, but nevertheless accepted his sentence like an unrepentant lifer.

In the five-year-interval between *The Late Great Townes Van Zandt* and the release of 1978's *Flyin' Shoes*, Townes met and eventually married a fifteen-year-old Texan named Cindy Morgan; rented a shack with acreage in rural Tennessee where he hauled his own water and cut the wood needed to keep it warm (even if he still made his daily visit to the liquor store seventeen miles away and continued to heedlessly gamble, once losing a gold tooth which was messily extracted on the spot); seldom saw his son or his mother; was prescribed lithium for his depression, which he occasionally took; periodically attempted to cut down on his drinking, once by having Cindy tie him to a tree with chains for twenty-eight hours; toured and toured, some-times to spellbound if modestly-sized audiences, sometimes to chatty crowds numbering less than ten. He also wrote— it was the last sustained bout of superior songwriting of his life—and even went back into the studio, the album that was to be *7 Come 11* ultimately not to be, Kevin Eggers, who was "financing" the sessions, unable to pay for the studio time, the tapes never released (not until twenty years later, anyway, as *The Nashville Sessions*).

By 1977, though, Poppy Records had become Tomato Records and Eggers and Townes were back in business. (Why did Townes stick with Eggers through thin and thinner? Why didn't he sign with someone else? Because no one else wanted him and Eggers did.) But before recording began on what became *Flyin' Shoes*, the newly formed Tomato released *Live at the Old Quarter*, a double-al-bum document of a three-night stand at the Houston club from July, 1973. It's just Townes and his guitar and a hun-dred hushed disciples and it's where any Townes neophyte should begin and where aficionados always return. He's old enough to have earned his battered craft, he's young enough to gush a gifted juicehead's *joie de vivre*, he's drunk enough to be loose yet sober enough to avoid being sloppy. His finger picking at its peak of powerful delicateness, Townes offers definitive versions of standards like "For the Sake of the Song" and "She Came and She Touched Me" as well as several brilliant new songs, the majority of which would later turn up on *Flyin' Shoes*. You can *hear* the swagger. (When Gram Parsons played across town at

Liberty Hall a few months previously, he'd been disappointed to learn that his show had run too late to catch Townes' gig at the Old Quarter. Maybe it's fortunate that the two never got to meet. Parsons only had six months left to live as it was; if he and Townes *had* gotten together, he might not have lasted that long.)

For the new album, for once Eggers hired an outside producer other than Jack Clement, and Chips Moman did a magnificent job with the new material in addition to bringing in matchless country-rock musicians like Philip Donnelly and Spooner Oldham and the Scruggs brothers, Gary and Randy. From the warm, rich sound of the relaxed strumming that introduces "Loretta," you know this is going to work, the agreeable ode to a barroom muse the template for a triumphant combination of song, presentation, and playing. Lyrically, "No Place to Fall" echoes the sentiments of "If I Needed You," but within a much wider context, faithfulness now not only deeply desired, but necessary in a coldly unsympathetic universe where time is a speeding train that won't ever come again. (Randy Scruggs' mandolin playing here and on the title track is mesmerizing.) "Flyin' Shoes" is introduced with mournful harmonica courtesy of Gary Scruggs that perfectly encapsulates the song's mood and message, the hackneyed wanderlust theme of so many songs rearranged and redefined, the narrator not so much running toward something as attempting to escape himself. The gentle "When She Don't Need Me" is a good example of Townes' ability to write a love song that actually deepens one's understanding of the subject as opposed to simply adding to the stock of clichés endemic to the genre. "Rex's Blues" is a superficially pleasant, chorus-free country song that surreptitiously manages to present several paradoxes of human existence in five finely chiseled verses:

satisfaction and discontent, love and aloneness, obligation and calling, hope and despair.

If *Flyin' Shoes* is Townes' most satisfying overall studio album, it also disclosed a troubling portent: of the record's nine songs, six had been resurrected from the aborted *7 Come 11* sessions of nearly five years earlier (and a seventh was a dispensable cover of Bo Diddley's "Who Do You Love" which had been in his stage act for just as long). Previous to this there had been six albums released in six years, a staggering feat of productivity for a songwriter of Townes' abilities even when factoring in the occasional filler and re-recordings, but this was more than a simple case of creative burnout. Or, if that was all it was, Townes never sufficiently recovered. In the eighteen years left to him, he'd record only two more albums of new material, little of it up to the standard he'd set during his songwriting prime. (The best cut from 1988's *At My Window*, for instance, the title track, was also originally recorded for *7 Come 11*.)

In creative compensation, perhaps, from this point on he spent more time on the road than off, usually winning new adherents one gig at a time (even if his set lists were becoming somewhat predictable), occasionally mortifying fans old and new. (Word was spreading, if not as quickly as he would have liked, about his music, making it possible for him to regularly tour clubs and small halls in the British Isles and Europe.) Cindy left him; he met, married, and divorced a third wife, Jeanene, who bore him two more children; his formerly worn but warm voice dropped a discomforting octave or two; his face began to resemble a scuffed and sliced old barstool; and while he was never seduced by good health and regular hours or drifted off into sterile professionalism, he made a renewed effort in the late eighties to confront both his depression (he sporadically took Zoloft) and alcoholism (entering detox several times, and once remaining sober for nearly a year). By all accounts, he was miserable while not drinking, and found that his songwriting muse hadn't returned, likely the major reason he'd attempted to straighten out in the first place. Once he began drinking again, it was apparent to friends and fans that this time it wasn't about encouraging the writing of good songs anymore or about having good times. An offer by Sonic Youth's Steve Shelley to produce a new Townes album for the imprint that their label, Geffen, had set up for them, was sabotaged by Townes being simply too drunk to work with. Townes' last great tune, "A Song For," is essentially a suicide note in song, the narrator confessing, as he collapses into a drunken sleep, that neither the world's pleasures nor his own formerly steadying art give any him reasons to bother staying alive any longer.

Songwriter and friend Peter Rowan remembered a gig they shared not long before Townes' death:

> The last show I did with him, I have pictures from it, was in Arkansas. They are the most moving pictures I've ever seen; Townes was almost transparent in them. We played together on stage that night and Townes was so fragile. I remember while we were playing together looking at him and thinking, "Brother, you're outta here."

Outta here turned out to be New Years Day, 1997, slightly more than a week after Townes broke his hip and, more afraid of the enforced detoxification that an extended hospital stay would entail than the untreated effect of a significant injury, refused to see a doctor. Eventually unable to stand the pain any longer, the hip was mended but he insisted on being discharged from the hospital far too soon and died within a few hours. It was the same day that his hero Hank Williams had died forty years before. It makes sense.

LITTLE RICHARD

Eternity was in that moment.

—William Congreve

I've said it before, I'll say it again: real rock and roll is metaphysical skin popping masquerading as unadulterated id music—shameless, feral, timeless. Real rock and roll makes you do things tonight you won't believe you actually did tomorrow morning. If it's not dangerous, in other words, it's not the real thing. And in spite of sixty years of artistically degenerative dilution, wanton trivializing commercialization, and simple overexposure, the best of Little Richard's music remains dangerous. Just as people need to pray, however, in order to remain in contact with what they consider holy, it's just that we need to be reminded occasionally. The tragedy of Richard Wayne Penniman's life is that he was taught that God and the Devil are two separate beings and that you have to choose who you're going to pray to; the triumph of his art emerged from the terrible tension created by this same ill-founded, if admittedly fecund, belief. And one out of two ain't just

115

not bad, it's as good as it ever gets, which, as everybody knows, isn't all that often.

Little Richard (he was the smallest of twelve brothers and sisters born to a moonshiner/juke-joint-proprietor/bricklayer father and a mother adored by all of her children, none more than by Richard, who would watch her make her face up and later sneak into her bedroom to do the same thing) was born in Macon, Georgia in 1932. The Pennimans were poor, and every year, it seemed, there was another baby to care for, but Richard's mother Leva Mae was adamant that Richard "was the most trouble of any of 'em. He was always mischievous, always getting up to tricks. He got a lot of whippings. He didn't get whipped for everything he did, mind, or he wouldn't be here now, cos he did something nearly all the time." One of the things he did was present an elderly neighbourhood woman with a nicely wrapped box containing his own feces as a birthday present. He also defecated in a jelly jar, after which he carefully screwed the top back on and returned it to the pantry shelf for his mother to discover. There's no truth to the rumour that this is where the title of his song "Tutti Frutti" originated.

In Macon, as it was elsewhere in the American South, church was the social glue that held poor families (black and white) and entire communities together. The first organized singing Richard was involved with was a children's gospel group organized by a neighbourhood friend of the family called the "Tiny Tots." Later, there were the "Penniman Singers," which included most of his brothers and sisters, who would travel from church to church and occasionally compete in "Battle of the Gospels." Baptist gospel music is extraordinarily fervent to begin with, but Richard's singing was so impassioned he earned the nickname "War Hawk" for his uncommonly loud and zealous presentation.

He especially liked to sing at the local Pentecostal church, where he would join in with the frenzied "holy dancing" and even attempt to speak in tongues. Richard's paternal grandfather, as well as his mother's brother, had been preachers, and it was his dream to be a preacher himself one day, preferably a performing one like the famous "singing evangelist" Brother Joe May. At the same time, he was also copping blow jobs from the local queen, Madame Oop, and getting up to all sorts of things with a grocery boy his own age, things that the Good Lord did not approve of, no matter how good they undeniably felt. His other father, the non-heavenly one, wasn't too happy with him either, unable to understand how a son of his could be so effeminate in speech and manner, telling Richard he wasn't a real son, was just barely half a son, before usually proceeding to smack him around.

High school was good for at least introducing him to the saxophone, which he got to play in the marching band, and the part-time job he had at Macon City Auditorium selling Coca Cola allowed him to see and hear a different kind of music from strict gospel, including big band jazz musicians such as Cab Calloway and, most importantly, his favourite singer, Sister Rosetta Tharpe, already famous for singing gospel lyrics to revved up tunes and playing a hot electric guitar, in the process fusing the spiritual and the secular like few had done before. When she appeared in Macon, Richard made sure he was hanging around the parking lot when the band arrived, and began singing one of her songs when they were unloading their equipment. Tharpe was impressed enough to invite him on stage that night to sing a song with her. Richard described the applause he got as the best thing that had ever happened to him. The thirty-five dollars Tharpe handed him after the show felt pretty good too.

School over by age fourteen (if everyone was the same—poor and black—*someone* had to be different and therefore ostracized, and a faggot-sissy-freak would have to do), and home—especially when his father was there—not feeling much like home, Richard began hanging around the travelling medicine shows that passed through town, freaks of a feather fluttering together. His first steady carnival job was singing loud enough (never a problem) to get people's attention so that the man wearing the turban could earn a few coins predicting people's futures. Eventually he got out of Macon with Dr. Hudson's Medicine Show and sang the only non-gospel song he knew from start to finish to help draw the crowd to whom the not-so good doctor sold his useless snake oil. One night, when Dr. Hudson *et al* happened to be appearing at the same venue as B. Brown and His Orchestra, whose singer was too drunk to perform, Richard grabbed the microphone and never let it go. Eventually, Sugarfoot Sam from Alabam's Minstrel Show, the Tidy Jolly Steppers, and the L.J. Heath Show, and frequently while in drag. Finally, a way to get paid, not abused, for wearing makeup and eyelashes.

Blues shouter Billy Wright also wore makeup—and outlandish clothing and flamboyantly curled hair—but was a popular recording artist who didn't have to wear a dress to garner attention. Not only was he a significant influence on the development of Richard's performing persona, he also helped the eighteen-year-old Richard secure a contract with RCA. The results were predictable—undistinguished R&B with obvious gospel undertones—but one of the batch of songs recorded with Wright's band received enough regional airplay for Richard's father to play it incessantly on the jukebox at his club. As another song says, everybody loves a winner, even if it's your formerly shunned, no-good faggot son. Around this time, while cruising the Macon Greyhound station late one night, Richard met a piano player named Esquerita, who taught him everything he knew about the instrument that would become almost as much a part of his identity as his towering hairdo and trademark "Whooo!" And life really is that tantalizingly, terrifyingly capricious: you show up for a blow job, you leave with the seed of a life-transforming musical gift.

A few more commonplace recordings even less commercially successful than the first set; the shock of his father's murder (shot at his club); more one-nighters across the South (both the kind with a band and the kind without); and a slow-building reputation as a mesmerizing entertainer. Musician and producer Johnny Otis:

> I was having lunch in the coffee shop at the Club Matinee when somebody came out and said, "Johnny, you just gotta come and see this dude in here." They were having some entertainment. So I went through and I see this outrageous person, good-looking and very effeminate, with a big pompadour. He started singing and he was so *good*. I loved it . . . He did a few things, then he got on the floor. I think he even did a split . . . I remember it as being just beautiful, bizarre, and exotic, and when he got through he remarked, "This is Little Richard, King of the Blues," and then he added, "And the Queen, too."

Even when the music isn't transcendent—and the formulaic, if spirited boogie-woogied-up blues tunes Richard was belting out each night at this point certainly were not—the performance can be. The right performer (or performers) on the right night have the capacity to move an audience to fits of rock-and-roll near-rapture regardless of whether the material is commonplace. A live album like Hound Dog Taylor's *Beware of the Dog* is, strictly musically speaking, predominantly composed of only average blues tunes; as performed by a magnificently incomprehensible, bottleneck-wailing Hound Dog and his potent two-piece band in a sweaty Illinois club on a well-lubricated Saturday night, however, these same just-okay songs are converted by an act of inspired, ecstatic execution into something more than the sum of their merely passable parts. Sometimes it's all about the shaman in the bright-red lipstick and floor-length cape doing the splits, not the song.

Another label (Peacock Records), another bunch of commercially unsuccessful and artistically unexceptional songs, but Richard's standing as a scintillating live performer paid off when bluesman Lloyd Price encouraged him to send an audition tape to his own label, Los Angeles' Specialty Records. California had undergone an influx of African-American immigration during the Second World War, and this new population had pocket money it wanted to spend on their own type of entertainment. Among the R&B hits Specialty had turned out was Price's "Lawdy Miss Clawdy." Richard wanted a hit, too—and his own Cadillac, just like Price (the only one in Macon belonged to the funeral home)—and he pestered anyone he could get on the phone at Specialty about his tape, although it wasn't until ten months later that he finally got the call to come to New Orleans to cut a few tunes.

While it may be impossible to determine which song was the first rock-and-roll recording (a maddeningly nebulous, impossibly indeterminate designation for such an inherently evolutionary form anyway)—whether "Rocket 88," "That's Alright Mama," Richard's own "Tutti Frutti," or some lesser known tune lost in the musical mists of time—the ingredients that came to make up what we now call "rock and roll" were there the day Richard stepped into the little New Orleans recording studio in 1955. Like every song that's a contender for rock and roll's prime-mover status, "Tutti Frutti" was basically blues with an uptempo beat performed by a young man accustomed to shouting gospel music. And like almost every genre-shattering artistic breakthrough, its originators had very little idea what they were doing.

"Tutti Frutti, Good Booty," a paean to anal intercourse that had been a staple of Richard's stage act in black nightclubs and white frat-parties, was *not* on the agenda the first day Richard recorded for Specialty Records. After a fruitless morning recording conventional blues that no one was particularly impressed with, however, the crew retired to the nearby Dew Drop Inn where Richard, always the show-off, commandeered the piano and proceeded to unleash the most ribald tune he knew. The song was subsequently cleaned up lyrically but left untouched musically, and "A-Wop-Bop-A-Lu-Bop-A-Wop-Bam-Boom!" the world of popular music was never the same. (On hearing "Tutti Frutti" for the first time, Keith Richards claimed that it was as though the world changed suddenly from monochrome to Technicolor.)

According to Bumps Blackwell, the Specialty employee who'd heard something in Richard's voice on his audition reel and who convinced the label's owner to buy out his contract with Peacock for $1000 and bring him into the studio, the key to "Tutti Frutti"'s success was Richard's raucous piano playing. (Although most people would argue that it's Richard's incendiary vocals—the screaming, shrieking attack of joy that led Jimi Hendrix to claim "I want to do with my guitar what Little Richard does with his voice"—that make the song so compelling.) There were only fifteen minutes left in the session by the time a new set of bowdlerized lyrics were completed. Blackwell again: "There had been no chance to write an arrangement, so I had to take the chance on Richard playing the piano himself [because all of the other songs had been cut using studio musicians] . . . It was impossible for the other piano players to learn it in the short time we had." All of which was enormously fortuitous: "You couldn't get a learned piano player to give you that simplicity and put that much energy and excitement into it." Even if you have all of the necessary ingredients, sometimes a little luck is needed to come up with the right recipe.

The song was a number two hit on the R&B chart — there wasn't such a thing as a "rock and roll" chart yet; Richard was still helping to invent such a thing — but of course he'd signed a lousy contract with Specialty, and naturally Pat Boone cut a crooning cover version of "Tutti Frutti" that drained every ounce of sex and excitement and menace from Richard's pulsating original (allowing Boone's rendering to outsell Richard's by a significant margin), and . . . But what the hell, his version *was* still a hit, he *was* making more money than he'd ever made before (he bought that Cadillac he'd wanted and his mother a new house), and there was a demand for personal appearances and steady cash to be made from doing what he'd always done, putting on the loudest, lewdest, most entertaining musical show anyone had ever seen. Richard didn't disappoint. Musician H.B. Barnum:

> He'd just burst on to the stage from anywhere, and you wouldn't be able to hear anything but the roar of the audience. He might come out and walk on the piano. He might go out in the audience. His charisma was just a whole new thing to the business. Richard was totally out of this world,

wild, and it gave people who wanted to scream a chance to go ahead and scream instead of trying to be cool.

My parents, then teenagers and just beginning to go steady in Chatham, Ontario, saw Little Richard in his performing prime at a record hop at the Kinsmen Auditorium in 1958. My mother remembers everyone dancing from the first notes of Richard's pounding piano; my father remembers Richard standing atop his piano and simulating masturbation with a microphone.

Barnum claimed Richard also single-handedly improved American race relations. Richard, he believed, brought

the races together. When I first went on the road there were many segregated audiences. With Richard, although they still had the audiences segregated in the building, they were *there* together. And most times, before the end of the night, they would all be mixed together. Up until then, the audiences were either all black or all white, and no one else would come in. His records weren't boy-meets-girl-girl-meets-boy things, they were *fun* records, all fun.

How can you feel funny (or something worse) about the colour of a person's skin when you're both jumping up and down beside one another? Having fun shall set you free . . .

In typical life-on-the-road fashion, Richard and his band played as hard as they worked (and this was a group that usually performed a gig in a different city every night for months on end). As with everything else associated with the band, Richard was in charge when it came to the after-show orgies, organizing it so that the different musicians in his employ would have sex with women while he watched. A very young Etta James would sometimes be on the same musical bill as Richard:

> I was so naïve in those days. Richard and the band were always having those parties and I'd knock on the door and try to get in. They'd say, "Don't open the door, she's a minor." Then one day, I climbed up and looked through the transom—and the things I *saw*!"

Something she probably didn't see—luckily, for the sake of her young mind—was the time backstage at the Paramount Theatre when Richard was masturbating standing up while a girl licked his nipples (Richard's preferred sexual activity) and Buddy Holly wandered into the room and pulled down his pants and began to have intercourse with the girl from behind while she continued to please the unruffled Richard. Peggy Sue had no idea what she was missing.

Charles White's *The Life and Times of Little Richard: The Quasar of Rock* (which he wrote with his subject's unabashed cooperation) is not only an indispensable compendium of biographical information, it's also an illuminating portal into Richard's deeply contradictory character. Richard embraced the opportunities for unfettered sexual satiation that came with fame and money like only someone who's been denied them his entire life can. Yet even while openly enjoying himself with a remarkable lack of reticence (and gleefully recalling his many exploits decades later), he simultaneously affirmed the sinfulness of his actions after virtually every orgasm, feeling not so much ashamed as angry at himself while insisting that homosexuality was "contagious." Even though the world (including human nature) is obviously a messy mix of this and that, Christian fundamentalism—like all forms of fundamentalism—is predicated on an either/or understanding of reality, particularly the ethical realm. For now, Richard satisfied himself with being dissatisfied with himself.

He didn't have time to do much more. In addition to the incessant touring, in just over two years Richard created not only the bedrock of his own musical reputation, but some of the rawest, most rapturous songs in the history of popular music. "Tutti Frutti" was quickly followed in 1955 by "Long Tall Sally," "Slippin' and Slidin'," "Rip It Up," and "Ready Teddy," all staples of the rock-and-roll canon. Successive singles like "The Girl Can't Help It," "Lucille," "Jenny, Jenny," "Keep A-Knockin'," and "Good Golly Miss Molly" all are bite-sized conduits to minor mystical delights, riotous reminders of our sacred selves, of our too-infrequently glimpsed metaphysical shadow lives. The best rock and roll—and it simply doesn't get any better than these scorching, pioneering songs—ambushes our everyday, ordinary consciousness and slams the brakes on interminable Time, allowing us to exist, if only for as long as the turntable continues to spin, in the uncommon eternity of *right fucking now*. Essayist Logan Pearsall Smith wrote that "It is through the cracks in our brains that ecstasy creeps in." A song like "Good Golly Miss Molly" supplies the much-needed head kick that cracks our humdrum brains a little wider open.

The dynamic, draining live performances; writing and recording superlative song after song; the sex and the money and the boozing: this much happiness is hard work. Instead of taking a mental and physical break, though—rock and roll circa the mid-fifties was treated like any other widget, you kept pumping it out until the public grew tired of it—Richard opened the door of his Los Angeles home on a rare day off the road to a representative of the Church of God of the Ten Commandments, who kindly reinforced Richard's fear that his songs were the devil's music, that his sexual predilections were evil, and that what he should be using his charismatic personality and prominent public platform for was spreading God's compassionate word. It was probably as much the appeal of a long rest as it was the acumen of the door-to-door missionary's arguments, but Richard began to contemplate packing away his piano and picking up a Bible. If only he could be sure, if only he had a sign . . .

On a flight to Australia in 1957, where he was going as part of a package tour that included Eddie Cochran and Gene Vincent, Richard panicked when he thought that the wings of the plane were on fire and that angels were holding the disabled craft aloft. Eventually calmed down and convinced he was only imagining it, when forty-thousand other people also saw a ball of fire shoot through the sky above Sydney's outdoor arena where he was performing a couple of weeks later, that was it, what more of a heavenly sign could he ask for? When he informed his band members the next day on the ferry from Sydney that he was quitting the sinful world of rock and roll to walk in the light of the Lord and they didn't believe him, he threw the eight-thousand-dollar ring he was wearing into the ocean. There's no record of whether or not his faith wavered when, not long after, he discovered that the fire he saw in the sky was actually the launch of Russia's Sputnik One, the first human-made object to orbit the earth.

Richard gave away his Cadillacs and enrolled at Oakwood College in Huntsville, Alabama, with the goal of becoming an ordained minister, and got straight and got married to a young woman he met at an evangelical meeting. Like Jerry Lee Lewis, another refugee Baptist wandering in the wilderness of rock and roll who would periodically excoriate himself for his sinful ways and perform penance by singing exclusively religious material, by 1960 Richard began recording gospel music. Except that whatever is holy is a hell of a lot more palpable in "Lucille" or "Great Balls of Fire" than it is in "Go Tell It on the Mountain," and the sacred isn't something you say, it's something you experience, goosebumps and a dizzying sense of blessedness the surest sign you've a hit upon a hallowed manifestation. (Watch any YouTube video of Richard in his rock-and-roll prime: it's a joyous energy that lifts off the screen, not unlike that of a wild-eyed, enraptured Baptist minister at his most beatific.) "Malt does more than Milton can/To justify God's ways to man," A.E. Housman wrote. Blazing rock and roll, too.

The path of righteousness wasn't as smooth as he'd envisioned. College classes were no less boring than those in high school (and a whole lot easier to skip); Richard talked a church deacon's son into letting him have a peek at him naked (who then told his father); he was arrested in a bus-station restroom along with several other toilet trawlers as part of a police raid; his marriage, not surprisingly, turned out to be like a lot of things that seem like the right thing to do at the time. Even the sanctified world of gospel music was still part of that other, often problematical world called "reality." Bumps Blackwell:

> We were recording one session on Sunday, and there were forty musicians in the studio on double time. Richard was due to arrive at 10 A.M. and he kept us all waiting around until 8 P.M., when he turned up to announce calmly, "The Lord does not want me to record today." Manny Klein, who had organized the session, broke down and wept.

When British promoter Don Arden invited Richard to tour his country in 1962 with new singing sensation Sam

Cooke, Richard jumped at the chance to be an adored entertainer again, although he made it clear he would only perform gospel music. Arden enthusiastically agreed — until the first show in Doncaster, where the audience's reaction was somewhere between inert incredulity and bewildered rage. Terrified of what adverse word of mouth was going to cost him financially, Arden begged J.W. Alexander, Cooke's manager and a friend of Richard's, to try to convince him to sing at least a few rock-and-roll songs. Alexander:

> We were late because of fog and had to be driven to the show and we missed the first one [in Doncaster]. When we got there Don Arden was having a fit. Richard had gone on the first show and done the religious thing and Arden wanted to know if we would talk to Richard and try to persuade him to do his Rock 'n' Roll. You know, if we would talk to him. I said, "Look, if I know this guy right he's a competitor. Don't need anyone else to say anything to him. Sam'll just go out there and he'll kill that audience. Richard'll come out and take care of himself."

If Cooke killed the audience, Richard — inflamed by envy, pent-up performing energy, and an unconscious craving for the return of his King of Rock and Roll crown — massacred them, leaving exhilarated corpses there and everywhere else he played in England. He kept the coronation going by agreeing to a two-month tour of Germany, where his opening act was a new band called the Beatles. It was the first time Richard realized what a deep cultural impact he and his music had had, the four reverent Liverpudlians testifying that without him and a few other first-generation rockers, they wouldn't exist. It might not have been heaven, but it was pretty damn close.

If there was any chance he might backslide into religious rectitude once he came home, Cooke's escalating recording success took care of that by making Richard resolute to return to the full gleam of the limelight (and, admittedly, all of the warm and wonderful material rewards that glimmered with it). He undertook another Arden-organized tour of England that proved as victorious as the first—this time the awestruck, recently formed Rolling Stones paying tribute to his rock-and-roll eminence—and, riding the wave of his triumphal return, recorded his first rock-and-roll songs in seven years once he was back in the United States. The King was back on his throne. Unfortunately, the majority of his subjects had left the castle.

Ironically, the very groups that were so willing to acknowledge their enormous musical debt to Richard were among the reasons the American public wasn't interested in his new material, like "Bama Lama Bama Loo," his first "comeback" single of 1964. While it is true that, with a few exceptions, American music was in a creative lull after Richard's religious exile—Jerry Lee Lewis' public ostracism for marrying his thirteen-year-old cousin, Elvis being drafted, and Chuck Berry being incarcerated for something a white man wouldn't have been—British bands like the Beatles and the Stones had turned their love of raw American rock and roll and R&B into something the media called "The British Invasion," an energetic, guitar-based take on the music they'd been so inspired by. Shaggy haircuts and funny accents didn't guarantee aesthetic success (see Herman's Hermits *et al*), but public taste is roughly equivalent to that of an easily bored seven-year-old for whom novelty is paramount. Now, when Little Richard went "Whoo!" it was passé; when Paul McCartney did it (after learning it from Richard), it was fresh and exciting. The Everly Brothers—a huge influence on the Beatles, particularly McCartney—knew their career was in trouble when someone innocently asked them if they knew that their harmonies sounded a lot like the Beatles'.

In addition, Richard claimed that racism was at work—white D.J.s were simply not playing his new records—and that "the establishment" didn't want to see his return to recording prominence. But if the first charge was true, it didn't explain how he sold millions of records when those same white D.J.s were even more entrenched in power less than a decade before; besides, a hit song, no matter who records it, makes a lot of different people a lot of money, something for which that same establishment is quite willing to overlook just about anything, even the hit-maker being African–American (in fact, they're quite adept at it). Aside from the image damage done by the British Invasion, the main reason why Richard's new songs didn't catch on is because they weren't the extraordinarily unique blasts of joyfulness his early hits were.

Realizing that public taste had changed, Richard abandoned the frenetic saxophone and piano-based sound of the fifties for, initially, a more "contemporary," guitar-heavy sound (and later, other popular "sounds," such as Stax, swamp rock, et cetera). The music was always energetic and mostly fine, but, aside from Richard's incomparable voice, incontrovertibly nondescript. A succession of different labels played up his still-outrageous persona in an attempt to recapture the public's attention (e.g., 1966's *The Wild and Frantic Little Richard* and 1967's *The Explosive Little Richard*), yet listening to these records is like being at an undeniably loud and lively house party, but without knowing whose home you're at or why everyone is there.

But even if there hadn't been his religious hiatus and the British Invasion to overcome, it's unlikely that Richard's string of recording successes would have continued much longer anyway. Given their fixed, nearly formulaic nature (he'd discovered a delight-delivering recipe; why wouldn't he keep repeating it?), it's actually remarkable that there are as many magnificent Little Richard songs as there are. It's a testament to the quality of the tunes, the power of the performances, and, most all, to Richard's matchless vocals and illimitable verve that he wasn't a one-hit wonder like other pioneer rockers like Johnny Burnette or Billy Riley, individuals who made one sound-defining (and career-defining) great track. "Tutti Frutti" is timeless. This makes up for a lot.

We exist in eternity, but that's not where we live. Any hesitation Richard might have felt about making a full-time return to the world of rock and roll was burned away by his smoldering indignation at every non-charting song. He might not have been able to control the fate of his records, but he knew he could still thrill an audience every time he stepped into the spotlight, so he put together a stage show that included a nine piece band, dancers, costume changes (heavy on regal robes), a throne for his Highness, and more camp than the biggest national park could contain. It was the dawn of the era of the self-contained "serious" group, so it wasn't what hip rock-and-roll audiences wanted to see, but Las Vegas loved it and encouraged him to push his love of spectacle right out of the stratosphere. The "Rock and Roll Revival" ethos of the late sixties brought some choice bookings (including the Toronto Peace Festival in 1969, where Richard shared the stage with elders Chuck Berry, Bo Diddley, Gene Vincent, and Jerry Lee Lewis as well as the Doors and a solo John Lennon), which, while well-meaning, nevertheless carried a career-stifling whiff of nostalgia. Bands like the MC5, Creedence Clearwater Revival, and Delaney & Bonnie knew the real deal when they heard it, though, and included passionate cover versions of Richard songs on their albums (the wild live medley on the latter's *On Tour* album being the best).

Little Richard relying on cocaine would have seemed irrational at one time — Richard *was* an energizing drug — but aging bones are springy young again and sluggish spirits wail to full sail with the ingestion of enough expensive white powder. Throughout the late-sixties and early-seventies, Richard was making a lot of money staying on the road most of the year, but what his enormous stage show didn't eat up, drugs did (eventually, not just cocaine either). Cost wasn't the only problem, of course — do enough coke, and crushing post-high depression, paranoia, and violent mood swings are more common than the longed-for euphoria the drug initially brings. After a close friend was butchered (literally), and his brother died unexpectedly of a heart attack while watering his lawn, and musician/producer turned drug dealer/pimp Larry Williams came very close to killing Richard over an unpaid drug debt, the formerly staid-seeming life of being just another one of the flock lying at the Lord's feet looked pretty appealing once again. There are no atheists in the midst of cocaine psychosis.

By the late seventies Richard had gotten clean and gone back to preaching — for awhile, even endorsed something called the Black Heritage Bible, which highlighted scriptural passages featuring black personages — and, once again, renounced not only rock and roll but homosexuality, shouting out Leviticus 18:22 and First Corinthians 6:9 liked he used to holler the magical gibberish of his songs. For thirteen years he refused to sing any of his old numbers, and even when he did—beginning at an AIDS benefit in 1989 (Richard always made clear that although he hated the sin, he loved the sinner)—it didn't matter anymore, his performances about as meaningful as his appearances on television shows like Full House and The Fresh Prince of Bel Air. Claiming now that rock and roll could be used to help spread the word of God, he finally achieved the synthesis of spirit and instinct that had eluded him his entire life, but at the cost of his art, his true spiritual calling. The oyster needs the irritation to produce the beautiful pearl. Little Richard created a rare handful.

ALAN WILSON

This long disease, my life.

—Alexander Pope

You'd think he would have been happy. Happy enough, anyway. He was the acknowledged musical force behind one of the era's most popular groups and the lead singer of two top-twenty, yet admirably individualistic singles. He not only had the respect of his peers, but—even more rare—the admiration of his initially-inspiring elders. No narcissistic rock star made still more solipsistic by too much unearned adulation, when the rest of his bandmates pursued drugs and groupies while out on tour, he searched out the nearest park to inspect and catalogue the local flora and fauna. He was twenty-seven years old when he died of a barbiturate overdose that likely wasn't intentional but might just as well have been for the indifference he frequently felt about living. If his early death was probably as inevitable as it was unfortunate, his life was as ultimately triumphant as it was undeniably troubled.

No bluesman's birth credentials could have been more suspect than Alan Christie Wilson's. Born in 1943, he grew up in the Boston suburb of Arlington, played the trombone in junior high, listened to Coltrane and Monk and East Indian music while leading a trad-jazz band as a senior, then briefly attended Boston University on a music scholarship before settling down to dedicate his life to the blues. Physically, he was pudgy, baby-faced, and bespectacled from an early age (was so myopic, in fact, his nickname was "Blind Owl"). And he was white. Which, of course, to a certain kind of well-meaning racist, meant, *ipso facto*, he could never actually *be* a bluesman.

Individuals who would never utter anything as obviously offensive as So-and-so "is a good poet for a *black* man," freely claim that some other So-and-so "is a good *white* blues guitarist." The implication in the case of the former is that there's real poetry, and then there is the inherently inferior efforts of an intrinsically second-rate poeticizing race. Which is nonsense, of course: a poem can be judged inferior or superior, but who its author is doesn't enter into the evaluatory process. Yet many of these otherwise sensible people—white *and* black, although it's usually the white, middle-class, vigilantly liberal sort who are the most vociferous—will claim that only African-Americans can sing or play the blues, and that while certain white people can passably imitate, they can never authentically duplicate. Underlying this argument is a sort of reverse racism: people with black skin are innately more soulful, passionate, funky, et cetera than people with white skin. Aside from the not-inconsiderable fact that this kind of misguided mythologizing leads to the inevitable stereotyping of an entire race as exalted performers (making them ideal as entertainers for the more "rational" races), it also presumes to judge a work of art—in this case, music—before even listening to it.

But not only does the Bible advise us to "Know them by their fruits," so does a more compelling authority: Sleepy John Estes. "The blues is a feeling. You get something happen to you, and then you can sing it off. It's a feeling that comes to you when there's anything you want to do and can't do. And when you can sing it off in a song, that gives you a thrill." In his *Poetics* Aristotle dubbed the purgative appeal of tragedy as *kartharis*; a good blues song does the same thing, and without a second act that drags and in a thirtieth of the time. Things happened to Alan Wilson; there were lots of things he wanted to do that he couldn't; he sang about them and gave not just himself a thrill, but everyone who listened. That's the blues.

Whiskey and women, the double-barreled blast that eventually scars every bluesman, weren't necessary wounds for a pre-pubescent Alan to know the blues. Preternaturally sensitive to the natural world from an early age, he came home in tears one crackling cold, limb-bending New England day to tell his mother that the trees were crying, the trees were screaming at him about how much they hurt. He also suffered from sleep paralysis. High-school friend David Maxwell: "When he'd wake up . . . [h]e couldn't move for twenty or thirty minutes . . . He would talk about the weird stuff that would happen while he was going to sleep, staring up at the ceiling. Then when he woke up, his muscles were without the ability to move for a long time, ten, fifteen minutes." You don't have to work in a cotton field to wonder why the hell everything always turns out wrong.

The first blues music that moved him was a Muddy Waters record, the distorted, filthy squall of Little Walter's harmonica setting the instrumental agenda for the rest of Alan's life. He soon learned, however, that not all "blues" music was sufficiently bluesy. Alan was drawn to Delta blues or country blues, the primal, pre-Second World War, acoustic-based music of Charlie Patton and Robert Johnson and Son House and Skip James, music that is instrumentally (usually just acoustic guitar, slide guitar, and maybe harmonica) ultra-elemental, is alternatively fiery and forlorn. A plugged-in exception was made for John Lee Hooker, who played an electric guitar, but was at his best performing solo, thumping out the beat with his foot and keeping the chords simple and sincere. Heavy sorrow needs heavy catharsis. Music doesn't get any heavier than Delta blues.

Alan's fixation on country blues and other modal, non-harmonic music like classical Indian ("Anything harmony-based, with chord changes, he couldn't get interested in," recalled friend David Polacheck. "No matter how good it was—if it wasn't modal in character, it just wasn't interesting to him") is indicative of his emotional character. Country blues is composed of blunt, minor chords played relentlessly—some would say monotonously—to aching effect. You can't play what you can't feel, and the near-absence of any other kind of music in Alan's life (either as a listener or as a writer) indicates either a deficiency and/or a denial of what most people would designate as ordinary, "happy" emotions. What cost Alan personally, though, assisted in elevating him artistically: remaining true to what he knew, he made a virtue out of his limitation of sentiment and narrowness of musical interest. We should never ask an artist to be perfect, only to be perfect at what they do.

University classes couldn't compete with staying at home and practicing the harmonica and the bottleneck guitar, however, and within a year Alan had dropped out of Boston U. and was living in the cheapest, smallest, dirtiest lodgings he could locate in Cambridge, Massachusetts, less money going out meaning less money having to come in meaning more time to do what he really wanted. Immersing himself in listening to, studying, and practicing the blues—he'd finally found a spiritual salve to rival the soothing narcosis of spending time in nature—it wasn't long before he'd become proficient enough at both guitar and harmonica to play the occasional coffee-house gig and to give lessons in what was (at least in folksy, early sixties Cambridge) still a deeply mysterious musical form. Some people—saints, industrious worldly successes, drunks, et cetera—only find genuine happiness in the total sublimation of tetchy selfhood in something bigger, better, self-blessed. Fellow blues-enthusiast Tom Hoskins:

> His apartment was pretty trashy . . . So was he, actually. But he was a cool guy. It was sort of like the absent-minded professor. He lived in his head, and his head just drove him. He didn't have time to think about personal hygiene and stuff like that, because there was so much going on in his head. He was a smart man. He was a nerd, but he was a very special nerd . . . especially when talking about blues or talking about music. Then I was kind of thinking, "Gee, maybe *I'm* privileged to hang out with *this* guy."

As liberating as absenting yourself from ordinary, everyday existence can be, however—self-consciousness shrinking as absorption in something (anything) other than yourself grows—God *does* intermittently recede, success *does* occasionally pale, sobriety *does* inevitably recur. And then you're left with disagreeable you all over again. As well as drinking too much, David Evans, a friend Alan had met at a record store around this time, remembered how Alan also "used to pull at his hair. He had a little bald spot where he pulled his hair out so much. It was somewhere

where he parted his hair. It was sort of a nervous thing."
Beautiful sunsets or the beauty of Son House's music notwithstanding, we always end up stuck with ourselves,
pissed off and pulling out our hair.

Simultaneous with Alan's discovery of the Delta blues
was the world's rediscovery of many of the same original
Delta-blues masters. Young white blues enthusiasts like
Tom Hoskins and John Fahey went from searching out
obscure records to seeking out the all-but-forgotten artists who had made them decades before. When Hoskins
managed to bring John Hurt up to Cambridge from the
Mississippi farm the sixty-two year old was working on,
Alan was invited to play harmonica at one of his gigs.
Fahey performed the same service by convincing another
aging Mississippian, Bukka White, that his music hadn't
been forgotten and that there were audiences in the north
eager to pay to hear him perform. Fahey needed to keep
costs down if White was to return south with the kind
of cash Fahey had enticed him away from home with,
so Alan volunteered to have White stay at his apartment
during the latter's week-long residency. In addition to taking his blues education to another level by learning from
White one-on-one during his week in Cambridge, Wilson
stumbled into his own part in what has come to be known
as the folk (i.e., acoustic blues) revival.

While playing White a Son House record one night,
the old man casually noted he had seen the great blues-
man not long before in Memphis. Alan tipped off room-
mate and fellow blues fanatic Phil Spiro, who, along with
Dick Waterman and Nick Perls, eventually located Son in
Rochester, New York, where he'd been living since 1943.
Son hadn't recorded since the year before he moved to
Rochester, where he'd worked as a cook and porter in

a restaurant, on the railroad, and in a department store. At the time he was unemployed, chronically alcoholic, and hadn't owned a guitar for twenty years. Undeterred, the trio booked the delighted-to-be-wooed Son to play a Cambridge club, where it was immediately evident that he wasn't yet ready for an audience, having forgotten the music and words to his own compositions and given to drunkenly ranting about God and the Devil and heaven and hell between "songs" (Son had been a Baptist preacher before exchanging a Bible for a guitar). Not much could be done about Son's imbibing (Waterman: "He could not be left on his own all day . . . [I]f he got out of your sight and found a bottle, there was no 'take a sip' or 'take a swig.' He would simply drink the entire bottle"), but he was encouraged to rehabilitate his deteriorated musical skills. Had he never done anything else of musical significance, Alan Wilson would forever be remembered by appreciative blues fans for helping make this happen.

Whether one believes that Waterman was telling the truth when he claimed that "Al Wilson taught Son House how to play Son House. I can tell you flatly that without Al invigorating and revitalizing Son, there would have been no Son House rediscovery," or the more restrained assessment of Spiro that "What really happened was that Al sat down with Son in our apartment, playing records and hearing Son's reactions. He played Son his old recordings and also played for him on the guitar. He was reminding Son of what he had done in the past, *not* teaching him how to play," it's undeniable that Alan's extraordinary musical knowledge (Son House's wasn't the only senior bluesman's catalogue he knew by rote) and simple musical prowess were invaluable to the launch of Son House's second career. When Waterman secured Son a deal with Columbia to re-record some of his classic songs, Alan ended up playing on two numbers (and two more on the expanded CD version of *Father of the Delta Blues*).

Feeling he had exhausted the Cambridge scene, in 1965 Alan accepted an offer from John Fahey to join him in California where the latter was a PhD student in music at UCLA (and where Alan could make a few bucks reading and writing musical notation for Fahey). Aside from periodically joining Fahey on stage, Alan practiced as intensely as he ever had (and quickly mastered Fahey's Indian veena, an instrument Fahey never learned how to play), read voraciously with the aid of a UCLA library card, and cut down on his beer intake in favour of a much more enlightening occasional acid trip. Assiduously tending to his soul, however, left little time for the care of his corporeal self. Fahey: "Wilson refused to take baths very often. And he usually stank. When he lived with me, I had to frequently fill up the tub with water and soap, and then threaten him, force him to take his clothes off and take a bath. And I'd buy him clothes and underwear and stuff." When a geeked-out Alan glommed upon recent country blues discoveree Skip James, the infamously caustic James snapped at the younger man, "Why don't you take a bath?" Too bad Alan never made a solo album; he could have called it *Alan Wilson: Dirty Blues*.

Alan hadn't been in California long before he met Bob Hite, a man who was the antithesis of Alan in every important way but one. Huge, hirsute, and loudly extroverted (his nickname was "The Bear"), Hite was also the owner of approximately fifteen-thousand blues records, and even though he didn't play an instrument on stage, was as much an amateur scholar (the best kind) of the blues, although not exclusively of country blues, as Alan. The two quickly formed an acoustic jug band with a couple of others (Alan coaxed out of his cocoon of passivity by Hite's aggressive, gregarious enthusiasm), and soon the ever-curious Alan was messing around with an electric guitar. A couple of personnel changes later, the now entirely electrified first Canned Heat line-up was set. The band's name was taken from a 1929 Tommy Johnson song, "Canned Heat Blues," a tune about the intoxicating potential of a certain kind of homemade hooch made from Sterno, a portable cooking/heating source.

Alan hadn't abandoned his love of country blues—he blew harmonica on most of the band's songs as well as playing bottleneck guitar—but Canned Heat, while founded on Alan and Hite's idea of electrifying (in all possible ways) country blues—as opposed to updating the uptown Chicago-blues sound, like, say, the Paul Butterfield Blues Band—was a more eclectic unit than Alan would have hatched on his own. Alan appreciated Henry Vestine's bright B.B. King-based guitar playing, which created an interesting fusion when combined with his own, darker Delta-blues style. And Hite's bawdily boisterous stage manner—modelled in part on the performing persona of Howlin' Wolf, although updated for the peace-and-love generation to include more smiles than sneers—provided Canned Heat with some necessary razzmatazz, complementing (and, to be honest, compensating for) Alan's stationary, if stately, aloofness. (To the same degree that Hite clearly revelled in being the centre of attention, Alan looked as uncomfortable on stage as he did off—not nervous or self-conscious, just slightly confused as to why he was physically *there*.) While it's undeniable that Vestine's increasing fascination with loud British blues (e.g., Cream) occasionally pushed the band into indulgent, near-parodic jam territory, and that Hite's hyperactive exhortations to "boogie" too often sounded like the over-excitable blather of a frat boy after too many beers, and that when Alan died, Canned Heat became instantly, irrelevantly one-dimensional, pure boogie-rock dunderheads, at their best, the band was a classic case of being more than the sum of its performing parts. Dark needs light to know it exists; ditto, light.

The new band quickly established a reputation as a powerful live act doing authentic blues, and were soon as busy playing LA clubs as they wanted to be. Hite's large — in every sense of the word — presence was what was naturally most conspicuous to concertgoers, but discerning attendees couldn't help but notice the band's pale, pudgy, virtually immobile guitar player. Early fan Roger Handy often caught the band at the Ash Grove Club. "Alan was just a total god to me," he recalled. "I always went to hear Canned Heat, and I'd park myself right in front of Alan's Super Reverb amplifier so I could hear him play harmonica and hear him play slide guitar to best advantage. He was just something else." It was at the Ash Grove that a Liberty Records executive caught their act and offered them a deal. Within weeks the band was in the studio recording their eponymous debut LP. Released in July 1967, unlike many of the incense-and-peppermint-saturated albums born in the "Summer of Love," *Canned Heat* sounds as fresh and invigorating today as it must have nearly half a century ago, its bedrock traditionalism ironically guaranteeing it perennial contemporariness.

Canned Heat reflects what the band's early shows sounded like (among non-bootleg recordings, *Live at the Topanga Corral* — although actually recorded at the Kaleidoscope Club — is the closest one can get to hearing the real thing). Hite agreeably bellows his way though ten of the eleven cuts, all of them covers of vintage blues songs, compensating for what he lacks in subtlety and range with guts and contagious glee. Even on down-and-out tunes like Willie

Dixon's "Evil is Going On" and William Harris' "Bullfrog Blues," Hite sounds like exactly what he was: a lifelong fan finally getting the chance to do it himself, and having a blast every minute of it. Alan's reverb-laden harmonica work and slippery slide guitar are the most impressive things about the album, especially the former. As with most serious blues harpists, Little Walter was Alan's biggest influence, the older man's brash, amplified sound taken further forward by Alan's extensive use of reverb, a sound simultaneously antediluvian and near-psychedelic, particularly on the slower, simmering numbers. And like any true master of his instrument, Alan never plays a boring note, never lazily repeats himself, never falls back on genre clichés.

Alan's sole lead vocal on *Canned Heat* is a version of Sonny Boy Williamson's "Help Me." Unlike Hite, who sounds like Howlin' Wolf before he hit full puberty, Alan, despite singing falsetto, sounds like himself, his startlingly high, surprisingly hushed, thoroughly somber voice accentuating his absolute individuality. (Though it's obvious Alan was inspired by the upper-register eeriness of Skip James, he proves it's possible to be inspired by, and pull from a tradition, without becoming buried in the source.) Like any other artistic form, the blues can easily get ground down in mannerisms, formulas, and clichés, and too many blues singers, regardless of race, believe that in order to come across as "authentic" they need to sound like they imagine an elderly, uneducated, usually southern black man would. Even those who understand that authenticity is born out of necessary personal expression and thereby sing *their* blues *their* way sometimes fall into this imitative trap. When the Gun Club's Jeffrey Lee Pierce sings about "the whiskey and the womens" instead of "the whiskey and the women" (as he would ordinarily say it) in the course of the band's otherwise wonderfully original, punked-up take on Son House's "Preaching the Blues," it doesn't sound more "authentic" or even like a post-modern, nudge-nudge-wink-wink homage. It sounds like a white man singing in blackface.

Being in a band and recording an album and playing before audiences kept Alan busy and from indulging his worst excessively-introspective instincts, but you're never so busy that you forget what it is to be human. Most, if not all people at one time or another, for instance, suffer romantic trauma; which, for a blues musician, isn't only not an unuseful thing, it's almost compulsory. (John Lee Hooker: "If it wasn't for women, there wouldn't be no blues.") But even among those for whom a worried mind and a broken heart constitute ideal working conditions, Alan's erotic travails managed to set new industry standards. Though he lived at the peak of an era when sexual promiscuity wasn't just acceptable, it was mandatory for anyone who was fashionably liberated, Alan's difficulties getting laid (never mind finding a fulfilling relationship) bordered on the tragi-comic. Frank Cook, Canned Heat's first drummer:

> He thought that he would be loved by women because of the art he did. That's not unusual, except there was a real desperation. He felt he was too dorky, too shy around women. He was incredibly naïve in that area. I think he was a virgin, or he'd only done it once or something along those lines . . . So I told him, "Okay, let me set this up." I remember the night very well. I told my wife at the time I was gonna go out on a mission to get Al laid. She said, "I think you ought to." [So] we [Cook and a female friend of his] got loaded together and he [Alan] was waiting in the car. I asked her if she could sleep with my friend, and

she said, you know, "Okay!" And so then I came downstairs. She was in an apartment house, and I came out the
front door and said, "Okay, look, Marilyn's ready . . . All
you need to do is go up there, it's apartment number four
upstairs. Push the door open, walk in, go up the second
floor, fourth apartment." So I leave him there and I see him
the next day. I said, "Well, Alan, how'd it go, huh?" And he
said, "Instead of pushing in on the door, I pulled back on
it, and it locked."

That one of the two front men in a popular sixties musical group suffered such sexual indignities might seem
implausible if the sufferer weren't Alan. Somatically, he
was almost entirely indifferent to his corporeal existence.
David Evans:

He just looked kind of like your all-American nerd, I suppose you'd say. He'd tape his glasses up when he'd break
them, the rim, the nose, or on the side. He'd take bandage
tape and tape it together . . . In a lot of ways, he was kind of
the classic nerd, I guess. He was the guy who was just out of
it. He wasn't concerned socially about things; he just wanted
you to take him as he was. He didn't try to put on anything
for anyone as far as how to look or present himself.

Socially, Alan was beyond introversion—his idea of
a good time when Canned Heat was on the road was
to investigate the botany in the nearest park. He even
brought his own food and cooking utensils on tour. Band
manager Skip Taylor:

We'd check into a Holiday Inn or a Hilton or whatever, and
he had his little hot plate kind of thing, and a little stove, and
he'd take his bagged food. That's his things, and off he'd go!

"Well," he'd say, "what time do I have to be back? What time
are we leaving?" I mean, right when we'd check in . . .

Every emotional slight was a burning psychological sore, no
rebuff too inconsequential not to be the source of a fresh
psychic cancer. "London Blues," from *Future Blues*, Alan's
last studio album with the band, is a slow-crawling litany of
amorous wrongs inflicted on him by . . . a groupie. A groupie!
When he half-sings/speaks in his trademark wounded war-
ble of how he can't believe she called him up to ask him
for free concert tickets, he really does sound shocked and
disgusted. Friend Marina Bokelman remembered how at
times like this "you could almost see the black cloud around
him. It was a visible depression, in his body language . . .
He would become more taciturn, not want to speak, and be
kind of listless. It's like the light would go out."

While touring their debut album, the band, sans
Alan—who was off collecting leaves while the others
were partying back at the hotel—was busted for pot
possession when such things meant potential jail time.
Undeterred, however, they were back in the studio
recording their next LP within months of their debut's
release. The differences between it and its successor, *Boogie with Canned Heat*, are striking. Most apparent is the number of original compositions, even if the
majority, as per the blues tradition, borrow freely from
other, older songs. "Whiskey Headed Woman No.2,"
for instance, is an amped-up, boogie-charged rewrite of
Tommy McClennan's "Whiskey Headed Woman" that
pays respect to the past while making sure to exist in the
present, a task not easily, or often, achieved, too many
blues purists often forgetting that too much studied rev-
erence makes for too little necessarily irreverent, essential liveliness. Alan's "An Owl Song" is noteworthy less

as a song than for containing his first all-original lyrics as well as the swinging melody and added instrumentation (horns and piano), Alan obviously becoming more comfortable working in the studio and willing to experiment further with the basic country-blues sound via overdubs. The songs that Alan wasn't significantly involved with are *Boogie with Canned Heat*'s weakest, including the LP's interminable nadir, "Fried Hockey Boogie," a portent of the death-by-boogie overdosing to come.

The album's unquestionable highlight is Alan's "On the Road Again." Although based on Floyd Jones' song of the same name (who modelled *his* song on Tommy Johnson's "Big Road Blues"), from the opening, droning buzz that is an Indian tanpura, but to Western ears sounds like nothing so much as the ominous whirr of an approaching cloud of malevolent cicadas, it's obvious that this is no deferential blues cover. After six deliberate descending plucks of a stringed instrument, we slide into a near-hypnotic harmonica- and bass-and-drums-driven groove that doesn't let up until song's end, at which time we hear a slow ascending trip up the same set of strings. Even when Alan employed another's lyrics, as he did here, because he lacked even an ounce of showbiz, they always had to represent his own feelings or point of view for him to convincingly sing them, and Jones' tale of loneliness, abandonment, and sorrow sounds comfortably uncomfortably lived-in, especially as delivered in Alan's fretfully high, forlorn tone. Issued as the B-side of "Boogie Music," a one-off attempt to create an upbeat, catchy tune after "Evil Woman," the first single from *Boogie with Canned Heat*, failed to sell, the strangely alluring "On the Road Again" had been a commercial afterthought until D.J.s began playing it between the usual Top 40 fodder. "On the Road Again" eventually made it to number eight in the

UK and 16 at home, an atypical wedding of good taste and popular acceptance.

With the unexpected influx of hit-record money, Hite bought a house in the hills of Topanga Canyon, Vestine bought guitars and drugs, and Alan bought biology books. He didn't even have a place to call his own, renting a small room in an apartment he shared with two college students who rarely saw him, sleeping on friends' couches or in his van, or, more and more frequently, crashing in his sleeping bag in a park or in Hite's heavily wooded backyard. While the others were enjoying the material benefits of having a top-twenty single, Alan, its author, became fixated on what he saw as the imminent extinction of the California redwoods (and, by extension, the earth's ecosystem). Marina Bokelman:

> He would be extremely distressed, distraught even, about the trees. He would come in and it would be like, "Do you realize? This is what's happening! And they're becoming extinct at the rate of this, and do you realize what's happening?" There was a sense of urgency and despair, that this thing was happening and there was nothing he could do about it.

In retrospect, Canned Heat manager Skip Taylor realized that Alan's growing depression was entwined with his apocalyptic environmentalism:

> His whole outlook on society and the environment, pollution and the growth of the cities, things like that—that's what was really getting to him. I think he had just locked himself into a kind of tunnel vision, that things were, excuse the word, fucked. And there was nothing he or anybody else was going to be able to do about it, and he didn't want to be around to see it all.

In the meantime, the only thing to do was to record a new album, the band's second of 1968. A two-record set, *Living the Blues* contains three-quarters of a single album's worth of first-rate music. All of side one is given over to some vigorously performed vintage covers (Charlie Patton, Jimmy Rogers) faithfully roared to life by the Bear (as well as a less successful Hite original, the generic, overlong "Sandy's Blues"); Alan's second all-original composition, "My Mistake (an excellent example of how Vestine's attacking style and Alan's soothing slide could compliment each other if the former kept his volume knob turned below ten); and another one of Alan's sparkling reclamation jobs, a reworked version of Henry Thomas' "Bull Doze Blues," here entitled "Going Up the Country." From its opening burst of flute, the latter announces itself as something unique in Alan's canon: a joyously celebratory song, an irresistibly catchy, lighthearted hymn of praise to nature, travel, and hope. Another improbable hit (compared to Alan's voice, Bob Dylan sounds like Frank Sinatra), it made it all the way to number eleven in the US. It's fortunate that Alan was long dead by the time the song was leased to a parade of corporations as TV-commercial background music (including Tide Clean Breeze, a product it's hard to imagine him comprehending, never mind using) — he might have been compelled to compose a sequel: "Going up the Country with a Gun to Kill the Sonofabitches to Whom Nothing is Sacred except for the Making of More and More Money."

There's not a lot to recommend over the remaining two-and-a-half sides of *Living the Blues*. After a credible, cranked-up cover of Blind Lemon Jefferson's "One Kind Favor" (sometimes known as "See That My Grave is Kept Clean"), there's the nearly twenty minute "Parthenogenesis," a group showcase meant to illustrate the essence of each group member's singular skills but which resulted in a confused mess of indulgent fragments. (Not surprisingly, Alan comes out best—particularly on the poignant "Childhood's End," the inclusion of a handful of chromatic harmonica workouts and jaw-harp ragas— one of which was recorded two years previous with John Fahey—impressive proof of his exploratory spirit, ragas sharing a certain mesmerizing modality with country blues.) The real genesis of this mess is likely revealed on the *Canned Heat '70—Live In Europe* album when a fan shouts out a request for "Parthenogenesis" and Hite replies, "Yeah, right. You got any acid?" The entire second album of *Living the Blues* is given over to a two-sided, forty-one minute live version of "Refried Boogie," just in case the pithy eleven-minute studio version on *Boogie with Canned Heat* wasn't enough. Boogie till you puke, indeed.

After recording a fine, highly inventive single, "Time Was," that was closer to blues-based pop than anything else Alan had ever done and which—surprise, surprise— chronicles his disappointment over how a relationship that had once seemed so secure had collapsed, the band began work on their next album, *Hallelujah*. Pulling back from the excesses of *Living the Blues* was one step in the right direction (a single LP; no forty-minute live jams; et cetera); another was Alan composing and singing four of the eleven tracks (Hite's efforts beginning to sound hackneyed in spite of, or maybe because of, his never-ending he-man hollering). In addition to the "failed" single "Time Was" (it rose only as high as sixty-seven, which was probably a relief—another hit and Alan might have had to perform on American Bandstand), there was "Do Not Enter," "Get Off My Back," and "Change My Ways," all of them, like "Time Was," using traditional blues forms as a springboard for something bracingly different.

Lyrically, Alan remained loyal to the classic *aab* stanza, but not only was he now singing in his own, non-falsetto voice, the actual words had become his own Alan Wilson vernacular. Both "Do Not Enter" and "Get Off My Back"—hurt, cranky, near-paranoid—are all the more disturbing because he sounds as if he's speaking directly to the listener. It's akin to what Nick Drake attempted to do on his final album *Pink Moon*, direct communication between performer and listener, just one soul talking to another, all of the potentially interfering artiness expunged from the art. The pathos of "Change My Ways"—a nice bit of self-advice (which he unfortunately never took) to open up to other human beings like he does with nature—is intensified by the fact that we can clearly hear Alan's ultimately futile desire to change. Musically, this latest batch of songs were livelier in tempo and richer in texture, a case, perhaps, of whistling a happy tune while walking past the gaping graveyard. (In fact, Alan is literally whistling on "Change My Ways.") *Future Blues* would be where he'd perfect this highly individual style of blues, but *Hallelujah* is where the template was first clearly formed.

In spite of this artistic breakthrough, it was at around this time that Alan attempted to take his own life. Speaking to a *Rolling Stone* reporter a year or so later, Hite remembered how at some point Alan

> stopped rappin' and laughin'. Everything got him uptight, the smog in L.A., what people were doing to the redwoods ... Everything ... He said to me, "I don't know what my problems are anymore. It's a drag gettin' up every day." One night he walked out of the Topanga Corral with a half pint of gin. He'd stashed fifty reds somewhere and he figured he'd do it that way. But someone'd stolen the reds. The next day

he wrecked his van, but with not a scratch on himself. He was so disappointed.

Hite and Taylor insisted that Alan seek professional help. Agreeable to the idea but typically apathetic about acting upon it, his lead singer and manager eventually took the unorthodox—but, to their minds, necessary—step of having Alan committed to a mental hospital, which he went along with willingly. When he was discharged he may or may not have been psychologically healthier, but he did have a wonderful new song he'd written while inside receiving treatment.

"Poor Moon" is yet another aesthetic leap forward. Subject matter-wise, its lamentation over the pernicious impact of human beings on the natural world—specifically, Alan's fear of what the impending moon landing would one day lead to—is certainly a blues-rock first, a blasting open of a lyrical domain usually reserved for the exclusively personal. Musically, too, it's a fascinating artifact; conspicuously solo-less and with a virtually a cappella break in the middle, the inclusion of beginning-to-end background vocals (overdubbed by Alan) are a Canned Heat first, the "Oh Well Oh Well Oh Well Oh Well Oh" chanting throughout a sort of Beach-Boys-gone-modal-mad technique that pulls the listener under and into Alan's obsession. In spite of its undeniable catchiness—for someone who was so grounded in country blues, Alan always brought an appealing, pop-like melodic touch to all of his compositions—the song, not surprisingly, failed to chart in the top one hundred. Oh well.

When Henry Vestine, citing his inability to continue working with bassist Larry Taylor (this, after Taylor said he'd never work with *him* again after a stoned Vestine played a particularly long, loud, and pointless solo live), abruptly quit the band a month or so after the release of "Poor Moon," for once the tumult surrounding the band wasn't all Alan's doing. A replacement, Harvey Mandel, was quickly found, and the band embarked on a long tour, including a stop at Woodstock, before ultimately departing for Europe. The tour, captured on the *Canned Heat '70—Live in Europe* album, is notable for a storming version of the band's new single, a Bob Hite-sung cover of Wilbert Harrison's "Let's Work Together" that features Alan peeling off some searing bottleneck lines, and Alan's performance of two of his own songs, one of which was at that point unrecorded and another that was never to appear on a studio LP. The aforementioned "London Blues" is Alan's new "argot blues" at its best, a plain-sung (almost spoken) tale of deceit and disappointment, blazing boogie rock for the pathologically sensitive. But it's the harrowing "Pulling Hair Blues" that sets the bar for creating confessional uneasiness in the listener. Accompanied only by Taylor's softly plunking bass and his own mournful harmonica, Alan enumerates the minutiae of his depression: how he's eating too much, how he can't get laid, how he's pulling out his hair, how he can't sleep, how he knows he should be enjoying himself as he travels around the world, but that it brings him no pleasure. It's as stark a portrait of clinical depression as anyone is going to live to give. (One only wishes it had been recorded again in the studio so that the distracting bass solo in the middle could be excised.)

Once home, the band began work on their next— and their last with Alan—studio album. *Future Blues* is Canned Heat's best LP not just because of Alan's quartet of superb songs, but because Mandel supplies subtler, more inventive guitar support throughout than Vestine ever had and because the tacked-on single "Let's Work

Together" is an ideal vehicle for Hite's let's-all-boogie bawl and the leadoff-track "Sugar Bee" is a perfectly inconsequential ditty perfectly shouted out by Hite with Alan and Mandel trading off twangy leads and Alan using so much reverb on his harmonica it sounds as if he's blown out your speakers' woofers. In addition to an even more disturbing studio version of "London Blues," there's the positively merry "Shake and Break It" (a tune Alan might have heard during the Son House sessions five years before), the equally cheery "Skat" (a lyric-less excursion into its title's genre, evidence both that, whatever else was or wasn't going on in his life, Alan's musical curiosity—and courage—never abated, and that he never wallowed in his ennui), and the staggering "My Time Ain't Long" (only slightly sullied by a pointless guitar-freak out coda). Its title cribbed from either Robert Johnson or Elmore James (or whoever *they* cribbed it from) and with a bottleneck hook worthy of James, one of that instrument's masters, the song is movingly oxymoronic, each stanza rhapsodizing about how beautiful things like the moon shining through some trees are, only to have such bucolic visions cruelly undercut by the claim in the chorus that the narrator knows he won't be around for very much longer to enjoy them. Inside the record's gatefold there's a long appeal from Alan entitled "Grim Harvest" for fans to get involved in the fight to save the disappearing redwoods, and a full-length picture of the band huddled in the forest, everyone looking morosely at the camera except for Alan who's standing between two dwarfing California giants, a tiny hand on each as he peers up through his thick glasses at the tops of the trees, staring in equal parts wonder and woe.

Sometime after *Future Blues'* release Alan entered the hospital again, this time voluntarily. Needing mental help is not good; seeking it out is, is an encouraging survival sign. Alan was well-enough to check himself in and out of the hospital while the band recorded their next album, one that wouldn't be released while he was alive. *Hooker 'N' Heat* is the new boys of boogie backing up the master, John Lee Hooker, on a justified two-record set. All of the songs were written and sung by Hooker, so a song-by-song breakdown is out of place here, but the album is still essential listening for fans of Alan's work because of his superbly sympathetic accompaniment, particularly on six of the non-band tracks, just Hooker on electric guitar and Alan joining him on either harmonica or piano (the only recorded instance of Alan playing the latter instrument). All that needs to be said here of Alan's work on *Hooker 'N' Heat* is Hooker's own assessment of his young accompanist three decades later. "I say that man was a *genius*," Hooker told his biographer, Charles Shaar Murray. "If you didn't know him, you couldn't get right into him. You didn't know how to get into that beautiful frame he had around him. Inside him, that was beautiful. *Beautiful*."

A couple of months after the Hooker sessions wrapped up, Alan took the band back into the studio to record his final song. "Human Condition" is a swinging, practically peppy account of what seems to be a conversation between Alan and a psychiatrist, with Alan coming to understand that the low-down feelings he's been experiencing aren't unique to him but are in fact endemic to his particular species. The only thing to do, he concludes, is to know it, to accept it, and to stand up to it.

And then it was time to hit the road again. It wasn't unusual for the rest of the band to show up at the airport for a tour and find Alan absent. They'd roll their eyes and maybe moan a little about *Who does he think he is that he doesn't have to play by the same rules as everybody else?* then wait for him to show up on a later flight, always there and ready to play by the time it was show time. But not this time.

Given Alan's most recent institutionalization and past suicidal tendencies, as well as his general despondency, drummer Fito de la Parra, for one, wondered if, when Alan didn't show up on September 2 for a European tour, there might be more to it this time than Alan just being Alan.

> [W]e were all in the limousine . . . outside the TWA terminal in LAX. There was no sign of Alan. Skip Taylor drove up and stuck his head in the limo window. "We can't find him. Nobody knows where the hell he is. If you guys don't get on that plane right now, you'll miss the festival, and we already cashed the deposit so we'd be in deep legal shit if that happens. Get on the plane." He stopped for a minute. "You know what I think?" "Yeah," Bear said. "We know what you think." "I think he's dead" [Taylor replied].

What Taylor eventually discovered was this: the day the band left for Europe, Alan had driven his van to Bob Hite's house and taken, as he often did, his sleeping bag with him into the surrounding woods. What Ed Marrow, Hite's wife's son from a prior relationship, discovered the next morning was Alan in his sleeping bag, his clothes folded neatly on the ground beside him, and that Canned Heat was in need of a new guitarist.

The coroner ruled it death by barbiturate overdose, which many have taken to mean suicide by the same. But while the authorities didn't find any suicide note, they did find four more pills in Alan's pants pocket, and if someone was intent upon overdosing, it's unlikely they would have hoarded four pills. Additionally, the classic death-by-downers formula is pills plus booze, and the coroner found no trace of alcohol in his body. What likely happened was that Alan, in desperate need of a decent night's sleep—hence his arrival at Hite's property, where he often ended up when particularly plagued by insomnia—took more pills than he should have to ensure that he got it.

He did. His body was cremated and his ashes spread amongst the California redwoods he worried over so much. He didn't have to worry about them, or anything else, anymore.

WILLIE P. BENNETT

Fame is no plant that grows on mortal soil.

—John Milton

Willie P. Bennett sang about coming down from Thessalon, how Toronto was not his home, but Toronto was where he was born, in 1951, and Toronto was where I saw him play for the first time, at the Free Times Café in 1985, thirty people—tops—jammed into a room no bigger than your living room, all of them knowing what they were in for except me. All I knew about country-folk was through my Neil Young albums, and even that puny war was dearly paid for, believe me, no high-school girl willing to find out if side two of *On the Beach*—the slow side—was a turn-it-up turn-on, no radio station out of nearby Detroit disposed to extending their idea of heavy metal to a steel-guitar bar.

One of the things I wanted to do when I left home for university and Toronto was to go to an actual folk club and see an actual folk singer. I looked in *Now* magazine under the listing for *Folk* and picked the Free Times Café because it was near Spadina and College, two streets I at least knew the names of. I forget who I went with — it doesn't matter who I went with — I forget who I went with because what I do remember is that on the way home back to my room in residence that night I had a song-buzzing brain and a self-financed, privately produced cassette tape that Willie sold for ten dollars at the end of the show out of the yellow cloth bag slung over his shoulder. It was self-financed and privately produced because, I later learned, the three albums he recorded in the seventies were put out by a small Canadian label that no longer existed, and by the mid-eighties, the darkest of the dark ages of popular music, anything un-synthesized and non-digitized was sonically suspect.

Anyone who I thought deserved him, I dragged off to see him. Girlfriends and friends became ex-girlfriends and strangers, but the years couldn't touch the music; even Time, the biggest bully of all, can never touch the music. Good music, I mean. And even though a hundred-dollar cut of the door was considered a very good night's take and it was usually only other musicians and freaks like me, who'd hunted down all of the out-of-print albums and traded bootlegs of folk-festival shows, who knew who he was and what his music meant, songs like "White Line" and "Storm Clouds" and "Down to the Water" and "Lace and Pretty Flowers" are as good as any of the best stuff John Prine or Guy Clark or even Townes Van Zandt were writing back then. And just because no one knows it doesn't mean it's not true.

He was sixteen years old when he dropped out of Danforth Technical School (now Danforth Collegiate and Technical Institute) and got his first job as a shipper-receiver and bought his first guitar and decided to become a folk singer, a fact so charmingly archaic-sounding, *it* could be the subject of a folk song. He eventually ended up in London, Ontario, in the early seventies where, more than Toronto, there was a lively folk and bluegrass scene. String-player extraordinaire David Essig, founder of Woodshed Records and the producer of the three brilliant albums Willie would record for the label, remembers how Willie "lived initially for a short time with Stan and Garnet Rogers in a one-bedroom apartment. Stan got the bedroom; Garnet slept on the chesterfield; and Willie slept on the floor in a broom closet that he outfitted as a makeshift bedroom."

Playing around town and elsewhere, whether solo or with a progressive bluegrass aggregate known as the Bone China Band, Willie's genuinely emotive singing (he always hit the high notes out of the corner of his mouth) and erudite yet earthy songs began to attract the sort of attention every genuine artist craves: life-altering adoration. Scott Bradshaw—aka Scott B. Sympathy, the Toronto folk-rock troubadour who helped keep acoustic guitars cool during the aurally ugly eighties—remembers how he "first heard Willie sing at the Snales Pace Coffee House on Talbot Street in London about 1976. I was nineteen or so. [From that point on,] I spent the next bunch of years trying to turn everyone I knew on to this *talent*. I remember buying . . . copies of *Hobo's Taunt* [Willie's second album] to hand out to friends." A major-label, high-powered, big-budgeted publicist might make you popular, but disciples handing out your work for free will help make your art immortal.

Eventually Ken Palmer, mandolin player and founder of the bluegrass Dixie Flyers (Willie played harmonica with the Flyers when he wasn't gigging on his own), took over his management, and Essig and Palmer, friends as well as fellow pickers, decided to turn Willie's fat batch of beautiful songs into 1975's *Tryin' To Start Out Clean*, even if that meant having to create a brand new record label—Woodshed—to do so. It was worth it for the sake of the music.

Music like "Music in Your Eyes," a song so sorrowfully delicate it threatens to break down right before your ears before its rebirth in the blooming chorus, everything alight and music in your eyes. Music like "Country Squall" and "Down to the Water" and "Willie's Diamond Joe," melodious acoustic prayers for redemption, understanding, release. *Tryin' To Start Out Clean* is no neo-folkie relic, however, the addition of the Dixie Flyers' expert picking and plucking (abetted by producer David Essig's warm mandolin and Ron Dann's sweet pedal steel) infusing the entire album with an irresistibly affirmative zest that makes such convenient catchphrases as *folk* or *bluegrass* or *country* (or any hyphenated combination thereof) meaningless. Oh, and the opening suite ("Driftin' Snow" into "White Line" into "Me and Molly") is the best album opener in the history of roots music—period—all of the hallowed household names in your CD collection not excepted. The LP ends with the title track (followed by a brief reprise of "Driftin' Snow"), and just *try* not to tap your foot and join in on the chorus. Sole music for the soul.

Despite receiving some nice recognition from fellow musicians (Maryland's Seldom Scene covered "White Line" on their *Live at the Cellar Door* album, as did, among others, David Whiffen, John Starling, and Jonathan Edwards), an unknown musician's debut (albeit astounding) LP on an idealistic Canadian independent record label meant more hard slogging on the club and folk festival circuit and making up the monetary difference building docks on Georgian Bay, playing on other people's records, and drywalling. There's a 3:55-second snippet on YouTube of a wild-haired Willie and band (featuring an equally hyper-hirsute Ken Whiteley on mandolin) performing at Hamilton's Festival of Friends in 1976 that conveys enough of the raucous joy they were clearly capable of delivering live to make you resent being merely virtually there. (The raucous joy wasn't limited to the music they made. Musician Tony Quarrington, who would go on to produce Willie's last album, *Heart Strings*, remembered following Willie *et al* at the Groaning Board in Toronto: "Willie and his band had been there the week before, and even though the gig was pretty well-paid, Willie and his cohorts drank so much on their tabs that at the end of the week they owed the club hundreds of dollars. Or maybe it was just Willie, and not the band.")

Two years after *Tryin' To Start Out Clean* came *Hobo's Taunt*, this time co-produced by Willie and again containing a disc full of superlative songs and impassioned singing and playing, although on his second offering the newgrass emphasis was played down in favour of a stronger folksinger timbre with clear traditional country touches. Instead of being a concession to the marketplace, however (what marketplace? Country-pap queen Anne Murray's fans weren't going to be interested either way), aside from the spry opener, "Come On Train" and the simply gorgeous "Lace and Pretty Flowers" (which Willie wrote at the bequest of a couple of betrothed friends an hour before their wedding), the songs are slower, sadder, and even more meditative than on the debut, befitting the less lively arrangements. Also new were the horns supplied by Chris Whiteley and Tom Evans that adorned a couple of tracks, not pick-up-the-tempo, Saturday-night-happy horns, but heartrending, Sunday-morning-after horns. Listening to songs like "Storm Clouds," which laments loss of nerve and wasted (chemical and otherwise) time, or the title track which bemoans a mind that won't do what it's told, or "Lonely Car Funerals," which wonders who it was that died and why no one showed up to say goodbye, it's easy to forget that Willie was only twenty-six years old when *Hobo's Taunt* appeared. Among three million other useful things, art reminds us that insight isn't proportionate to age, and that personal pain is the itch that helps make the impersonal pearl of lasting artworks.

None of the songs on *Hobo's Taunt* are self-pitying paeans to then-fashionable singer-songwriter solipsism, nor do they have a depressing effect upon the listener. This is partly because of Willie's always highly melodic songwriting, and partly because, like all good art, the songs *explore* melancholy and loss of meaning as opposed to merely reveling in them. "Poetry is the spontaneous overflow of powerful feelings . . . recollected in tranquility," Wordsworth claimed, and Essig and recording engineer Daniel Lanois and Willie recollected masterfully inside the tranquility of the Lanois brothers' Grant Avenue Studio in Hamilton.

A flawless, entirely filler-free first album is rare (*Music from the Big Pink*, *The Violent Femmes*, *Willis Alan Ramsey*, *Paul Siebel*, and maybe a few more), but not unheard of; after all, there'd been a lifetime to write and polish the songs and perfect the sound that comprises the inaugural LP. But when it's time, a year or two later, to head back into the studio and do the whole thing all over again, the song quality tends, understandably, to drop off. Again, there are exceptions (the Band's eponymously-titled sophomore effort, for instance), but the exceptions are even more exceptional the second time around. Willie not only managed to avoid the sophomore jinx with *Hobo's Taunt*, but with his third album in just four years, 1978's *Blackie and the Rodeo King*, he pulled off that rarest of musical career rarities (so rare, in fact, no others come to mind), a tour de force hat-trick. He was only twenty-seven years old, and there were more good songs to come, but it was the last time he'd bury one deep in the back of the net, no instant replay required.

Blackie is a continuation of the sound and sense of its predecessor: a primarily folk-based, country-rock palette augmented by astute dabs of Chris Whiteley's trumpet and Essig's mandolin, with lyrics highlighting the loneliness, uncertainty, and regret that come with belonging to the human species. Again, it's not a lyrically morose or musically lugubrious listening experience—W.H. Auden said that if someone is writing a love poem, they're thinking about their prosody, not the love object of the poem, and Willie *et al* were too accomplished as artists to overlook the importance of memorable melodies, sympathetic musical accompaniment, et cetera—but it's obvious that around this time Willie was suffering through some serious romantic travails that were to his music's, if not his personal life's, benefit. (Willie's heartache resources ran deep: was married and divorced, had girlfriends and breakups, and at the time of his death called Linda Duemo more than a girlfriend if not legally a wife.)

Both "Has Anyone Seen My Baby Here Tonight?" and "(If I Could) Take My Own Advice" bemoan the kind of love that revolves around women who the narrator knows are cheating on him, but whom he can't help loving (and forgiving) anyway. The title track, a true story about two characters Willie met on a Greyhound bus trip from London to Hamilton, while ultimately affirmative in the way that the two outcasts in the song's title look out for one another, is, after all, about a heroin addict and a dying drunk, while songs like "This Lonesome Feelin'" and "Standing By the Highway

(No Place in Mind)" convey their emotionally isolated essences by their titles alone. Even the lone cover tune on the album, the indestructible "Stardust," is about a love that *used* to be—today's only solace coming not from a living person, but from the song that gets written about her. And "Pens and Papers," distinguished by a moving Keith Whiteley organ solo, succeeds in upping the aloneness ante by starting off being about a failed love affair before turning into a disquisition on the artist's ultimately futile attempt to make sense out of things like, well, failed love affairs. If Willie thought his ink was running in the rain at this point, with three dazzling albums to his credit, one shudders to think what he felt over the next dark decade.

Ah, yes, the eighties. You remember them: an epoch when otherwise-intelligent people routinely referred to Madonna and Prince as geniuses, and *Born in the U.S.A* was considered stirring roots music. Scott Bradshaw testifies to how "It was a tough go for a folk musician at that time. I was one of the only ones playing acoustic guitar on Queen Street in those days. Hard to believe now. I do remember drum machines and sax players were plentiful." As an indication of just how far Willie's already modest commercial standing had fallen, music journalist Chris Vautour recalled how

> I first heard about Bennett when a band called Varis Tombley started playing an amphetamine-fueled version of his song "Blackie & The Rodeo King" in the summer of 1988. Later it turned out that a co-worker of mine was a friend of Bennett, so I asked my colleague if he could buy some records from Bennett for me. He came back and told me that Bennett didn't even have copies of his own records, and that if I could find some, Willie would buy them from me.

Even if venues weren't as welcoming and audiences weren't as large, Willie still gigged, of course (sometimes in the company of Colin Linden and his scintillating slide-guitar and yelp-on-top background vocals), it being his primary income source, and continued to win new converts (like me) one underpaid show at a time. *Live at the Nervous Breakdown*, a compilation record recorded at a London, Ontario club you'll have a hard time finding and which will cost you a small fortune if you do, includes a rare recorded document of Willie playing solo in front of a live audience around this time. His single contribution to the album, a typically poignant version of "Has Anybody Seen My Baby Here Tonight?", is everything Willie live was like in his prime: nerve-end honest, yet somehow deep-tenor soothing. Rick Danko once described band-mate Levon Helm's voice as something that heals people. Amen to that, brother, just be sure to add Willie P. Bennett's name to that very short list as well.

Along with a few brave others out on the lonely acoustic trail, Willie continued to write, if (frustratingly) not record, introducing new songs into his already classics-packed sets. He also served as an inspiration to younger artists foolish enough to try and make a living giving the world the beautiful, affecting music it's never really had much use for. After being stirred by Willie's performance at Snales Place years before, Bradshaw later had the opportunity to come full circle and not only meet, but perform with his hero:

I first played with Willie in the mid-eighties at the Princess Theatre in Waterloo. I opened the show and spent a couple of hours before hanging at a pub and letting Willie know what a fan I was. For me it was like meeting Dylan or Neil Young. We played darts (Willie had his own darts in tow) and I beat him fair and square first game, which seemed to amuse him a bit. He didn't hold it against me and Willie was warm and encouraging. He played harmonica on my first two albums and drove to Brantford for a cameo in a video we made. Always encouraging. We had the pleasure of Willie taking the stage with us on many occasions. During the eighties I booked Willie to play two nights at the Cameron House in Toronto, his first Queen Street gigs. I knew Willie would blow them away and he certainly did.

Yes, he did—I know, because I was there, having coerced a sort-of girlfriend and two of her friends into attending Willie's first foray onto Toronto's then (pre-Urban Outfitters, pre-Foot Locker, pre-Gap) most modish street. It was a good choice of venue, as Handsome Ned had been the Cameron's in-House flag-bearer for the twangier end of roots music for years, so the regulars weren't entirely unfamiliar with the strum of acoustic guitars and the wail of a harmonica, but it was, once again, Willie's amazing catalogue of songs and his passionate vocal performance that won over the crowd. I think one of what's-her-name's friends even bought the independently made cassette tape Willie was selling at the show, the same one I had purchased a few years previous after *my* first time experiencing Willie live.

The Lucky Ones, as the 1985 cassette was called, was one side Willie solo, one side Willie with band, in retrospect probably as much a demo meant to interest record labels as it was a self-contained musical statement. Several of the acoustic songs were absolutely first-rate—the tender title tune; the resilient "Sometimes It Comes So Easy," a frequent show opener during this time; "Rains on Me," a drippingly melancholic meditation on despair; the uncommonly acerbic "Living in a Dirty Town"—and some were never recorded elsewhere, meaning only devotees like me get to hear them (it's the sole reason I still own a cassette player; in fact, it's the only cassette I own). Then there's the other side . . .

"Patience of a Working Man" would live to find a place on Willie's official return to recording after eleven years, 1989's also-titled *The Lucky Ones* on Duke Street Records, but the problem wasn't as much the songs (although "Heart Headlines" is almost as mawkish as its title, and "Our Love, Our Love" isn't far behind), but the production, which borders on MOR mush, a sound as far away from the pristine picking of the three Woodshed records as the north shore of Hudson Bay is from downtown Nashville, where Willie would travel around this time to discover that many are called to Music City, USA to get rich selling their songs, but few are chosen. I play the first side of the cassette a lot. Then I rewind it.

In 1988, while Willie was busy in the studio finishing up the mixes on his Duke Street comeback, a friend and I, who I'd successfully converted into a Willie fanatic, attended one of his shows in Toronto's east end (I forget where exactly). I also forget the circumstances of the gig, but it was something along the lines of Toronto Live Music Week, with different performers playing all around town at a variety of venues. Brad had never heard Willie play live, so I was excited for both of us, sharing things you're proud to know about being something you do as a useless under-graduate in lieu of actually doing things you yourself are proud to have done. We got to the bar early, eager to get a table up front near the small stage, and were on our second drinks when I noticed something was wrong.

By this point I'd attended five or so of Willie's shows, and chatter amongst the crowd while he was perform-ing wasn't one of their characteristic features. Willie was

LIVES OF THE POETS (WITH GUITARS)

doing his usual outstanding job up on stage, but the audience seemed more interested in each other than in what he was up to musically. Then I caught on: as part of Toronto Live Music Week, or whatever it was called, pass-holders were allowed to venue-hop from event to event, to sample, buffet-style, who was playing and to linger or amble along as the mood struck them. For the majority of attendees that night, the mood was Saturday-night chatty, maybe just a little more of this particular serving of song and then a pop down the street to see what was cooking there. I was annoyed, even embarrassed, but Willie was angry. At first he put his fury into his playing, singing the low and high notes with extra urgency, slamming his strings and blowing his harp with increased intensity. In return, the audience simply talked louder.

At one point, I heard myself say toward the stage, "I guess they figured they bought their tickets, they can do whatever they want," and was surprised to hear Willie answer back that if that was the case, then they could have their money back. Emboldened, Brad and I made sure to hoot and holler and clap our hands red after every song. Discouraged by the rest of the audience's response, Willie began to drink bourbon between songs. The liquor blotted out the boors in the audience, allowed him to concentrate on making the music, which was as magical as always, with the added bonus, on our end, of making him drunk enough that by the end of the night he accepted a couple of bedazzled university students' invitation to come back to my house in Kensington Market and keep the party going.

There, it wasn't long before his guitar was unpacked and his harmonica belt laid out on the cracked glass coffee table and Willie played for us all night long, right through until unwelcome morning. He led the way in drinking up every drop of alcohol we had in the house,

including one of my absent roommate's bottles of cooking sherry, and smoked all of his cigarettes and then all
of Brad's, and when the dope dealer and his emaciated,
coked-out girlfriend from three doors down knocked on
the door at three A.M. and wondered if we were having
a party, smoked all of his hash; but what he mostly did
was play all night, playing as if he were performing at a
packed Massey Hall and not for two awestruck U of T
philosophy students and a couple of clueless drug casu-
alties just happy not to have to get high alone. What I
remember best, though, is after we first arrived and were
sitting around the kitchen table drinking beer and listening to one of my many Kitchen Tapes (mix tapes I made
of favourite artists that were to be listened to while getting drunk at the kitchen table), I thought Willie would be
thrilled to hear, sandwiched between a Pogues song and a
Tim Hardin number, one of Willie's own tunes come blaring out of the cheap boom-box speakers. When he proceeded to talk right through it, and I asked him what it felt
like to hear his own music in such good company, he said
it was flattering, of course, but that it didn't make him feel
like it made other people, like myself, feel. For him to feel
that good, he had to be making music, not listening to it. It
wasn't long after that that we moved into the living room
and out came the guitar.

When *The Lucky Ones* was released a year later, my
happiness that there was a new Willie album to buy was
undercut by it having to be *this* particular album. It's not
a write-off — Willie was incapable of an insincere vocal
performance and the lyrics are authentically lived-in, if
less richly resonant than on his Woodshed records — but
it's not quite right, either, the production too rooty-toot
punchy here (as on the horn-heavy lead-off track, "Train
Tracks"), too string-section schmaltzy there (as on the

closing number, "Andrew's Waltz"). There are a couple of songs that don't get suffocated in the production — the newgrassy "Don't Have Much to Say" and "Ain't Got Notion," in large part because neither has reverbed drums on them, the blight of most albums recorded in the eighties — but on the whole, *The Lucky Ones* sounds like Willie and his producer Danny Greenspoon attempting to sound like what was on "new country" radio at the time (particularly painful is the needless, stiff remake of "Tryin' to Start Out Clean," all of its delightful jagged-ness polished smooth). Looking back, you can always tell on which albums an artist was attempting to sound "contemporary:" those are the ones that always end up sounding dated.

More welcome was a 1991 compilation (*Collectibles*) of selected tracks from the three Woodshed albums brought out by the short-lived Dark Light label, an attempt to make some of Willie's long out-of-print seventies music available to a brave new CD world. It was a valiant enterprise and it included revealing song-by-song reflections from Willie himself. It too was out of print within a few years. His Dark Light follow-up, 1993's *Take My Own Advice*, was basically *The Lucky Ones* Part Two: a couple of glossy remakes from the back catalogue; a good song or two ("Step Away" being the stand-out) overwhelmed by inappropriate (read: "up-to-date") production touches, a few songs that, in their grating sentimentality and lyrical obtuseness, it's hard to believe came from the same pen that wrote "Storm Clouds" or "Country Squall."

When I moved back to Toronto in 1997 after living in the American South for four years, I was shocked to spot an album called *Blackie and the Rodeo Kings: High or Hurtin'* on the CD rack at Sam the Record Man. He's dead, I thought, unaware, in that innocent pre-internet age, of the tribute album Canadian musicians Colin Linden, Stephen Fearing, and Tom Wilson had recorded, not for a dearly departed Willie, but for a master songwriter still alive but unacceptably unknown by most music listeners. The trio's versions of such Willie standards as "Faces" and "Come On Train" didn't add anything to the originals, but were energetically performed and imbued with the deep respect the artists clearly shared for Willie's work. As for Willie himself, I discovered he wasn't deceased, but was something almost as bewildering: a Flying Squirrel.

In one sense, Willie's longtime (fifteen years) tenure as a multi-instrumental sideman and backing vocalist to another elite Canadian songwriter, Fred Eaglesmith, made sense. To begin with, it was obvious that Eaglesmith knew he had something very special when Willie took his place on stage with him every night, which perhaps was quietly rewarding enough. Recounting the first time they played together, "We were at a festival one time and he said, 'Hey, can I play harmonica with you today?'" Eaglesmith remembered. "And I said 'Really, you want to play harmonica with me?' and he said 'Yeah,' and he never left." In addition, Eaglesmith routinely played two-hundred-and-fifty shows a year, so Willie was able to put some money in the bank for one of the first times in his life, a not insignificant development for someone approaching middle age. He was also on record as saying he was tired of chasing after the brass ring of solo success, was weary of a recording industry that valued all of the lowest things the highest.

"Willie was bored with his own career," maintained Washboard Hank, the dynamic human percussion section who anchored Fred's band during its touring peak, "and he was having lots of fun playing with Fred and he was developing his own totally new sound on the mandolin. In a way it was a free ride: lots of gigs, steady pay, interesting places to travel to, and no worries." On stage, it was obvious that Willie revelled in being a full-time musician highly valued by both Eaglesmith and his large and adoring audience of "Fredheads" for his innovative mandolin playing (I, for one, had never heard a mandolin played with the aid of a tremolo pedal before) and signature harmonica work. The albums he appeared on as a member of the band, particularly1994's *Live at the Paradise Hotel* and *Lipstick, Lies and Gasoline* from 1997, are among the best of Eaglesmith's career.

Some of Willie's older fans, however, wondered if he was selling himself and his talent short, trading in the stress and strain of an ultimately more fulfilling solo career for the congenial anonymity of sideman status. Maybe it was part of a bigger philosophical impulse to further erode his earthbound ego, a process that began when Willie became interested in Buddhism ("He had some scriptures that he would quote now and then," Washboard Hank recalled, "but he was not attracted to the religion so much as the philosophy"). Greg Quill, a fellow musician and longtime Willie supporter (he wrote about him more than once for the *Toronto Star* and provided the liner notes to *Collectibles*), admitted that he

> was always mystified about why [Willie] gave up his own career to play harmonica and mandolin in Fred Eaglesmith's band. Nothing against Fred—he's a spectacular artist, genuinely talented, a hard worker and unique—but so was Willie (well, maybe not such a hard worker). One summer about 10 years ago, I was performing at Fred's annual fundraising picnic camp, and bumped into Willie backstage. He was

putting new strings on Fred's guitar. He did it before every performance, he told me, without explaining why. No one replaces strings after just one show, and most guitarists hate new strings. It was not something he'd been asked to do, he added, in case I got the wrong idea. I gathered it was some sort of Buddhist/Taoist exercise in humility and service to a friend. He admired Fred's fierce independence, his determination to live and work his own way, off the established music grid. He loved the gypsy caravan life, too, skipping from one gig to the next, never sure what was waiting at the end of the day, never standing in the spotlight, but helping make Fred sound better than he might have. That's probably the most admirable quality a musician can aspire to: selfless musical generosity.

Slumping baseball players will tell you that even if you're not hitting very well, you can always play good defence.

Washboard Hank remembers Willie as a mesmerizing performer right to the end (even in his reduced role as sideman on another man's songs), as well as a beneficent teacher; and, like all of us, someone not above needing to be occasionally reminded of a few elemental lessons.

Playing with Willie was hair-raising, the hair on your neck would stand up when he would play a passage that was just so impossibly perfect. There are moments like that in all great art—with Willie it was every night. Of course he was a total pain in the ass when it came to sound checks, sometimes they would take three hours. He reveled in his position of total power and would tell the sound man to adjust a certain frequency and the sound man would shove a dial and Willie would know by ear what dial he had shoved, and then say "not 570, I said 560" or something like that. As a roommate he was very respectful and aware. At first he would lecture me on being "mindful" and eventually I became better behaved. We would talk a lot about spiritual stuff and philosophy. Willie seemed to have a natural intelligence and he would ponder things. Sometimes a conversation would have huge gaps in it and we would talk about something over a number of days. I would ask a question and the next day out of nowhere he would answer it. Willie would sometimes get drunk and act in a very un-Buddhist fashion, he would not be mindful. This would be my chance to protect him and try to keep him out of trouble. I would have given my life for him because I loved and respected him.

Still the occasional modest solo show when not touring with Eaglesmith (and probably too much and too hard—he was the oldest member of the band by far); a collection of pleasantly unexceptional, primarily acoustic, all-new songs recorded with a variety of friends and admirers (1998's *Heartstrings*) that was middling enough to win a Juno Award for Best Roots/Traditional album; rumours of a collection of stunning originals taped live from the floor, no overdubs, just Willie and his guitar and harmonica-in-a-rack, recorded in Winnipeg in the last year of his life; then a heart attack that finally got him off the road; then another one a few months later, February 15, 2008, that put him on the one road that no one ever travels back down.

I can still remember the thrill of listening to my new secondhand copy of *Tryin' to Start Out Clean* for the first time, incredulous that this remarkable music could have existed for so many years without me knowing about it. I remember Willie leaving Brad and me behind on Spadina Avenue after we'd walked him from my place in

Kensington Market to the *7-11* so he could buy a fresh pack of cigarettes, the taxi pulling into the sunny Saturday morning traffic, Willie rolling down the back window to give us a raised-thumb goodbye.

GRAM PARSONS

A perfect tragedy is the noblest production of human nature.
—Joseph Addison

C lothes may not make the man, but they are a fairly reliable indication of what the man underneath is up to. And if the man in question is attired in a white silk jacket and equally iridescent bell-bottoms emblazoned with artfully embroidered depictions of poppies, marijuana leaves, LSD cubes, plenty of Seconal and Tuinal tablets, a naked woman, and a flaming red cross surrounded by radiating shafts of blue-and-gold scarlet flames, chances are he's made up his mind to make trouble, both for himself and whoever he happens to come into contact with. In the twenty-six years and ten months he was with us, Gram Parsons made lots and lots of trouble. Which is precisely why we're still singing his songs and talking about him today, more than forty years after his death.

Born in Winter Haven, Florida, in 1947 (although the main family home was in Waycross, Georgia), Cecil Ingram Connor III was the maternal grandson of a wealthy citrus magnate and the life-long beneficiary of a substantial trust fund. Rich, good-looking, southern, and with a family history as sensational as anything even Tennessee Williams could have come up with, some of the familial highlights (or lowlights) of Parsons' life story include: his father killing himself with a shotgun blast to the head; the man his widowed mother married reputedly giving his alcoholic, hospital-bound wife her fatal last drink; his stepfather dying from cirrhosis of the liver soon after his stepson's infamous overdose in the Joshua Tree Inn in 1973 and the hijacking of his dead body from the airport and its partial immolation in the nearby desert. And that's without even mentioning the most interesting thing, the music.

Elvis was still six months away from compelling the Ed Sullivan Show cameramen to film him from the waist up only when nine-year-old Gram saw him perform at the Waycross City Auditorium and discovered what he was supposed to do with the rest of his life. (Also on the bill that night were the Louvin Brothers, the high-lonesome counterpart to Elvis' hip-swiveling contribution to Gram's eventual musical identity, the soul to go with the body.) Louise Cone, the Connor family's housekeeper's younger sister who was hired to act as Gram's sister's nanny, remembered how

> Gram was a sweet child as long as you let him be Elvis Presley. He loved Elvis Presley, imitating him and playing the piano. Even as a little boy. Our favorite thing was waiting for The Ed Sullivan Show. Gram would crawl onto the floor and watch and get up and go right along with Elvis. He had his guitar and he got right along with him. He'd shake his hips; he was an Elvis imitator, one hundred percent. Gram came up with Elvis in his heart.

Elvis in his heart and a big fat silver spoon stuck in his mouth that throughout his life threatened to gag him. B.E.

(Before Elvis), Gram got any toy he wanted and a chauffeur to take him and his friends to play mini-putt whenever they felt like it; A.E. (After Elvis), he received every musical instrument and record he desired ("Gram would get anywhere from ten to fifteen 45s a week," childhood friend Dickey Smith recalled. "Coon Dog [Gram's father] had a charge account and Gram picked up whatever he wanted").

Coon Dog also had a drinking problem to match his wife's and a hole in his soul from being, officially, the vice president of his wife's family's citrus empire, but unofficially (often the more meaningful designation) just Avis' husband, ol' Coon Dog—Oh, a nice enough old boy, all right, but not someone you'd want to leave at the controls for too long, if you catch my drift. His wife also may or may not have been having an affair—it doesn't really matter if she was if her husband thought she was—and one year just before Christmas when the rest of the family was in Winter Haven (Coon Dog was supposed to join them there a couple of days later) he blew his head off with one of his shotguns. Before he did, though, he made sure to first buy his music-loving son a very expensive Christmas present, a reel-to-reel tape recorder, a rarity at that time. Gram was twelve years old.

Coon Dog's widow had the help pack up the house and moved with the children into the family mansion in Winter Haven where she could hide from her late husband's ghost and where within a year she'd meet and marry Bob Parsons, a conman to some, a nattily dressed, alcoholic ne'er-do-well and cut-rate Don Juan at the very least. He was the closest thing in Gram's life to a strong male figure, though, and helped to carry on the long family tradition of giving your children lots and lots of stuff in lieu of actually spending time with them. One of Gram's girlfriends from this time remembered Gram, then barely a teenager, having his own mini-apartment within the family mansion while "his mother stayed at the other end of the house, drinking. He had lots of instruments [and his own bathroom, fridge, and television], and that's where he hung out with all his friends. He had a private entrance and didn't have to go through the main door to get into the house." No one feels sorry for the poor little rich boy, and no one should—there are far worse fates to suffer from than opulence—but we don't end up who we are all on our own. If Gram the adult would not tolerate second-best anything and always had to be the centre of attention and could act like an entitled brat who never hesitated to howl when he didn't get exactly what he wanted, it's important to remember how he got that way, even if knowing this wouldn't have made him any less of an entitled brat.

Because he's the alt-country king and he's from the American South and he didn't exactly discourage the impression that he'd grown up listening to Hank Williams on the family's dusty old wireless, it's surprising to some that Gram wore the exact same musical training wheels as many other late-sixties roots innovators, such as Gene Clark. Early on there were rock bands (the Pacers, the Legends) like thousands of other rock bands (Chuck Berry and Ventures covers mostly); later on there were folk-revival groups (the Village Vanguards, the Shilos) modeled on the likes of the Kingston Trio and the Journeymen, sterile folk reacting against shallow pop. Not a lot of country music, though; Pacers bandmate Jim Carlton recalled how

> I played this version of "Steel Guitar Rag" for him and he said, "What the hell are you doing?" and started playing this Floyd Cramer country piano, mocking me, making fun of country music. Gram did not cut his teeth on country music;

his dad wasn't a country singer. He was no shit kicker—he was an urbane, polished kid.

As Gram became a better musician and began to write his own songs, Bob Parsons was the most encouraging family member of his stepson's musical aspirations. He bought the Legends a VW bus and had the band's name painted on the side; he bought all of the Vanguards matching outfits; he hustled hard to get Gram's various bands booked at his and Avis' frequent parties and at country club dances and teen clubs and proms. He may have been an alcoholic parasite who couldn't keep his pants on, and part of the reason he was so supportive of Gram was undoubtedly because he had nothing better to do and he enjoyed the buzz of being a part of even low-level show business, but even as all of Gram's mother's people wanted Gram to slow down and get a part-time job to keep him occupied after school, Bob Parsons was the one who helped him believe in himself as a musician. Every scoundrel has a silver lining. And given that most of us aren't the flawless individuals we like to think we are, this is heartening.

Abetted by Bob Parsons (relative Rob Hoskins: "Gram's mother was dying, and, pardon my French, but that motherfucker brought her a bottle of scotch into the hospital. Does that tell you what he was like?"), Gram's mother died the same day that Gram graduated from high school. He'd wanted to go east and applied to only one school—Harvard—and, although academically unqualified, Bob Parsons made it happen. There, with earnest neo-folk quartets on the wane nationwide and the Beatles clearing the air for real rock and roll again, Gram quickly lost his student card and put together what eventually became the International Submarine Band (the name was borrowed from the Little Rascals TV show). Although Gram wouldn't have been able to avoid hearing country music growing up where he did, it was Submarine Band guitarist John Nuese who helped remove the redneck stigma the music carried and to make it Gram's driving passion:

> I started right away to teach him some country music and turned him on to Merle Haggard and Buck Owens. It became apparent to Gram that this was the music that he should be doing. The folk stuff was nice, but it didn't have any *cojones*. Gram knew nothing about what was going on with country music in the sixties and he quickly became an avid fan of the modern country sound, which was Merle Haggard and Buck Owens. He took that music and made it his own.

On the International Submarine Band's first and only album, *Safe at Home*, it's apparent twenty seconds into the lead-off track, "Blue Eyes," what Nuese meant by Gram making country music "his own." Mainly by supplying a pronounced rock-and-roll backbeat to traditional country and western song structures, the band put itself at the vanguard of what has come to be known as "country-rock."

As with most things worth talking about, there's not much consensus about how and when it began or even exactly what it is. When it comes to the origin of country-rock, most people point to either *Safe at Home* or Gram's only album with the Byrds, *Sweetheart of the Rodeo* (both released in 1968, although the former was recorded a year earlier and both primarily Gram's twangy creation), although Roger McGuinn's "Mr. Spaceman," Chris Hillman's "Time Between," Gene Clark's "Tried So Hard," Richie Furay's "Child's Claim to Fame," and Michael Nesmith's "Papa Gene's Blues" all predate or are at least contemporaneous with anything on either of these two seminal albums. As for the term "country-rock" itself, Parsons himself preferred the more expansive "Cosmic American Music." In the end, it's probably best to simply drop the whole topic and to heed Townes Van Zandt, who wisely opined that there are really only two kinds of music: the blues and zippity-do-da. From this point on, Gram Parsons played the blues. *White* blues.

Although there was plenty of black music in Gram's musicological colour wheel (especially evident during his time with the Flying Burrito Brothers, when R&B and gospel were featured items on the musical menu), country music in its embryonic form was hillbilly music: poor, white North American immigrants playing indigenous string instruments such as fiddles brought over from Scotland. As the immigrants began, unavoidably, to intermingle, their chosen old-country instruments commenced to do the same, the Italian mandolin, for example, mixing it up nicely with the Spanish guitar. Of course, the rural Caucasian purveyors of this new music were singing about the same things as their black brothers and sisters at the bottom of the economic food chain—being poor, being lonely, being drunk, wishing they were somewhere else (usually safe at home in heaven dead)—and eventually the two musical forms could no longer resist one another and broke through the colour line, spawning all sorts of new musical offspring (the banjo, for instance, so central to country music, is African-American in origin). What's Buck Owens and the vaunted Bakersfield sound, for instance, but hill music amped up with drums and electric guitar? What's Chuck Berry, for that matter, but urban folk music you can dance to? (And what was "Maybellene," his first hit, but an overhauled version of Western swing-master Bob Wills' "Ida Red"?)

But country music, even when altered by interactions with this or that non-traditional element, is still, at source,

country music, is still primarily ballads with strong harmonies performed with stringed instruments. It's the
Louvin Brothers, in other words, not Sam and Dave.
Gram Parsons loved Ray Charles, Little Richard, Stax,
and too many other African-American artists to mention—and by the time he was with the Burrito Brothers
these influences found their way into his music—but the
longing and sorrow and loneliness and ultimate spiritual
emancipation he compelled his listeners to experience for
themselves was accomplished by a country singer singing
country songs. There was plenty of country-and-western
music around my working-class home when I was a kid,
but it was bad country, Countrypolitan mush no different
from its pop-pabulum cousin. Hearing Gram Parsons for
the first time was the difference between reading about
God in a mimeographed pamphlet stuck underneath the
windshield wiper of your car at the shopping mall versus
staring into the roaring eyes of the Almighty. It was like
discovering I had a muscle I'd never used before. Oh, so
that's what people call a soul.

Safe at Home is an apprentice work, but an extremely
compelling one. Although the original Submarine Band
had splintered and now included only Gram and John
Nuese from the original group, top-notch session men and a
few friends pitched together to help them record an album
for Lee Hazelwood's new label, LHI, with Hazelwood's
then-girlfriend, Suzi Jane Hokum, producing. Not surprisingly, though, it was essentially Gram's show, three of
the four originals on the LP having been written by him,
the fourth a co-write with Electric Flag keyboardist Barry
Goldberg. The overall sound wasn't that much different
from what Gram's musical mentors Merle Haggard and
Buck Owens were up to at this time—lean Bakersfield
country music with the accent on Jay Dee Maness' stinging

steel guitar—but there were subtle differences that pointed toward both Gram's more mature work and to why his enormous influence wasn't purely musical.

If the lyrics on *Safe at Home* don't go much beyond being about loving, not being loved, and wishing to be in love, they're also uncluttered and often clever and always cliché-free, a popular music anomaly, then as now. More importantly, Gram delivers them with his trademark trembling tenor firmly in place from the get-go. What I wrote in my novel *Moody Food* about the voice of the character Thomas Graham, heavily based upon Gram Parsons, I repeat now about its real-life inspiration: Like a back rub on the brain. Like drinking velvet out of a glass. Like hearing God hum. More than on the buoyant originals and the fresh Haggard and Cash covers, however, it's the last song on the album, "Do You Know How It Feels to Be Lonesome," that best exemplifies what Gram could do with a ballad and indicates what a stupendous singer he could be. Between the honest ache in his delivery and the wonderfully melancholic melodicism of the song itself, it's impossible, by song's end, not to know how it feels to be lonesome. No one—not even Gram's heartbreaking hero, George Jones—could sing a sad song better. And the medley of "Folsom Prison Blues" and "That's All Right" slyly utilizes the same loping shuffle for both songs, the transition from country-and-western classic to rock-and-roll standard *boom pop boom pop*, *boom pop boom pop* seamless, the musical lesson obvious. This is where country and rock come together for really the only time on the album, and the effect is understated but palpable: maybe these two musical planets aren't so far apart in the universe after all.

The non-musical impact of the album is just as subtle but no less tangible. Most conspicuously, there's the record's cover, which has the shaggy-haired boys decked out in antebellum duds like a *Sgt. Pepper's Lonely Hearts Club Band* cover shoot transported via a time machine to the American Civil War era. Next, it's easy to imagine Merle or Buck performing the sprightly lead-off track "Blue Eyes" until you come to the line where Gram sings of how he might as well get stoned (one look at the album cover, and you know he's not talking about being drunk). It's an entirely casual reference, but the effect is immediate: this is most *definitely* not a Buck Owens song. It's touches such as these that help disarm the potential country-music skeptic. If these guys smoke dope and don't wear crew cuts and obviously have a sense of humour about what they're doing, maybe it's okay to whistle along to "Luxury Liner" and "Strong Boy" and perhaps it's even all right to be emotionally moved by "Do You Know How It Feels to Be Lonesome." One of Gram Parsons' most significant accomplishments was simply making it okay to like a genuine American art form that for too long had been almost exclusively the property of right-wing, redneck, dim-witted yahoos. The syllogism was as simple as it was mind-shattering: 1. Gram Parsons is cool. 2. Gram Parsons loves country music. 3. Therefore country music is cool.

How Gram ended up discarding his own group and their just-completed album to not only join the already well-established Byrds but to take over the actual reins of the struggling band and herd them in the direction of doing a straight country album is prototypical G.P. Roger McGuinn and Chris Hillman, the two remaining original Byrds after the 1967 firing of David Crosby, knew they needed to flesh out their live sound, so they ended up auditioning Gram, who Hillman "met . . . in a bank. We shared the same manager. The Byrds were scattered at that point so we grabbed Gram. He was hired for six months as a side guy, with my cousin Kevin Kelley on drums. We were just trying to keep the thing going." Gram helped keep the thing going all right, but going in a direction that the other two never would have headed. McGuinn: "We just hired a piano player and he turned out to be Parsons, a monster in sheep's clothing. And he exploded out of this sheep's clothing. God! It's George Jones! In a sequin suit."

In recent years Chris Hillman has attempted to debunk the prevalent misconception that Parsons alone was the "father of country-rock." Unfortunately, it's not enough for him to be aware that those in the know know the true musical score: that the genre's paternity will forever be in doubt, if the genre itself can even be said to exist. Hillman's bitterness regarding not only Parsons' perceived role as country-rock forefather but his entire posthumous fame is so palpable that it at times borders on the near-pathological. (In the book he co-wrote with respected rock journalist John Einarson, *Hot Burritos*, rarely does a page pass without some acerbic swipe from Hillman about how Parsons did too many drugs and drank too much, or how Parsons was personally selfish, or how Parsons didn't rehearse enough, or how Parsons wasn't professional enough, or even—incredibly, delusionally—how Parsons never wrote any good songs after he quit collaborating with Hillman.) It's not just observers like producer Jim Dickson who claim that "Chris Hillman never got over how much more credit Gram got than he did." As *Hot Burritos* makes painfully clear, Hillman himself believes that "Unfortunately it's all 'Gram, Gram, Gram,' and I face that every day."

Part of the reason for Gram's posthumous renown is undeniably a matter of, as latter-day Burrito bandmate Bernie Leadon observed, "How can you compete with a dead guy? You just can't. It's a martyr thing. Gram fell on his sword so he's a dead hero. He's mythic." (Although even when he was alive there was something undeniably mythic about Gram. Roger McGuinn: "I felt like I was in a movie when I was with Gram Parsons. It was surreal in a very disturbing way. It was almost like you could feel his impending doom coming on. Like life and death. I got that vibe a lot when I was with him.") Of course, the other part is the way his southern-honeyed voice simply haunts, his songs sting with sweet sorrow, and his personal charisma still sparkles four decades after he's been gone. Every time in *Hot Burritos* (and there are several) Hillman proudly invokes the achievements of his lengthy, post-Parsons career with such very professional, very boring outfits as the Parsonsless Burrito Brothers, the Souther-Hillman-Furay Band, the Desert Rose Band, or his own insipid solo career as a way to illustrate how he's the more accomplished artist and how Parsons was just a talented kid who blew it and who never lived up to his potential, one can't help but be reminded of Ludwig Wittgenstein's definition of genuine art: "a wild beast—tamed." Fair or not, it's the tamers we're thankful for, but it's the wild beasts we remember.

Lead singer McGuinn has fully admitted, "I was into experimentation and did not want to get involved in pure country," but that's exactly what the hit-making group Gram was a part of for less than a month—a month!—were convinced to do when they went into the studio to record their next album. Admittedly, Hillman had been playing authentic bluegrass when Gram was still performing Journeymen rip-offs and was keen to follow Gram's trip to the country, but it's impossible to imagine the then-diffident bass player persuading McGuinn to do a full-out country record like *Sweetheart of the Rodeo*. But Gram could. And did. Within weeks, McGuinn recalled, "We got into the whole country thing: playing poker every day, drinking whiskey, wearing cowboy hats and boots." And once the band entered the studio, "Gram was the boss of that whole thing," Jay Dee Maness testified. "Chris was only the bass player. I think Chris got a little attitude from that, because he wanted to be more than just the bass player . . . Gram was calling the shots. He wasn't nasty about it. He was just a strong personality."

A *strong* personality cuts both ways, of course. While former Submarine member Ian Dunlop allowed, "With Gram's energy and enthusiasm, you could see how he made the sale [of country music] to the Byrds. His enthusiasm was contagious, because he always went into everything believing without reservations," when Gram suddenly left to join the Byrds, "I felt, 'Holy mackerel, man, you haven't finished the god damn record with the other band!' The Byrds were big but still . . . Gram would jump on anything new until it didn't pan out or the novelty wore off. Of course the ISB were left sitting on a dud and were trying to figure out what to do." Adds Bob Buchanan, who'd been roped in by Gram at the last moment to play on *Safe at Home*, "Gram used the ISB as a stepping stone. That was the bad side of Gram—he didn't think of the rest of the band." Speaking of Anton Chekov, V.S. Pritchett defined genius as "spiritual greed." Fanatical, relentless, and deeply self-serving: spiritual or not, no one ever said greed was pretty.

To a great degree *Sweetheart of the Rodeo* is *Safe At Home* Part Two, only better (the songs, the performances) and bigger (the Byrds were only two years removed from a nationwide number-one hit, so the band's C&W detour was rock media news). Contrary to the contemporary cliché that it's a "country-rock" cornerstone, *Sweetheart* is similar to *Safe at Home* in that it primarily consists of traditional country songs ("You're Still on My Mind," "The Christian Life," "Life in Prison," "I Am a Pilgrim") performed as close to the sound and feel of the originals as possible (among the elite Nashville session players on the record are Earl Ball on piano, Lloyd Green on steel guitar, and Roy Husky on bass).

The cultural impact of the "Eight Miles High" Byrds flying through the country was huge, much more so than that of the Submarine Band, who were relative unknowns. Writing in the newly ordained hippie bible, *Rolling Stone*, Jon Landau praised the Byrds for "doing country as country, show[ing] just how powerful and relevant unadorned country music is." In an age (Vietnam, urban uprisings, student unrest, political assassinations) when young and old, "straight" and "head," left and right, seemed unalterably antagonistic, hearing country music and all of its off-putting connotations (redneck, reactionary, racist) praised in the same hippier-than-thou magazine that sold IMPEACH LBJ! bumper stickers and marijuana grow-op kits in its back pages was revolutionary.

Almost as pioneering were the more ambitious songs on *Sweetheart*. The delightfully jolly lead-off track, "You Ain't Going Nowhere," is, if we do use the term (and it is an admittedly convenient tool for stylistic differentiation), archetypal country-rock: a series of Dylan's most Dylanesque non-sequiturs strung together and sung by McGuinn in his inimitable nasal with help from Gram and Hillman on the familiarly Byrdsy chorus and with lots of Lloyd Green's sweet pedal steel in the forefront. The album's closer, the other Dylan tune, "Nothing was Delivered," also features the steel guitar, but with conspicuous heavy rock drumming during the chorus. Gram's were the only band originals on the album, his "100 Years From Now" distinguished by very un-country lyrics (eschatological love song?) and prominent cymbal crashes and busy tom-toms during the fade. Gram's other original, "Hickory Wind" (actually a co-write with former Submarine mate Bob Buchanan) is *Sweetheart*'s indisputable highlight, a perfect fusion of words (homesickness for a home that doesn't exist anymore, if it ever did), music (beguiling melody), and performance (mesmerizing vocal performance from Gram, sorrowful fiddle and steel guitar throughout). It's Gram's finest composition and could only be improved upon by him, which he did when he re-recorded it on his second, and last, solo album (Emmylou Harris' soaring vocals replacing the faintly generic background vocals on the *Sweetheart* version, Gram's vocals somehow even more forcefully vulnerable).

While the Byrds were in Nashville recording their album, Columbia, the band's label, used its considerable corporate muscle to secure them a gig at the Grand Ole Opry. No rock band had ever set foot on the hallowed Opry stage before, so they were allowed only two agreed-upon songs, both placatory Merle Haggard covers. After performing "Sing Me Back Home" (to, depending on whose memory you trust, either muted derision or almost total silence or a bit of each), Gram pulled a Gram and announced to the crowd and to everyone listening at home on the radio that the band wasn't going to do "Life in Prison," their previously announced second number, but, instead, his own "Hickory Wind," which he wanted to dedicate to his grandmother. The Opry officials were livid because (a) you didn't perform songs that hadn't been okayed first; and (b) you weren't allowed to personally dedicate songs on the Opry. The other Byrds were taken aback as well, but went along with Gram's unexpected executive decision because, really, they had no other choice. Gram saw an opportunity and took it. Disrespectful? Undeniably. Selfish? Unquestionably. A pure rock-and-roll moment? You bet.

Gram's Machiavellianism wasn't limited to matters exclusively musical; put another way, his vision of what he wanted to accomplish musically was so utterly thoroughgoing, it permeated virtually every aspect of his life as an almost foolproof formula for professional success and personal failure. Bob Buchanan on Gram's disinte-grating relationship with Nancy Ross, his girlfriend and the mother of his child:

> As far as Nancy and the baby, as far as how he took care of them, Gram had no clue. Give her some money and tell her to go shopping. Yell at her when she got in trouble. She got in trouble a lot because that brought her affection. He was too busy with his own self. If there was something that he enjoyed or someone that he liked, he'd give them attention. Nancy and the baby were a load to bear.

Byrds roadie Carlos Bernal on Gram as share-and-share-alike hippie:

> I had a sniffer of cocaine and Gram asked me if I had powder. I had a bottle with a little glass cap and a long glass tube. We called them high hats. They were about an inch and half high. I gave him my high hat to go to the bathroom to have a snort. He comes back from the bathroom and gives me the bottle and it was empty. He said, "Oh, man, it fell in the toilet." The bottle wasn't wet, but there was no blow in it. He took it. He snorted all my blow or put it in a thimble or something.

British disc jockey Jeff Baxter, who met the *Sweetheart*-era Byrds on the first of their two trips to the UK, and who had offered Gram a ride to Stonehenge, where Mick Jagger and Keith Richards had organized an impromptu stoned sight-seeing outing: "Gram came over and said, 'I'm not going with you, I'm going with *them* [Jagger and Richards].' . . I felt a bit miffed but I suppose if you're a rock 'n' roll star you want to go with other rock 'n' roll stars."

Probably the best-known case of Gram doing what was best for Gram was his de facto quitting of the Byrds, a band he'd been with for a little over five months, when he refused to fly with the rest of the group from London to South Africa for a planned ten-day tour on the morning of their planned departure. Hillman: "People to this day go on the premise that Gram did not want to go to South Africa because of racial reasons [Parsons claimed he didn't go because of his distaste of apartheid]. That's not true. Gram wanted to stay in England and hang out with Mick and Keith . . . [T]he closest [Gram] came to black people was the servants he had in his home." Added Bernal (who was drafted to take Gram's spot in the depleted line-up — with predictably disastrous results): "Gram wasn't going on the tour because he couldn't have things just exactly as he wanted. The things he wanted, he could have had after a while, but he wanted them immediately. He wanted a steel guitar to do a lot of his tunes and things that the band wasn't prepared to jump into overnight."

Gram's trust-fund-abetted selfishness is undeniable; the preternatural sense of entitlement that came with it no more contestable. But neither is the colossal amount of self-confidence he carried, which, combined with his palpable passion for music that truly mattered and his restlessly innovatory spirit, helped create the charismatic Pied Piper of Cosmic American Music which he became. History is full of pampered children of the wealthy and parentally indifferent, but few go on to enrich and even change entire strangers' lives with their vision and their voice. Gram did.

Just how charismatic Gram could be is evinced by who he formed his next band, the Flying Burrito Brothers (he stole the name from ex-Submarine band mate Ian Dunlop), with. Gram officially flew the Byrds' coop the morning of July 9, 1968. February 1969 — *seven* months later — saw the release of Parsons' and Hillman's new band's, The Flying Burrito Brothers', first album, *The Gilded Palace of Sin*. "He probably got me in a weak moment," Hillman reflected, as if still slightly dazzled how it all came together, and came together so remarkably quickly. "He made friends with me in his charming manner. We hadn't planned the band yet. It wasn't premeditated that I would quit the Byrds and Gram and I would start a band the next day." Yet that's pretty much what happened. "There was a brotherly kinship we had in those first few months [in the Burrito Brothers]," Hillman acknowledged. From despised pariah to brotherly close collaborator: that was G.P.

Gram courted Hillman for good reason: the latter was an important ingredient in the Burritos' winning recipe. A versatile instrumentalist (bass, guitar, mandolin), a first-rate harmony singer (his stabs at solo vocals, then and later, are thin and unauthoritative), a briefly effectual songwriting partner, he was also the guy who could be counted on to hold it all together when Gram got a little too out there, whether in the studio or on stage. Every baseball team needs a solid shortstop, even if he's a light hitter who doesn't get half the attention that the home run-hitting clean-up batter does. Rounding out the Burritos line-up was bassist Chris Ethridge, a friend of Gram's with a southern accent thicker than his own, who'd played on *Safe at Home*. (In typically thoughtless Gram fashion, "After he left The Byrds," Ethridge remembered, "Gram and Keith Richards would call two or three times a week in the middle of the night [to talk about plans to form the Burrito Brothers]. Of course it would be daytime over there in England.") Finally, there was the Burritos' undisputed instrumental ace, "Sneaky" Pete Kleinow, on pedal steel guitar. Not only did Gram finally have a full-time steel player in his band, but because both he and Hillman were only adequate rhythm guitar players, all of the leads were to be taken by Kleinow, giving the band an extremely unique sound. Even the Buckaroos and Merle Haggard's band the Strangers had, respectively, Don Rich and Roy Nichols on lead electric guitar.

Of the unorthodox, but immense contribution Kleinow made to the Burritos' inimitable sound, Ethridge, still amazed, recalled: "It was unbelievable. He could sound like a whole symphony orchestra on that little one-neck steel." Bernie Leadon, who would replace Ethridge on the Burritos' second album, was just as overwhelmed: "There was no way you could get your brain around what he was doing . . . So you had to laugh sometimes. It was like watching an acrobat. 'How the hell did he make that leap from here to there?' Like the Flying Burrito Brothers music itself, Kleinow was contentedly outside the musical mainstream. Hillman:

> [A]ll of the other steel players looked at him with a wary eye. They didn't quite understand him. He was different. The steel guitar requires a very anally retentive personality. It's clean, it's shiny, it's tuned. Sneaky would set up his steel and it had all sorts of junk on it and it was never in tune. He had an old single-neck Fender and he'd made his own fuzz-tone, this big black metal box with a toggle switch. He'd hit the toggle switch and your fillings would fall out it was so loud.

Of course, without the magically still-fresh collection of songs Gram and the band came up with for their first album we wouldn't know about Kleinow's wildly inventive steel playing. At their best, the Flying Burrito Brothers obliterated any of the usual distinctions between rock and roll, country and western, and rhythm and blues (plus a dash of psychedelica). What they ended up creating was Flying Burrito Brothers music—not quite *sui generis*, but as close to it as anything in art can be. It simply didn't—and doesn't—sound like anything else.

With two ex-Byrds in the group, it wasn't hard to secure a record deal, and because Gram and Hillman were living together (both were suffering through serious marital troubles) in a three-bedroom ranch house out in the San Fernando Valley, the songwriting chemistry they'd been building had a day-in, day-out chance to develop. And though there were plenty of chemical and romantic high jinks going on at the house dubbed Burrito Manor (legendary rock groupie Pamela Des Barres remembered how, visiting the pair with a female friend, Hillman and Parsons "greeted us with a grocery bag full of pot and played us a bunch of country forty-fives on a portable record player"), the emphasis was on writing the songs that became *The Gilded Palace of Sin*.

A significant component of many of these new songs was rhythm and blues, another reason why the band's (and Gram's) reputation as prototypical "country-rockers" is superficial and misleading. Hillman:

> We were more than aware of Percy Sledge and Robert Carr [Hillman surely means "Dark End of the Street" singer James Carr] and things like that. Those kinds of singers and those kinds of songs like "Dark End of the Street." We were consciously welding the two. That was the merging of the black and white blues . . . taking those R&B songs and putting a light country and western arrangement to them. We were aware we couldn't try to be two black soul singers and try to do "Dark End of the Street." Not like Percy Sledge would do it anyway. So we did our own interpretation.

Not only "Dark End of the Street," but "Do Right Woman" (a song best known by Aretha Franklin) was Burritotized. And the Saturday-night/Sunday-morning love songs "Hot Burrito #1" and "Hot Burrito #2" (co-written by Gram and Ethridge), meanwhile, feature plenty of gospel-inspired organ and funky piano, Kleinow's steel guitar the only country thing about either track (and even then, the sounds he coaxed out of his instrument are closer to a science-fiction-movie soundtrack than country and western).

Similarly, the more straightforward country compositions are only ostensibly so: lyrically, "Wheels" is a *carpe diem* take on Bach's "Come Sweet Death," with Kleinow making his instrument sound, on the chorus, like an unemployed pedal steel player operating a dentist drill; "Sin City" has the Everly Brothers-like harmonies that typified much of the album, but is about greed, underage groupies, spiritual poverty, mohair suits, and the end of the world; "Christine's Tune" is a sprightly, acoustic-guitar-driven shuffle à la "Wake Up Little Susie," but isn't about the kind of girl you'd take to the movies (at least not to watch the film), and with howling Kleinow pedal steel work on the solo and the fade. The most traditional sounding song on the entire album might be the bluegrass-with-drums "My Uncle," but, being an anti-Vietnam, pro-draft-resistor ditty, it passes the album's lofty iconoclasm test with flying freak-flag colours. "Hippie Boy" is, admittedly, filler, but the most whacked-out piece of fluff ever cooked up to pad out an album. Over steady gospel organ and minimal bass, drums, and pedal steel, for nearly five minutes Hillman recites — not sings — in his best holy-roller imitation, the story of the little hippie boy who learns you should never carry more dope than you can eat. Gram said it was a protest song against what went down at the 1968 Democratic Convention in Chicago, but Gram said a lot of things, especially when he was high and thought he could get away with saying them. Still, by the time the wonderfully off-key choir, composed of clearly inebriated friends and studio hangers-on, sneaks in the chorus to the gospel standard "Peace in the Valley," it almost makes sense.

The next step was to use a chunk of A&M's modest advance money to have the entire band outfitted by legendary Los Angeles tailor Nudie Cohn, who'd already fashioned rhinestone-encrusted, protective eyewear-inducing stage-wear for the likes of Roy Rogers, Hank Williams, and Gram's prime-mover hero, Elvis. Nudie's clothes were pure country gaudy, and Gram insisted that everyone help design their own theme-based suits—haute coutre-perfect for the Burrito's skewed brand of C&W. The others chose things like rising suns and blooming roses and various favourite animals; Gram chose pills and pot and a burning cross. The album cover that resulted from the photo shoot was decadent dandy wonderful, as Hillman acknowledged, just the boys and "[t]wo models we wanted to look like hookers. It was out in the middle of the desert. It was freezing and we were loaded . . . outlaw band, yeah."

Suitably nattily Nudie-attired, once they hit the road to promote the album (with former Byrd Michael Clarke having been made a permanent member on drums and sporting his own off-the-rack Nudie suit), it was the usual fate of a profoundly unique band making timeless music: small crowds now, a big influence later. Ian Tyson and his folk-singing wife Sylvia caught the Burritos when they made their New York debut. Tyson:

The volume, which was deafening, I remember. They were right up there with Cream for loudness, tremendously loud and you couldn't hear what they were doing over this gigantic wall of drawl and twang, but Gram was a real charismatic kid [there's that word again]. I really liked what they were doing. After that I started persuading Sylvia that we should move in that direction.

Not long after, the pair formed their own steel-guitar-heavy band, the Great Speckled Bird. They weren't the only ones watching—Hillman recalled how future Eagles co-founder Glenn Frey "was just in awe of Gram. He learned about stage presence and how to deliver a vocal and don't think Glenn Frey wasn't in the audience studying Gram." But let's not hold Gram responsible for the birth of the Eagles: no soul deserves that degree of damnation.

Besides, one doesn't have to look too far to find things he *can* be held accountable for. Whatever room he was in, Gram tended to set the tone, and the tenor for the Burritos was decidedly laid back. Not California laid back—comatose laid back. The abstemious Kleinow remembers:

Our first showcase after we did the debut album was at the Whiskey a Go Go. Jerry Moss and Herb Alpert [the respective M and A of their label, A&M], all the bigwigs and suits were sitting downstairs waiting for their new act to come on stage. We came out and started playing. Gram was so stoned he couldn't play the piano; he was in one of his invalid moods. Chris Hillman was right up there plugging away but Chris Ethridge had smoked a little too much of something. As we started to play, after about three or four songs, Ethridge got to the point where he wasn't able to stand up any more and he flopped down. Our little roadie Frankie came up and put a chair behind him and Chris plopped down in the chair. As he continued to play he got more and more stoned and finally passed out and fell out of the chair and dropped his bass on the ground. Little Frankie came out, he couldn't even play the bass, and picked it up and started plunking away on bass. It would have made a great comedy routine if it had been done for Hollywood. But the suits from A&M were getting up from their table mid-concert and walking out.

If their leader was setting a less-than-exemplary chemical example, he was also calling the shots regarding rehearsing; or, rather, wasn't. Between usually being blitzed and above doing anything as mundane as practicing their set, the Burritos tended to be a sloppy live act (ragged tempos; flubbed lyrics; excepting Kleinow's scintillating pedal steel work, tending toward the sonically monochromatic), if undeniably soulful and exciting (if for no other reason than it was absorbing to see if they'd make it through the entire gig). If you were expecting a tight, professional show, you would have been better off paying to see Poco; if you wanted to hear a group who clearly took the music, but not themselves, seriously, the Burritos were your band. The Burritos were C&W hoodlums, and they didn't care who knew it. Hillman:

> One night Hank Thompson, the big country star, sat in with us. He's a wonderful singer. So he did one of his big country hits and Michael was on drums. By that time of the night Michael was feeling no pain. He wasn't playing the shuffle the song required so Hank turned to Michael and shouted, "Drummer! Shuffle!" Michael yelled "Fuck You" back at him. I just shrugged and thought to myself, "Aw perfect. There's that Burrito attitude."

Naturally, it's easier to go with the pharmaceutical flow and refuse to make any concessions to what constitutes a prudent career move when, as Gram did, you received a biannual trust-fund payment of around $50,000. The mettle necessary for naming your album's prettiest, most radio-friendly song "Hot Burrito #1" doesn't come cheaply. And because he had an independent income that allowed him to do whatever he wanted, whenever he felt like doing it, it isn't surprising that, once *The Gilded Palace of Sin* missed the charts by a country-rock mile and the band (after a promotionally disastrous, if socially stimulating tour by train) had resigned themselves to playing half-full LA-area clubs, Gram began to lose interest. Meaning a declining concern for creating new Burritos material and even shoddier live shows. And sometimes—as when the Stones and drug buddy Keith Richards were in town—declining interest in attending even his own shows. Hillman:

> Gram was hanging out with the Stones and almost being a pest. We had a gig one evening and I had to go find him. I finally found him at the Stones' session! I go in there to get him and he's going, "I don't wanna go." And Jagger got right in his face and told him, "You've got a responsibility to Chris Hillman, the other band members, and the people who come to your show. You better go do your show *now*". . . So Gram got up and went to the show.

Although the band was in debt to A&M, the label opted to pull the hit-record lottery lever one more time and asked for another album. Only trouble was, the group had no new songs and an increasingly absentee lead singer. By now Chris Ethridge had tequila-ed himself out of the group (although not before helping them record the majestically shambolic, one-off single "The Train Song," a crunching piece of fuzzed-out country-funk), and former Dillard & Clark sideman Bernie Leadon took his place (Hillman switching to bass, and the Telecaster-toting Leadon giving the band a more versatile, if less distinct sound). New member Leadon recalled the atmosphere around the making of what would become *Burrito Deluxe*: "It was like, 'Here's a chord progression,' or 'How about this chord?' 'Got any ideas?' 'It's sunny outside and . . . my old lady's mad at me . . . How am I doing?'"

Not surprisingly, apart from "High Fashion Queen," a rollicking slice of satire left over from the first album, the best songs on *Burrito Deluxe* are the ones the band *didn't* write. If the harder-rocking "Older Guys" and "Lazy Days" are enjoyable froth, and the accordion-driven Tex-Mex pastiche "Man in the Fog" is goofy enough to get by, it was the stone-country cover of Harlan Howard's "Image of Me" that reminds one of just how affecting an instrument Gram's voice could be. The album's highlight is the group's cover of the Stones' "Wild Horses," a song Gram first heard when Keith Richards asked him to ask Kleinow to add some pedal steel to it. Much has been made of just how much of an impact Gram had on the Stones' music, but the question is ultimately irrelevant, as the Stones' rare forays into country music ("Sweet Virginia" excepted) were compromised either by Jagger's hopelessly disingenuous vocals (as on "Wild Horses") or rendered entirely ineffectual (as on the parodic "Dear Doctor" or "Faraway Eyes"). "Wild Horses"—which was written by Richards—is a good song made magnificent by Gram's tremblingly poignant, near sobbing vocal. If Otis Redding had been white and sung country music . . .

When the new album, as expected, died a quick commercial death, Gram knew it was time to move along again and began to pull away from the group as only a passive-aggressive prima donna can. Jim Dickson, who co-produced *Burrito Deluxe*: "Chris [Hillman] used to get pissed off because Gram wouldn't try. We'd go out and play, in [Topanga] Canyon or something, and if enough people showed up, then he'd entertain. But then he'd come in the studio and be lifeless again." Leadon, on what became disturbingly routine behavior during their live shows:

He [Gram] would sometimes just start playing, no intro, no nothing and we'd have to figure out what he's doing. Or we'd have the famous stuff that would happen at places like the Topanga Corral where we'd start a country shuffle number in one key and then Gram would start this really slow singing . . . in another key and tempo altogether, that slow, heroin groove. We'd be going, "What's he doing? What key's he in?" and we'd have to change up mid-song to what he was doing.

Things only got worse when a bad motorcycle accident encouraged a predilection for prescription painkillers. (Returning from a gig in Seattle, for example, a wheelchair-marooned Gram was denied entry to the plane because he was a slobbering mess.) Finally, in June 1970, Hillman, the band's co-founder, had had enough:

He showed up late and stoned out of his mind on something. We kick off an up-tempo song and Gram starts singing a ballad. It was like the Keystone Cops crashing into a wall. In the middle of the shuffle we had to suddenly stop as Michael slowed the time down on his cymbal to Gram's pace. That was it. There was steam coming out of my ears. Michael and I had both had it. He was as mad as I was—and Michael usually didn't care about anything. So afterward, backstage between sets in the dressing room I said to Gram, "You're all done." And Gram whines, "What are you talking about?" and Michael yells, "Hey Parsons, you're out of this fucking band. You're done. You're through." I was so mad at Gram I broke his guitar.

Unlike art (when it's good), life—good and bad— is rank with clichés. Once Gram got his wish and was free of the Burritos, he wasn't careful so he got what he wanted. The solo album he was given the opportunity to make, but which he wasn't ready to record, turned into a chemically-induced debacle. John Beland, a friend of country-rock's greatest guitarist, Clarence White, remembered visiting one of the sessions for the abuse-defused, never-released record:

> About four thirty in the morning it started wrapping up. Clarence introduced me to Gram, who was loaded . . . Gram threw his arms around me and he gives me this great big bear hug. He wouldn't let go and I'm looking over his shoulder and there's Clarence with his eyes rolled. It was embarrassing. Gram said, "I want to tell you, brother, you played your ass off tonight." I wasn't even playing on the session. I was only listening in the control room.

He got the freedom from being forced to simply suck it up like working musicians without a trust fund do—playing poorly paid, poorly attended gigs and growing the Teflon skin necessary for making worthy art in a world that prefers its opposite—and wasted most of it, spending nearly two years on and off heroin; following the Stones around on tour with his new teenage girlfriend, including to France, where the band were recording their last good album, *Exile on Main Street*; singing background vocals on a few friends' albums (Jesse Ed Davis, Delaney & Bonnie, Fred Neil); packing on the pounds like his old idol, Elvis, when he was off the smack and drinking heavily; being introduced to the woman, Emmylou Harris, whose shimmering vocals would make his own stirring voice that much more compelling; marrying his girlfriend at his stepfather's house (who had almost immediately remarried after Gram's mother's death—to the family babysitter); and, whether he knew it or not, getting ready to record his first solo album, *G.P.* Indolence—even lavishly indulgent indolence, like Gram's—can be forgiven when it's turned into goodness. There are so few genuine good things in the world, it simply has to be.

G.P. is good—very good. Part of it is the band. (That Warner Brothers, whom he'd signed a two-album contract with, supplied him with only a relatively modest recording budget didn't stop Gram from fulfilling his dream of hiring Elvis' ace regular musicians to play on the sessions; he simply dipped into his own bank account to make up the difference.) Part of it is his new singing partner. (To Chris Hillman's credit, he overlooked Gram's and his falling out and insisted Gram call up a young female folk singer he'd heard who he thought would perfectly complement Gram's voice. Harris remembered Gram's typically thoughtless overture: "So I got a phone call from him and he said, 'I'm in Baltimore, could you come pick me up?' And I said, 'No, that's fifty miles away!' And he said, 'Oh, is that far?' Typical, too, was the spell she eventually fell under: "There is a quality to his voice that was just so, so special . . . [H]is voice had a truly deep affect on me. I also think he had a way of incorporating culture into his songs. Country has always been a traditional, cut-and-dried form and he was always injecting incredible poetic images that were so down to earth. It's like taking Hank Williams' stuff forward.") The biggest contributors to the album's success, however, were the songs Gram wrote for the sessions and the commitment he brought to his vocals.

In grand G.P. fashion, the first day's session had to be cancelled because its main man was too messed up to record. Fiddler Byron Berline: "The first night Gram got pretty wasted. We all told him, 'This isn't going to work.' He was stumbling around. He dropped a guitar pick. We said, 'We'll be ready to play with you when you are ready.'" Soon, though, Elvis' players (James Burton on guitar and dobro, Glen D. Hardin on keyboards, and Ronnie Tutt on drums) and the rest of the session men (among them, Berline, Al Perkins and Buddy Emmons on steel guitar, and Barry Tashian on guitar and vocals) were as impressed as the neophyte Harris, thrilled both with the songs they were working on and Gram's refreshing attitude to recording, which encouraged the musicians to create their own unique instrumental contributions to the material. Even the sad songs sparkle with the players' obvious joy in what they're doing.

Unlike with *Burrito Deluxe*, the last time he was heard on vinyl, *G.P.*'s original songs (of which Gram wrote or co-wrote six) are its standouts. The covers ("We'll Sweep Out the Ashes in the Morning," "Streets of Baltimore," and "That's All It Took") are trad-country tunes lovingly performed, but vehicles, foremost, for the magical meshing of Gram and Harris' voices. Gram's model, when he was looking for a female singer to complement him, was always George Jones and Tammy Wynette's duets, but these simple country songs reveal a duo that do more than simply sound very good together: at their best, they become something entirely different, a perfect blending of high and low, strength and weakness, exaltedness and sorrow. (The fourth cover, "Cry One More Time," is for some reason sung by Tashian with Gram and Emmylou on background vocals.)

From the instant Berline's vigorous fiddling jumps out of the speakers on the album's opening track, "Still Feeling Blue," you know everything is going to be all right, that Gram's taken care of business. With bubbling banjo by Alan Munde and sparkling pedal steel, it's just a well-written hurtin' song, but one that possesses so much pleased panache it's also a proud declaration of aesthetic intention. "A Song For You" is a spookily beautiful ballad that only

Gram could have written, an ontological disquisition that's country at its musical core, but something else—something movingly original—altogether. "She," a co-write with Ethridge from the Burrito days that the other members vetoed for being too slow, is probably Gram's greatest recorded vocal, confidently faithful one moment, quiveringly uncertain the next. The Burritos, for all of their wonderfully whacked-out charm, could never have pulled off something as subtly gorgeous as this. I remember the first time I heard "The New Soft Shoe." When Gram drops in the reference to a shopping mall, it immediately changed the way I thought about music with fiddles and steel guitars. "Kiss the Children" and "How Much I Lied" are C&W weepers that become so much more than that because of both the taut, tender lyrics and Gram's gut-punch singing (with lots of help from Harris). While Gram's vocals are usually tremendously moving, it's important to note that he knew when not to sing and when not to sing too loudly or too emphatically. As Harris noted:

> By singing with Gram I learned that you plow under and let the melody and the words carry you. Rather than this emoting thing, emotion will happen on its own. As you experience life and know more, then [emotion is] gonna come out almost unconsciously as you sing. You have to have restraint in how you approach a song.

Album-closer "Big Mouth Blues" serves as a droll denouement, a funky-country R&B number that Gram sings with rowdy glee.

Making a record album is like writing a book: you have the time and controlled conditions to reflect upon what works and what doesn't and to edit out the superfluities and the mistakes. This is why nine times out of ten art is preferable to life. When you're promoting your latest labour out on the road, however, the full-on human factor can get in the way of the art. Gram's one and only solo tour was a success in that those who had the ears to hear what he was doing went away different people from who they were when they came, but he would have changed a lot more people's lives if he hadn't been the exalted fuck-up he was. Then again, if he hadn't been, maybe he wouldn't have been the melodious soul sage that he was, either. Anyway, after the band (competent, but not exemplary like the players on the album, who were either too expensive or too busy to tour) discovered that they hadn't rehearsed nearly enough (a Gram trademark, and, as their boss, his responsibility) and were fired from their first gig, they worked up a strong set and, during the subsequent month on the road, were terrible some nights and transcendent others, depending on their leader's chemical constitution. There were nights when, as band friend Kathy Fenton remembered, "They went *crazy* for Gram and Emmylou"; there were also nights like those in Houston when, according to journalist John Lomax,

> Gram was blasted out of his gourd, and it was pretty sad. He was putting everything into his system you could get, without regard to anything. Kaufman [Phil, Gram's road manager] had more on his hands than he could handle with Gram alone. One night Gram was so plowed he backed up and knocked Neil Flanz and the steel guitar flat off the side of the stage. Poor ol' Neil was sittin' there lookin' at his steel on the ground. Gram never even knew what he'd done.

Along the way Gram managed to get arrested, maced, and beaten up by the police in Blytheville, Arkansas, to constantly fight with his young wife, who everyone on the tour claimed was fiercely resentful of the obvious chemistry between her husband and Harris, and to perform a show in Hempstead, New York, that was simulcast on an FM radio station and which was released ten years later as the album *Gram Parsons and the Fallen Angels Live 1973*. It's raw and garage-band raggedy in places, but full of great songs and magnificent vocals and oozes with charm when Gram talks to the audience and the program's host. If it's perplexing how Gram could manage to be so obviously odious in some ways yet come across to so many people as so captivating, pay attention to *Live 1973*'s between-song chatter.

The tour over and back in LA, Gram occupied himself with writing songs, surviving his house burning down, separating from his wife, and doing lots of drugs, including heroin, again (as much as a decadent rock and roller, his day-long dosing resembled his mother's own 24/7 self-medicating alcoholic habit). He also attended the funeral for Clarence White, who'd been killed by a drunk driver while loading out his equipment after a gig with the Kentucky Colonels. At a Mexican restaurant afterward, Gram and Kaufman made a pact: in the case of either man's death, the surviving friend wouldn't allow the other to be sent off to eternity with the sort of stiff, conventionally functional funeral White had gotten. When the time came, the survivor was to immolate the other out in Joshua Tree, the California desert spot where Gram liked to go and, depending on his mood, either detox or get stoned and look for flying saucers.

When Gram entered the recording studio in the summer of 1973 to record his second solo album, Elvis' band and a couple of key players (Berline and Perkins) from the first album were back on board, but there was no repeat of the first-session debacle for *G.P.* Gram had cut back on the drink and drugs in preparation for recording and stayed relatively straight throughout the entire month they spent in the studio. Like many chemical bingers, Gram usually knew when he could afford to mess up and when he couldn't, and album-making time wasn't one of them. Once again, Gram wrote or co-wrote six songs on the album, and overall they're even stronger than the originals on *G.P.*

"Return of the Grievous Angel" sets the tone for the rest of the record: with lyrics by a fan named Tom Brown (who'd slipped them to Gram at a gig) and music by Gram, it's literate but never affected, musically majestic yet never cluttered or overblown. High art is rarely this damn hummable. The covers "Hearts on Fire," "I Can't Dance," and "Cash on the Barrelhead" are good fun, but, again, mostly notable for the superlative dual vocal treatment brought to each. The vocal symbiosis between Gram and Harris that was so apparent on *G.P.* is even more pronounced the second time around. "Love Hurts," the Boudleaux Bryant song made into a hit by the Everly Brothers, is a cover song of an entirely different standing. I played this song repeatedly after discovering Gram's music, and was infuriatingly flummoxed as to how he and Harris could take clichés like love being like a stove, it'll burn you when it's hot, and making them sound like a line lifted from English literature's greatest love poetry. I'm just as befuddled nearly thirty years later, only now I spend my time trying to make others feel the same way.

"Brass Buttons," a song written years before about his mother, is so delicate it could break, but which, being art, doesn't; instead, the listener does. Like "She" on the previous album, "$1000 Wedding" is a doleful tale of high hopes and tragic endings and is musically unclassifiable. Soul singer-songwriter country & blues? Reprising your own work is rarely a good idea, but linking "Hickory Wind" with "Cash on the Barrelhead" as a faux-live medley was genius. The note Harris hits at the start of the song's last line was worth the do-over alone. "Las Vegas" shows that Gram, in spite of his penchant for the slow sad stuff, still knew how to rock and roll, Burton on electric guitar and Perkins on pedal steel trading off smoking solos. "In My Hour of Darkness," a song as lovely as it is weary with loss, would have been the obvious album closer even if Gram hadn't died before the LP came out.

But Gram did die not long after the sessions wrapped up, and what better way to celebrate a stunning album in the can than to check into a low-rent motel in the Joshua Tree desert and stay wrecked on tequila and morphine, the same stuff that ended Hank Williams' life before he hit thirty. Gram was three weeks away from turning twenty-seven when he faced his own hour of darkness.

Kaufman kept his promise — sort of: stole his dead friend's body from the airport where it was to be shipped back to Gram's stepfather for burial in New Orleans — Bob Parsons' home and a city that had no significance to his stepson — and set fire to Gram's body in the desert, although managing to only partially burn the corpse. There was enough left over for Bob Parsons to bury it in a charmless New Orleans cemetery near a busy highway out by the airport. Bob Parsons outlived his stepson by a little over two years, dying of cirrhosis of the liver, the same disease that had killed Gram's mother.

Referring to W.B. Yeats, W.H. Auden wrote, "You were silly like us; your gift survived it all." Gram's old friend Chris Ethridge said, "He was a good Southern boy, loved to rock and roll, sad all the time. He wanted to go out like Hank Williams, and he did. He rock and rolled out, and it was his fault."

Amen.

HOUND DOG TAYLOR

There is nothing which has yet been contrived by man, by which
so much happiness is produced as by a good tavern or inn.

—Samuel Johnson

Even the most misanthropic and solipsistic of us
has difficulty denying the joy of another's joy.
Happiness, yes—that implies a steady level of
earned contentment that, actual or (more likely) affected,
is too much for our frequently fractured minds and bodies
to easily accept. But joy—episodic, euphoric, bequeathed
rather than assiduously acquired—we not only can believe,
we *need* to believe. Without oxygen and water there can be
no life; without at least the prospect of intermittent grace,
there remains little desire to go on living. That Hound
Dog Taylor was able to achieve, more often than not, this
uncommonly rarified state of bliss-kissed existence and to
reach it while playing the *blues*, is extraordinary. The fact
that he, his band, and most of his audience were usually
pie-eyed when it occurred certainly didn't hurt.

Theodore Roosevelt Taylor was born in 1915 in
Natchez, Mississippi, and God Bless the President of these

United States of America and if you always tell the truth and work like a mule and do as you're told you too can grow up to be the President one day, the fact that you're rural poor and invisible black and born with six fingers on each hand never you mind. He claimed that when he was nine years old his shotgun-toting stepfather escorted him from the family home with instructions not to return, but even if this is just the kind of story a bluesman likes to tell, it is known that at around this time he moved in with his older sister across town. He stuck around the South long enough to drop out of school and to work at a bunch of jobs somebody has to do and to pick up the guitar and to even get good enough to appear on the King Biscuit Flour radio show with Sonny Boy Williamson; also, for the local Ku Klux Klan to burn a cross on his front lawn for the sin of sleeping with a white woman. He left the South for Chicago when he was twenty-seven years old and never went back.

Because of World War Two there were plenty of factory jobs—even for Klan-fleeing, functionally illiterate black southerners—and for fifteen years he worked during the day and gigged whenever possible at night, sitting in on jam sessions and sometimes playing his own sets (as well as playing for tips in the Maxwell Street Market on Sunday mornings). It wasn't until 1957 that he quit his last straight job building television cabinets and decided to risk making his living playing the plentiful, if low-paying South- and West-side Chicago bars, his good-time electrified Delta-blues style making him a popular tavern act. Two other life-changing events occurred that year. Theodore Roosevelt Taylor became Hound Dog Taylor after a friend dubbed him so after observing him professing eternal love while ardently pursing two different women around a bar over the course of the same night. And whereas previously his guitar playing could be described as minimalistic and raw—not for the first time, technical limitation turned into stylistic advantage—now, after falling under the musical spell of the stinging sound of Elmore James' slide-guitar, it was simply ferocious: a wild, wailing, barely controllable electric beast. Aided by a cheap guitar and an even cheaper, distorting amplifier and a slide made from the leg of a kitchen table, for the rest of his life he'd play bottleneck almost exclusively. Not so life-changing, but characteristic of his life nonetheless, it was also around this time that a tipsy Hound Dog used a straight razor to saw off the tiny sixth finger—more of a stub, really, that kept catching on things and had no feeling anyway—from his right hand, leaving him a six-finger southpaw for the remainder of his days.

Even if your style is anti-style—even if you think your business isn't making art, but only making people smile and shout and dance—that's art too, maybe the purest (and most necessary) kind there is. And art isn't ready-made, it takes time to evolve and find its form. In 1959, Brewer Phillips, another ex-Mississippian, joined Hound Dog on second guitar; a drummer, Levi Warren, completed the two-piece backing combo dubbed the HouseRockers soon after. Hound Dog continued to thrill local audiences and even record a couple of singles for small labels that manage to sound like him but without the bite that make him so alluringly original—the dog defanged—and it wasn't until 1965 that Ted Harvey—who Hound Dog had first encountered drumming for seminal influence Elmore James ten years earlier—took over behind the drum kit for Warren and the final HouseRocker line-up was set.

It was this trio that twenty-three-year-old Delmark Records shipping clerk Bruce Iglauer saw perform one Sunday afternoon in the spring of 1970 at Florence's

Lounge on Chicago's southside. Iglauer was stunned not only by what he heard, but by what he saw:

> [T]heir equipment [was] on the floor, [and there was] no bandstand—they moved a table out of the bar [to make room]. They played for three hours straight. People were dancing in the aisles and on the seats and lots of people were sitting in. Lots of people were really drunk and they were shooting dice outside and the energy level was fantastic. Everybody knew Hound Dog and the music was totally raw and absolutely infectious . . . [In between songs] he'd tell these incomprehensible jokes, crack up in the middle of the joke and bury his face in his hands. He'd light a Pall Mall, tell another weird joke, put the Pall Mall on the mike stand, [and] start into another song . . . [H]e used a second guitar [Phillips] for bass lines. There was a drive that you couldn't get out of a Fender bass. The sounds were so raw and distorted—Hound Dog played on fifty dollar Japanese guitars through Sears Roebuck amplifiers and cracked speakers. The whole attitude was "Who gives a damn? We're just playin' for fun." No finesse. There was a lot of blues feeling but there was no attempt to be the least bit smooth, the least bit sophisticated. The music basically could have been played at a juke joint in Mississippi next door to where Muddy Waters was playing in 1949. It was totally unvarnished by virtue of the energy level and the distortion . . . [Plus,] he was so funny looking—a tall, gawky guy, very thin, huge toothy grin. Everybody naturally loved him.

Everybody now included Iglauer, who pleaded with his employer at Delmark to sign Hound Dog to a contract and get the most raucous, most real non-performer he'd ever seen or heard down on vinyl (Hound Dog didn't perform; Hound Dog simply played). His boss declined, so Iglauer did the only sensible thing: he started a record company with his own money (including $2,500 he'd inherited) just so he could ensure that Hound Dog Taylor and the HouseRockers would be recorded for posterity. Although Howlin' Wolf, who still occasionally played the Chicago clubs when he wasn't touring nationally or internationally, was a fan of Hound Dog's, and Canned Heat had name-checked him on the back of their first LP, the album Iglauer and co-producer Wesley Race recorded, 1971's *Hound Dog Taylor and the HouseRockers* (at a cost of $900 and the newly formed Alligator Record's inaugural release), was the fifty-six-year-old Hound Dog's first national exposure.

The list of wonderfully raw talents turned into glossy, gutless product by the record industry is dishearteningly long; Iglauer and Race are to be commended for one of the greatest non-production production jobs ever achieved. Iglauer:

> [O]ur goal . . . was to capture the club sound and feel as much as possible. That's why we didn't get Hound Dog a nice clean amp, why we recorded everything live . . . why I had them hear themselves on the studio monitors rather than headphones and why I set them up in a row, just like on stage. We had a list of all our favorite songs and we asked them to play each one once or twice (mostly once), not too many times to get tired of them.

Hound Dog Taylor and the HouseRockers opens with "She's Gone," a chugging piece of distorted filth that is John Lee Hooker-hypnotic and a fine introduction to the world according to Hound Dog: a loud, lustful, lonely place that's slightly menacing even when you're supposedly having a good time. "Walking the Ceiling" is a typical Hound Dog instrumental, powered by scorching, amp-bursting bottle-neck and a rhythm section that gets so caught up in the fun they rock-and-roll their way into a full-blown boogie. Hound Dog and The HouseRockers were always too busy getting off to concern themselves with what genre of music they were playing. "Held My Baby Last Night" slows things down, just like they'd do in a club, a Tampa Red song that Hound Dog sings with complete conviction (just because somebody says they miss their baby doesn't mean we have to believe that they do), blazing bottleneck accenting his every exhortation, complaint, and plea. Another instrumental, "Taylor's Rock," is both Saturday-night satori music and the first indication that, like all instantaneous delights—an orgasm, a drug rush, a slug of good cheap whiskey—Hound Dog's appeal is potent, visceral, and limited. But then no one ever said nirvana is supposed to be complicated.

There are three more cover songs, but to Hound Dog's considerable credit they don't stand out from the originals, the music of Hound Dog's masters so thoroughly seeped into his own sound, his inimitable style transformative of every song he ever played and sang. And if *Hound Dog Taylor and the HouseRockers* sounds better played very loudly in a kitchen full of drunken, dancing people than it does through headphones with your feet up on a stool, well, only a fool would ask a spoon to do the job of a fork.

Alligator's inaugural release didn't chart or win any awards or even become an underground sensation, but it did become a turntable hit on a few progressive rock stations that rarely played black bluesmen and sold well enough (around nine thousand copies the first year, which is a lot for a blues record on an independent label) to keep the company in business and to convince Iglauer that there was an audience for Hound Dog's music beyond the

Chicago bars he'd been playing for the last twenty-nine years. When offers to appear at out-of-town clubs and colleges began to come in, Hound Dog was happy to hit the road. It was at this time that Iglauer became more than Hound Dog's label boss and producer.

> After I began to realize that he couldn't read maps or road signs and couldn't get anywhere by himself, I began doing the booking, negotiating deals, issuing contracts. I still had my day job at Delmark at the time. He started going out to shows on a weekend then during the week for a day or two at a time, sometimes with me. He played some clubs, college dates and rock and roll shows. I remember him opening up for Mitch Ryder and Detroit. He did some shows with Big Mama Thornton in New York. We did one tour of Australia with Freddie King and did a lot of big venues. He worked quite a bit. Not as much as he wanted to — he would have been on the road all the time . . . He did some shows with Muddy, one at a New York Folk festival in Buffalo. I remember that because Buffalo was dry and Hound Dog and Brownie McGhee, who was also on the show, were both alcoholics. I literally had to break into a liquor store and steal some bottles of whiskey for them because they were too shaky to perform. I remember that we did leave some money.

Not that the audience in Buffalo that night knew or cared that Hound Dog's manager had to risk arrest (or possibly getting shot if caught by the owner) just to ensure that his charge didn't suffer a case of the DT's that would render him unable to play his guitar because of trembling hands or worse — they got what they'd come for: a furiously entertaining show starring a physically pulsating, emotionally affecting, always engaging Hound Dog who ritually began every show with the same ardent declaration: "Now—let's have some fun." Everyone suffers when living with an alcoholic, though, not just well-meaning, law-breaking managers. Iglauer:

> Hound Dog was very moody, probably mostly due to the alcohol. He had to have a double shot in his morning coffee just to keep his hands from shaking. He was mostly very cheery and laughing all the time, and loving to be the center of attention. But he could get angry in a flash . . . especially to the guys in the band. He had a very short temper. I saw the guys in the band pull knives on each other at various times. But sometimes he'd also attack them [verbally] as amusement. One time when we were driving across the country (I'd usually drive since I was the sober one), Ted was in the front with Brewer and Hound Dog in the back. Hound Dog woke up at six in the morning with a cigarette in his hand and slapped Ted in the back of the head and yelled "Wake up and argue!"

No one has it harder than the addict himself, however, and Hound Dog paid the price for his dependency on his beloved red water both physically (a dipsomaniac's inevitable day-to-day corporeal difficulties; the danger of violent involuntary withdrawal; the steady destruction of the major organs) and mentally (mood swings; physiologically induced depression; narrowing of emotional involvement with the outside world). Although he died of lung cancer, a drink without a smoke was unimaginable, so it might as well have been the bottle that killed him. One wishes it could have been different for Theodore Roosevelt Taylor. As for Hound Dog Taylor, one can't help but be thankful. Yes, thankful. Christ without the cross is no one's saviour. An authentic martyr must pay for his martyrdom. Hound Dog lived the way he did—and died because of it—so that we might boogie, so let us give thanks and do as he would have wanted us to do: keep on boogieing. And listening to his disciples. Toronto filmmaker Alan Zwieg, for example, remembers seeing Hound Dog and the HouseRockers at Toronto's El Mocambo club in the early seventies:

> When my friends and I started going to the El Mocambo, our experience of music, of rock and roll and blues, of the music we loved, was mostly limited to records and magazines and the rare appearances of something truly cool on TV. . . It was just so foreign to us but it was also glowing with something we were lusting after at that point, which was for lack of a better word, authenticity. This was the way music felt in the blues clubs of Chicago we'd only read about on the back of a John Mayall record. Into this scene came Hound Dog Taylor. We'd never heard of him. But if he was American and black and played the blues, we were there. And as soon as he sat down and plugged in, we knew we were going to love him. [Adding to the physical oddity of a Hound Dog show, he usually played sitting down.] A lot of it had to do with that authenticity thing. He didn't look like a star; more like a gravedigger. And maybe like that gravedigger showing up for work, he sat down, plugged in and cranked it out. And you could imagine this was what it might have sounded like if you'd been around the clubs in the days Elmore James or Lightnin' Hopkins were playing. He played loud guitar and lots of it and we loved loud guitar and the more the better. And he was raw. As raw as the punky white stuff we were loving like Iggy and The Stooges. He was everything we'd missed because we were young and white and in the suburbs and afraid to venture downtown to Yonge Street back when we might have been able to hear music like this. It wasn't too late. There was still real blues to be heard.

Natural Boogie (1974) offered more of the same, and that's as it should be. Musical diversity was never Hound Dog's intention. He knew what he liked (even if only because he liked what he knew), he tirelessly did what he liked, and he loved that other people liked what he did. What's more valuable: incremental aesthetic growth culminating in mid-dling achievement or consistently doing exceptionally well the single thing you enjoy doing and consistently making many people happy and even occasionally illuminated? "Only mediocrities develop," Philip Larkin wrote.

Opening track "Take Five" blows in on a squall of exquisitely stinky bottleneck and never lets up, the pro-saic lyrics just an excuse for Hound Dog to slide and scratch his way to Hound Dog heaven. The instrumen-tal "Hawaiian Boogie" was another chance to pay hom-age to Elmore James' existence-altering guitar styling (with added volume and flurry). "See Me in the Evening" is borderline humdrum twelve-bar blues salvaged by some delightfully rude bottleneck. "Sitting at Home" is the obligatory tempo-changer, a simmering, crawl-ing blues that allows Hound Dog to sob and shriek the way he knows best—with his guitar. "Sadie" is a surpris-ingly restrained near talking-blues that rides a six-minute modal lope to slow mojo hypnosis. But it's another Elmore James tune, "Shake Your Moneymaker" (here performed as "Roll Your Moneymaker"), that, surrounded by enjoy-able but pedestrian boogies like "You Can't Sit Down," "One More Time," and "Goodnight Boogie," highlights the undeniable one-dimensionality of the majority of Hound Dog's songwriting. "Shake Your Money Maker" and other James classics like "It Hurts Me Too" and "The Sky is Crying" are raw gut-punches and bottleneck explo-sions, but which, because of their memorable lyrics and attractive melodies, are more than that too.

But it doesn't really matter because of *Beware of the Dog*, the posthumously released live album that Iglauer and

Hound Dog had assembled in the months before the latter was diagnosed with inoperable lung cancer. No other concert LP except perhaps Jerry Lee Lewis' *Live at the Star Club* or the Ramones' *It's Alive* is as joyfully jagged, as invigoratingly raw with the simple exhilaration of being alive. Every song brims with blistering bottleneck and delirious singing and barely-maintained, off-the-rail rhythms. Album tracks such as "Give Me Back My Wig" are like water to champagne when compared to the versions contained here, the crazed combination of a frenzied audience and a shaman-shaking Hound Dog making for some genuine house-rocking music indeed. Ezra Pound claimed that just as "poetry begins to atrophy when it departs too far from music . . . Music begins to atrophy when it gets too far from the dance." To which Hound Dog would have surely added, "I'm wit'cha, Baby."

It's *Beware of the Dog*'s previously unreleased material, though, that shines the brightest, whether it's the runaway-freight-train version of "She'll Be Coming Around the Mountain" (yes, *that* "She'll Be Coming Around the Mountain"); the monumental, fuzzy freak-out "Let's Get Funky" (a hilarious horror story relating Hound Dog's real-life reluctance to perform oral sex pushed along not only by his bandsaw bottleneck and Brewer Phillips' percolating Telecaster, but also by Hound Dog's shouts, whoops, and maniacal laughter, himself as happily lost in the rocking rave-up as the audience clearly is); or album-closer "Freddie's Blues," a smoldering slow one about good love and bad love and the difficulty, sometimes, of telling the two apart. (It's also memorable for the superb job Hound Dog does of ignoring a clearly inebriated heckler during this rare quiet number—more than superb, actually, when you consider that the drunken heckler was his own drummer, Ted Harvey.)

227

Although, as Iglauer pointed out, "Usually the guys got along well. If anyone gave any of them any trouble, the other two were there for him. It was very much a family thing . . . they fought with each other except when someone from outside was causing a problem. Then they banded together," they were a family not above occasionally pulling knives on one another. Another common occurrence was the ancient male art form of claiming that, either by implication or outright avowal, someone's wife or girlfriend had been flagrantly unfaithful (usually with the claimee). It was probably just such a "joke" that led Hound Dog to shoot Brewer Phillips one day while they were juicing it up together. Iglauer:

> Brewer Phillips was over at Hound Dog's apartment. Son Seals, who was a friend of both of theirs, was there too. Brewer was making his usual remarks about fucking Hound Dog's old lady, Freda Horne (called "Freddie" by everyone). This was improper etiquette. It was fine for him to make this claim in the car on the way to a gig (when Hound Dog would claim to be fucking Phillip's lady in rebuttal). But Freddie was within earshot. And . . . I think Hound Dog's [undiagnosed] cancer was affecting his sexual performance. (This is based on my sharing a room with him in Toronto some months before. He took a girl back to the room so I vacated for a while. I returned after a time and found Hound Dog dozing on the bed in his shorts while the girl was taking a shower. Based on the attitude of both of them, I gathered that nothing had happened, but not for lack of trying.) So, Hound Dog left the room and returned with a .22 rifle. Based on the angle of the shots, I'm guessing that Hound Dog was aiming for Phillip's crotch. He hit him twice, in the forearm and thigh. Then Son wrestled the gun away from Hound Dog. The police were called and

Hound Dog was booked for attempted murder [and eventually released on bail].

Live by the bottle, die by the bottle. Ditto and then some for your dick.

Like his life, Hound Dog's death was fast and to the point. One day he was coughing a lot and feeling like he didn't have his usual amount of energy, the next day he was in the hospital that he'd never leave alive. He held on until Phillips came to the hospital and forgave his former bandleader for shooting him. Igaluer:

> On the weekend of December 13 and 14, [my then-wife and I] visited the hospital. We left at the end of visiting hours. As we waited for the elevator, the door to the stairs opened, and out came Brewer Phillips. He was finally coming to see Hound Dog. Phillip told me later that Hound Dog hugged him so hard that his fingernails cut Phillip's back.

Families fight; families forgive; family members say goodbye and help to bury their own.

Even before he was sick with the disease that claimed his life on December 17, 1975, Hound Dog liked to say that when he died he didn't want a funeral—he wanted a party. There was a funeral, but every time someone listens to his music, there's a party too. There should be, anyway.

PAUL SIEBEL /
WILLIS ALAN RAMSEY

Beware the fury of a patient man.

—John Dryden

A spoken-word promotional 45 exists—get your own, you can't have mine, they're rare and expensive—that was sent to the media to help promote the release of Paul Siebel's debut LP, 1970's *Woodsmoke and Oranges*. One of the questions the interviewer asks Paul is if he's afraid of being famous for only one or two songs and thereby stifled in his creative growth by a public made myopic by this sort of theoretical mainstream fame. This is what's called a champagne problem, akin to "If I win the lottery, will it make me a different person?" and "Is too much sex bad for my soul?" But to be young is to be awash in endless possibilities, unlimited potential, undiluted idealism. I'm sure that there were times on the road when Jerry Jeff Walker wished he didn't have to perform "Mr. Bojangles" for the eleven-thousandth time, but I'm equally sure that some people were exposed to other songs he wrote and other directions his music took over the years precisely because of the siren song of the ubiquitous "Mr. Bojangles." Anyway, being a one-hit wonder was one thing Paul Siebel didn't have to worry about.

Paul Siebel was born in Buffalo, New York, in 1937, where he learned to love country and folk and what was then called "continental" music (Irish, Polish, German music, et cetera), primarily through the radio, in particular the CBC, whose signal carried across the border from Toronto. A working-class kid in Buffalo illuminated by Hank Williams and Woody Guthrie via a transistor radio has just as much right to his roots as the son or daughter of a corporate lawyer growing up in Texas. How the seed gets planted doesn't matter; how deep in the soil it goes and what kind of soul crop it yields, does. Paul taught himself to play guitar, lived in New York briefly before being drafted, and then, upon being discharged from the army, returned to Buffalo in 1962, where there was a small but burgeoning folk scene, Eric Anderson and Jackson Frank being among his contemporaries.

But hometowns are for leaving, not for fostering your dreams, and Greenwich Village was where you needed to be if you wanted to be a folksinger, so that's where Paul ended up, playing basket-houses (clubs where you were paid, if at all, by what ended up in the passed basket) like the Four Winds and the occasional church basement. To stay alive he worked as a darkroom assistant to a commercial photographer and in a baby carriage factory in Brooklyn, where he spent his days fashioning wooden spokes. Like most aspiring folk singers, his set list was initially stocked with traditional songs of the "Fair and Tender Ladies" variety, but eventually he began to distinguish himself not only by his highly literate original material (as for so many, Dylan the obvious inspiration), but by the way country, bluegrass, and other elements made their way into his music, which instantly differentiated him from the already rapidly dated balladeers crowding Village stages.

Believe it or not, once upon a time there were major publishers who purchased books because their editors believed them to be superior pieces of literature, and not just because their sales teams smelled a bestseller; ditto for large record companies, such as Elektra, the Doors' label. It's true that the early seventies was the dawn of the singer-songwriter era (James Taylor, Cat Stevens, and Joni Mitchell all released bestselling albums the same year as Paul's first record), but when Elektra employees Paul Siegel and Paul Rothchild caught Paul's act at a New York coffee house one night, they had little trouble convincing label head Jac Holzman to sign Paul up simply because they thought he was a wonderful songwriter with a unique sound. (Danny Sugarman did the same thing the year before *over the telephone* when he sold Holzman on both the MC5 and the Stooges in the same conversation.) Holzman hadn't built a highly profitable record company being an artistic philanthropist, however, and the deal he offered Paul was, as euphemism-spouting agents like to say, modest; specifically, four three-hour sessions of studio time. Paul roped in guitarist David Bromberg, bassist Gary White, and keyboardist Jeff Gutcheon, and the four friends worked out tight arrangements that made recording the album in such a short span of time feasible—so much so that in addition to the ten songs that made the album, a handful of uncompleted songs were left over that remain unreleased.

But when one is blessed, it's best not to get too greedy; every life is allowed only so much beauty, joy, and contentment, and *Woodsmoke and Oranges* offers up so much of each that to ask for more is to commit a spiritual sin and to tempt cosmic retribution. "She Made Me Lose My Blues" is a fine opener, not just because of its jaunty joy and witty lyrics celebrating the revitalizing remedy of good music and good loving, but also because it encapsulates the breadth of Paul's musical vision, Weldon Myrick's pedal steel guitar dominating throughout and certainly twanging things up nicely yet not turning it into an outright country song (or even "country-rock") despite Paul's enthusiastic yodelling at song's end. So many hyphens are required when attempting to describe the musical make-up of Paul's songs — "She Made Me Lose My Blues", for example, is best described as jump-blues-country-folk-rock — that it's probably preferable to just accept the fact that complementing Paul's reliable acoustic guitar on almost every track is every possible variation of roots music that can co-exist within the same song, and that what we're hearing is simply Paul Siebel music.

"Miss Cherry Lane" is a silky piece of social satire (and like all superior specimens of the genre, as valid now as when it was written) rooted in an instantly memorable melody with an unexpected but delightfully germane violin break in the middle courtesy of former Sea Train stringman Richard Greene, the jazzy solo another reminder that this isn't just another earnest folk record but a piece of art whose form and content are as indivisible as needle and thread. "Nashville Again" is as close as Paul comes to average — an above-average love-gone-wrong song that most songwriters would lie and steal to have written (David Bromberg covered it on his *Long Way from Home* album) — while "The Ballad of Honest Sam" is such a compelling tale of a crooked small-town card shark that it's possible to overlook the fact that it's really about the inescapable evil of unfettered capitalism, *Das Kaptial* made flesh and spilt blood in just over four minutes. Side two closes with "Then Came the Children," as fine an argument for patchouli-scented hippie mysticism as exists, a mesmerizing melody carrying along its message of cosmic celebration in the face of everyday anxieties and concerns. Jerry Jeff Walker—a connoisseur of choice cover tunes who would dip into the Siebel song bag more than once— took a crack at it on his *Too Old to Change* LP, but couldn't touch the tenuous beauty of the original, its honest optimism subtly belied by its sadly beautiful music.

A songwriters' songwriter (almost as career damning as being a writer's writer), Paul's most covered tune is "Louise," Bonnie Raitt, Leo Kottke, and Linda Ronstadt all having had more commercial success with their respective versions than its author ever did with his, but Paul's rendering is still the gold standard, his nasally, aptly-imperfect voice the perfect instrument to convey the story of a young prostitute who dies alone, used up and forgotten, and whose body is sent home on the mail train. Amateurs think art is constructed out of ideas; people like singer-songwriter Mandy Mercier know that its essence lies in Swift's definition of style: "Proper words in proper places":

> I remember [singer-songwriter] Steve Forbert talking to Paul Siebel one night. He couldn't get over that song "Louise." The legend said he wrote one line a month and it took him a year to write that song. Forbert [kept] saying, "Louise rode home on the mail train." Like that was so important, that she be perceived as so unimportant that she had to ride the mail train.

The heartbreak ride of side two of *Woodsmoke and Oranges* continues with "Bride 1945," a sung short story in song of Chekhovian perfection married to a deceptively breezy arrangement about young suburban dreams and their tendency to turn to middle-age nightmares. Paul's satire isn't of the one-dimensional, finger-pointing variety, however, and he manages to make us feel remorse for his characters' fates (and ourselves as human beings) even when our initial instinct is to merely judge. "We make out of the quarrel with others rhetoric," Yeats argued. "but of the quarrel with ourselves, poetry."

By the time "My Town" is over, it's almost too much. To call it the best anti-war song ever written is to belittle its power and depth. "Blowin' in the Wind" and "Masters of War" are about good *us* versus bad *them*, as easy and as useless a starting point for any serious discussion of any topic as there is. Paul's achievement (with expert assistance from David Bromberg on spine-shivering dobro) is to make flag-waving Miss Delia a tragic figure and not an object of ridicule. "Any Day Woman" turns down the tragedy, thankfully, but not the intensity, Paul's reminder of the rules of unrequited love another favourite of Bonnie Raitt's, who turned in a convincing version on her self-titled debut a year later. Honky-tonk piano and steel guitar plus proto-feminist lyrics — "Any Day Woman" is that kind of song because Paul is that kind of artist. Paul and Bromberg's weaving acoustic guitars are all the musical underpinning "Long Afternoons" requires, a gentle remembrance of a youthful affair that is simultaneously sensuous, nostalgic, and wistful (as love affairs tend to be when recalled several years on). It's as close as folk music can get to lyric poetry, it's Keats you can hum.

Critical raves led to only nominal sales — Why? His voice not A.M. radio reassuring, his face not magazine pretty, his songs not cozily comforting — but his club gigs, as always, continued to be well received, and Elektra came though with some limited tour support, as when they secured him a high-profile spot opening for The Band on a couple of occasions, even paying for Bromberg, White, and Gutcheon to beef up the sound. But mostly the folk club circuit and fine-tuning the songs that would comprise 1971's follow-up, *Jack-Knife Gypsy*.

"Jasper and the Miners" announces a tweak in Paul's music—the sentiment more cynical, the sound a little more nuanced (six-string session ace and latter-day Byrd Clarence White lending his string-bending skills to the opening cut)—but with no detriment to the end result, by the time Jasper walks away through the snow with his boots on backward at song's end the listener wanting to immediately hear it again, so as to both re-experience the music and to reconsider the tale. Keyboardist Ralph Schuckett is the standout instrumentalist on "If I Could Stay," his insistent piano and moody organ overdubbing complementing the song's anguished personal speculations. Not for the last time on the album would Paul sound utterly alone, confused, and angry (usually at himself for his personal incomprehension). The title song is the tough saga of a backstreet hold-up with a twist that has nothing to do with the knife the mugger holds, and is the closest Paul ever comes to rocking out. The unexpected musical stridency is unforced and entirely appropriate. A pagan prayer to the earth buttressed by an ethereal arrangement (spare acoustic guitar; Buddy Emmons' sighing pedal steel; returnee Richard Greene's soaring strings; French horn), "Prayer Song" is less a soothing supplication, however, than a plea to the rain and the wind and the animals and the rest of the natural world to continue to console, sustain, *save*. If Kierkegaard had been an agnostic with pantheistic sympathies and with a superior sense of rhythm, this is what he would have come up with. "Legend of the

Captain's Daughter" concludes side one, a Cajun stomper as pleasantly derivative as most examples of the form, but a slight letdown nonetheless.

"When the Chips Are Down" sets things right—a clever catalogue of existential do's and don'ts floating on a waltz-time bed of nimble pedal steel and violin that, in the end, don't leave you any further ahead even if you pay attention to them anyway—but something's not quite right, the bracing satire of before having given way to something slightly sour. It's debatable whether Neil Young's *Tonight's the Night* or Alex Chilton's *Like Flies on Sherbert* is the drunkest LP ever released, but *Jack-Knife Gypsy* has to be the most hung-over-sounding album. You can almost smell the morning-after gloom. The remainder of the album is all competent country-rock denouement, verse-verse-chorus-solo enjoyable, but it's not particularly memorable. Oh, well: five instant classics, six more perfectly-fine forgettables, and all of it just a year after producing *Woodsmoke and Oranges*, a bona fide masterpiece. Maybe after a decent amount of time letting the field lie fallow he'd harvest another one.

Except—go ahead and pick your preferred agrarian metaphor—the land became barren, the tree refused to bear further fruit, spring did not follow winter. Always a popular club act, Paul continued to play and please and build a matchless reputation among his fellow songwriters who would turn others on to his albums and frequently cover his songs, and they and his few fans (*Jack-Knife Gypsy* fared even poorer commercially than its predecessor) waited for his third LP to appear. And waited. And waited.

It's a question that has haunted philosophers for centuries: what came first, the chicken or the substance-abuse problem? Later, after he got sober, Paul seemed unsure whether the alcohol and the late nights (which turned, as such nights often do, into *all* nights) contributed to the drying up of his songwriting ability, or were just the ultimately self-destructive solace he took to when that facility had already gone. Regardless, he played solo shows, he drank and drugged and drifted through a series of ephemeral relationships, he lived on gig money and the infrequent royalties generated from other people's versions of his songs, and began to resemble one of those unfortunate baseball pitchers who find themselves routinely throwing the ball twenty feet over the catcher's head because they tell themselves not to throw the ball over the catcher's head. (When I handed a copy of one Paul's albums to David Bromberg to sign after one of the latter's gigs, Bromberg sighed—literally sighed—saying only, "Oh, Paul," as he scribbled out his name.) Paul also tired of people asking him when they could expect him to make a new album. Like that was something that was up to *him*.

Paul's only other LP, a live album that captures him (assisted by old pals Bromberg and White) at a gig at LA-roots-bastion McCabes in 1978 (and released on the micro label Rag Baby in 1981) is disturbingly indicative of Paul's increasingly ambivalent relationship toward his back catalogue of original songs. Of the ten numbers, only half are his; and though they're ably performed, it's only on the covers that he really comes alive, Jimmie Rogers' "In the Jailhouse Now" and even the unlikely "You Are My Sunshine" obviously a lot more fun for him to play than his own compositions, which perhaps reminded him of what used to be so easy and enjoyable. (Significantly, on the only other places you'll find Paul's music—a 1980 benefit album entitled *Bread and Roses* and *Woodstock Mountain: More Music from Mud Acres*, a sort of folk-music collective souvenir—his contributions are affecting versions of Blind Lemon Jefferson's "Lonesome House" and Hank Williams' "Weary Blues.") Although he agreed to *Paul Siebel Live*'s release, when the label sent him a list of the songs set for inclusion and their proposed running order, he didn't bother to respond. When an animal stops cleaning itself, you know it's dying; when a songwriter stops caring about his or her own songs . . .

By the mid-eighties Paul had quit drinking and quit playing live and took a job working for the Parks Department and didn't like to talk about his music career. He also worked as a baker for a while, preferring the company of rolling pins and bags of flour to well-meaning people wanting to hear him play songs he wanted to forget because he couldn't write any more of them. A 2004 British CD-compilation of the first two albums brought him some much deserved attention among the alt-country crowd, but the composer of the liner notes, music writer Peter Dogget, observed that Paul—while clearly pleased, if slightly bewildered, by the renewed appreciation for his work—seemed "a little unsure as to whether he had actually been that talented in the first place." Today he lives in Maryland and enjoys sailing and restoring old violins.

When hotshot young director Michael Reeves was directing the film *Witchfinder General*, Vincent Price, the movie's veteran star, grew so frustrated by the twenty-five-year-old's continual reprimands that he was overplaying the role, that he eventually blurted, "Young man, I have made eighty-four films. What have you done?" To which Reeves answered, "I've made two good ones."

Compared to Willis Alan Ramsey, Paul Siebel was prolific. Twenty-one years old when he released his first album, "precocious" doesn't begin to do him justice. 1972's *Willis Alan Ramsey* is an album that someone tells you that you *have* to listen to or else forces you to hear, the best kind of promotional push there is. That it's also his only album is frustrating, is fascinating, is ultimately irrelevant.

A popular Texas bumper sticker reads I WASN'T BORN IN TEXAS, BUT I GOT HERE AS QUICKLY AS I COULD, and Willis Alan Ramsey wasn't but did, was born in Birmingham, Alabama in 1951, but grew up in Dallas, moving there when he was ten. He was in both the obligatory high-school rock-and-roll cover band and a folk duo, aesthetic antecedents to his fully mature sound: highly literate, deeply rhythmic acoustic music. A couple of failed attempts at college later, he was playing his own solo-acoustic material around Austin, when he heard that Leon Russell, who'd recently co-founded a supposedly art-and-artist-first record label, Shelter, was in town for a gig supported by the Allman Brothers. Willis hunted Russell down at his motel room and said he'd like a record contract, please. When Russell pointed out that it was customary in such matters to audition first, Ramsey happily obliged. On the spot. Pain-in-the-ass brashness often goes hand-in-hand with astonishing precocity. We forgive the first because of the existence of the second. But it doesn't mean that so-and-so isn't still a pain in the ass.

Russell and Gregg Allman, who listened in on the on-the-spot try-out, were equally stunned by the teenager's bag of songs, and Ramsey did indeed get his name on a Shelter recording contract. Album sessions began not long afterward, and isn't life wonderful the way things always work out just the way they're supposed to? Entirely justifiable sarcasm aside, sometimes they actually do. For a little while, anyway.

Sliding the record out of its sleeve for the first time — Willis' impossibly youthful face on the album cover, an impossibly cocksure grin on his face — you can't help but notice on the back jacket the number of recording studios—five—that were used to capture *Willis Alan Ramsey's* eleven songs. Later, Willis was prone to muttering dimly about all of the "shit" he had to go through when recording the album, as well as the whole year it took to get it done—a process that engendered a lifetime's distrust of the music industry—but the studios are all first-rate (Sunset Sound Studios in Hollywood, Beautiful Sound Studios in Memphis, et cetera), the varied session players the best in the business (Jim Keltner, Russ Kunkel, and Kenneth Buttrey on drums; Tim Drummond, Leland Sklar, and Carl Radle on bass; Red Rhodes on pedal steel guitar; Leon Russell himself chipping in on everything from piano to vibes); and the end result is stunning, so one can't but wonder about mountains and Texas-sized mole-hills and the petulance of youth, particularly monstrously talented youth accustomed to always getting what they want whenever they want it.

Ironically, one of the benefits of employing so many different recording locations and musicians is that, while indisputably a unified, organic effort, *Willis Alan Ramsey* is almost a sampler of Willis' sundry sounds and styles, as if he knew this selection of songs would have to suffice for the next four decades and counting. In addition to the delicate, ominous acoustic guitar that introduces it and the accordion that provides much of its musical colour, lead-off track "The Ballad of Spider John" also utilizes an understated but highly effective string section and some sobbing saxophone: mid-afternoon A.M.-radio balladry for an alternative, superior universe. The narrative economy and emotional poignancy of this tale of an aged con-man reduced to riding the rails and who only wants someone to listen to his story of misplayed love is remarkable no matter who wrote it; that it was composed by someone who didn't have to shave yet is astonishing. "Muskrat Candlelight" *was* A.M. music—not Willis' original, but via a cover version recorded by the Captain and Tennille (I know, I know), who renamed it "Muskrat Love" and also cutified it musically to the point that Willis' clever use of a couple of lonely muskrats to explore the banal beauty of domestic happiness is utterly submerged in sugary schmaltziness. No matter: what Elizabeth Barrett Browning did with enumeration in "How Do I Love Thee?" Willis does with rodents in "Muskrat Candlelight."

"Geraldine and the Honeybee" toughens things up considerably, Willis acting as a one-man band (drums excepted) on a funky little ditty about a honeybee that can't get enough of a certain chrysanthemum's sweet, sweet pollen, even if, poor thing, she's living in a compost pile. Because "Baby, I want you so bad" may be true, but, by virtue of its threadbare linguistic facileness, we don't register its truth, we need pop poets to give us uncommon ways of saying it so we can feel it. The right words in the right place aren't about being a fussy grammarian; Willis' radish-fresh language allows us to more completely own our own lust. "Wishbone" is Tinker-Toy blues, a caution- ary tale about the price of success in which the staccato piano and goofy vocal make it clear that tumbling from the top is only a slippery banana peel away. "Satin Sheets" is another musical detour, Willis back in coffee-house mode, alone on acoustic guitar and mixing up wobbly theology and sexual fantasy to charming effect, praise the Lord and pass along those little white pills, dear. Side one sighs to an end with "Goodbye Old Missoula," a ped- al-steel-smoky farewell to something more than a mere place or person. Need it be added that every one of these six expertly word-chiseled songs is as melodiously catchy as the flu?

"Painted Ladies" and Dusty Rhodes' merrily sawing fiddle takes us in yet another musical direction: stomping country-rock melded to a thinking rocker's lyric about nostalgia for a past that never existed, but which nevertheless needs to be believed if the too-real present is to be endured. "Watermelon Man" is gut-bucket folk that successfully fuses a filthy, fruity double entendre and a nasty slide guitar, courtesy of Robert Aberg. Woody Guthrie—or any other hero—never received a finer tribute than "Boy From Oklahoma," an all-that's-essential-inclusive biography-in-song that leaves no doubt in the listener that great men and women die, but they never go away. The acoustic guitar and cello duet that Willis and Cathy Pruitt play on "Angel Eyes" is as beautiful as the lover Willis conjures up with his words; in the end, a beautiful soul the finest aphrodisiac. And the entire thing wraps up with "Northeast Texas Women." In addition to guitar, bass, drum, and fiddle, the musician credits on the closing tune include "Coke crate," "bottle," "south wall," and "carpet and hallways," and every one of these is needed to create the magnificent cacophony that sounds something like the Band's "Up on Cripple Creek" stumbling home at four A.M. on downers and cheap red wine, the hooting and shrieking that accent Willis' paean to the glories of his adopted state's women the ideal un-harmony. Five silent seconds after the glorious mess that is "Northeast Texas Women" comes to an end, it lumbers back to life, some final bottle clinking, wall pounding, and discordant chording before someone clears his throat and someone else announces, "That's it."

Whoever it is, they had no idea how right they were.

There was cool-crowd adulation (Lyle Lovett: "I learned every song off his record. I went to see him every time he played, got tennis shoes like his. I wanted to be

Willis Alan Ramsey"); there was peer group admiration (covers by Jerry Jeff Walker, Jimmy Buffett, America); in time, there was even money (courtesy of the Captain and Tennille cover, a number four hit), more money than any commercially negligible performer (his album tanked) could imagine; but there wasn't any more music. Even the music that did exist was shrouded in a Willis-cast shadow: reportedly asking Shelter *not* to promote the album (he didn't believe in playing the music-busi-ness-hype game); cancelling a nation-wide club tour at the last minute because he decided he didn't want to play high-profile gigs in mega-media spotlights like New York and LA; being young and wild and stupid (Lovett again: "I'll never forget my first conversation with Willis. It was at the fanciest restaurant in Bryan [Texas.] While I inter-viewed him [for the student newspaper at Texas A&M, where Lovett was a journalism student] he was eating a filet mignon — out of his hand").

Once the cosmic-cowboy scene began to dry up in Austin, Willis moved to (among other places) Nashville, LA, Woodstock, London, and, eventually, to Scotland, where he lived in a lighthouse near Edinburgh and explored indigenous music and soul-searched, something he was able to do quite easily with the aid of his Muskrat royalty windfall. It sounds like every hippie musician's dream (par-ticularly one of Scottish heritage), but as much as they can be a nightmare at times, work-world responsibilities and deadlines keep us rooted to the earth and other people and even ourselves, particularly to the things we sometimes for-get we're here for. Sadder than the idea that Willis only had one album in him is the prospect that there was more exqui-site music within him that never came out simply because he lacked the worldly compulsion to get his hands dirty and go in and get it. Sometimes inspiration needs a push.

Michelangelo's frescoes on the ceiling of the the Sistine Chapel began life as a glorified house-painting job.

When he came back to America in the late 1980s to renew his visa he met his future wife, songwriter Alison Rogers, who apparently sparked his long-dormant song-writing flame, co-writing "That's Right (You're Not From Texas)" with Willis and Lyle Lovett, which the long-time admirer and now well-known performer recorded on his 1996 album *The Road to Ensenada*. Willis and Lovett collaborated on another song, "North Dakota," and Lovett recorded Willis' "Sleepwalking." Willis also contributed two new songs to Jamie Oldacker's *Mad Dogs and Okies* LP. All of which are completely fine, absolutely okay, thoroughly competent.

The beautiful loser cliché would be that Willis is a mad-genius recluse who spends all of his time obsessively tinkering with his never-ready masterpiece, likely high as a coot owl and living with a house full of rare, hairless cats. The truth is more mundane and a lot stranger. He's happily married and living in Colorado, and there *is* a new album (it even has a working title, *Gentility*), and in the periodic interviews he does—usually with local newspapers to publicize infrequent Texas club shows—Willis often matter-of-factly states that he's not a perfectionist by any means, that the album is almost ready, that they're actually in the mixing stages, and that it should be out any time now. Except that he's been telling this story for several years. (The album is entirely self-financed because he claims he doesn't want to risk any record company power plays compromising the integrity of the music—because everyone knows how disastrously that worked out on *Willis Alan Ramsey*.) And, yes, Willis does do the occasional public performance, usually in Texas or its environs. He's gained some pounds and a beard and his voice has lost some of its upper-range register and its tenor-tender vulnerability, but he puts on a professional show — often joined by his wife on background vocals — and is a surprisingly comfortable between-songs interlocutor.

If you're a Willis Alan Ramsey fanatic, however — and anyone introduced to his music eventually becomes one — maybe it's for the best that the longed-for follow-up to *Willis Alan Ramsey* has yet to appear (and if does appear, it will be so long after its predecessor it can't really be said to be the product of the same person). Part of the cost of knowing perfect things is realizing their rarity. Instead of asking why there isn't more, perhaps we're better off spending our time being thankful for what there is.

JOHN HARTFORD

For loveliness
Needs not the foreign aid of ornament,
But is when unadorned adorned the most.

—James Thomson

You don't *have* to shoot heroin into your eyeball or jump off the nearest bridge just because your art is undersold or undervalued. If John Hartford's music was about anything, it was about happiness. Except that's not the right word—happiness isn't a big enough word. *Joy*. John Hartford's music was about joy. *Is* joy.

Not that he didn't have his commercial heyday—he did write an American standard, after all; he had appeared regularly on a popular television program, the closest contemporary thing to immortality—but that was before he began making the music he was meant to make. Inevitability is not only not inevitable, though, it also takes however much time it needs to take. A then B then C then the John Cowan Hartford project began on December 30, 1937. Every mighty musical oak is born half-blind and bawling and wondering what the hell a lonely acorn

is supposed to do with itself, and even if one of his grand-
fathers helped found the Missouri Bar Association and
his own father was a prominent St. Louis surgeon, John
wasn't any different.

The usual growing up stuff, and then two extraordinary things: a summer job as a teenager working on
a steamer on the Mississippi River, and Earl Scrugg's
brand-new three-finger banjo-playing technique as heard
on the Grand Ole Opry radio show, the Damascus sound
that got him walking on his life's plucking path. At the
time in their lives when all most teenagers want is a clear
complexion and to be like everybody else, John had
already begun his lifelong love affair with steamboats and
rivers and was an accomplished fiddler and banjo player
who led his own high-school bluegrass band. It probably
cut down on the amount of action he got on Saturday
nights, but then precocity and simple worldly pleasures
rarely intermingle.

He dropped out of university, he worked as a disc
jockey, he pedalled product for a record distributor,
he played in country-and-western bands for drunks
and tips during the week and with a bluegrass band
called the Ozark Mountain Trio on the weekends, he
met and married Bonnie Hartford, who gave birth to
two children, and he began writing songs that were
one part contemporary country, one part Beatles, one
part post-Beatnik wit and wisdom, and in 1966 Chuck
Glaser helped him get signed with RCA and John put
together his first album, *John Hartford Looks at Life*. The
six records he made for RCA over the next five years
are sometimes lovely and frequently funny and usually
never less than inimitably hummy, but can't help being
what they are: albums recorded for a major record label
in the late sixties by a very idiosyncratic musician and

songwriter who was nonetheless recording for a major record label in the late sixties. No one beats City Hall. There's no such thing as revolution from within. If you lie down with dogs, you're going to get fleas. There are dogs who would find this offensive, but that doesn't make it any less true.

The endorsement from Johnny Cash on the back of 1967's *John Hartford Looks at Life* notes how "He can't, rather, *won't* change to become something he isn't. We all need to eat, but John Hartford is ready for the worst, as long as his music and lyrics—his whole philosophy—can be part of him." As if to emphasize this point, the opening track, "I Reckon," is a brief spoken word meditation on commercial success versus personal expression, but the overall effect of songs like "Untangle Your Mind" and "Like Unto a Mockingbird" is cuddly counterculture, a crafty company's idea of harmless, generic protest music, smooth, uptempo MOR for people who like to think themselves sophisticated because they watch restricted movies, John sounding like a hip Roger Miller who's firmly against such innocuous boogeymen as intellectual conformity and sexual prudishness. Bookending these are the ballads: velvety, often overly-wordy paeans to love like "The Tall Tall Grass." Perhaps the most genuinely individual thing about his inaugural album is the placing of John's relaxed banjo playing forefront in the mix and the conspicuous absence of Nashville-trademark sweetening strings or Jordanaire-like backing vocals.

The two succeeding LPs—*Earthwords & Music* (also from 1967) and the following year's *Gentle On My Mind and Other Originals*— demonstrate a marked improvement and are full of plentiful pleasures to be ferreted out from the still-occasional examples of empty rebellion and amorous froth. "Good Old Electric Washing Machine (Circa

1943)" is a hymn to solid everyday objects rooted in the shared past that we can see and hear and smell, and that enable us to better know who we are, too—unsolid things that we seem to be—groovy puddles on the floor notwithstanding. John's vocal imitation of the difference between an old hand-cranked washing machine and the new electrified model is evidence of true artistic eccentricity, authentic innovation born of genuine necessity. "I Would Not Be Here" is similarly cerebrally giggly, a first-person account of the infinite regress of the purely coincidental that leads to the only seemingly necessary accidents that constitute our lives. Addressing philosophical questions with plainspoken, backcountry language and imagery, John is something new in contemporary music, the industry's first Beat-hick. Musically, songs such as the above and others, like "Natural to Be Gone", show a loosening of line (by often eschewing strict *abab* rhyme schemes, for example), a stretching of song structure and melody beyond conventional country or ballad forms, and the employment of more varied instrumentation, including drums and finger-picked guitar. He wasn't yet making on record the music he was hearing in his head, but that he wasn't content to accept this aesthetic impasse is evidence of an artist at work and not an entertainer on the make, a rarity in sixties Nashville.

Then there is the title song of album number three (which had previously appeared in identical form on *Earthwords & Music* as well, such was RCA's hope for its success), which Glen Campbell heard and thought could be a hit if sufficiently polished and pimped. And he was right—it won four Grammys and went on to become one of the most widely recorded songs of all time. A soothing slice of pop balladry even in its original, Hartford-recorded form (it easily slides into the bathetic in other, less hardy hands), "Gentle On My Mind" is what A.M. music would sound like in a perfect world, a delightful little piece of calming craft that sticks in your head without bothering your brain. We occasionally need diversions; there's no reason when we reach for them that they can't be dignified.

A hit record doesn't always mean a great record, but it does mean that people will hear about you that wouldn't have otherwise, the kind of people who like to be associated with people who compose hit records. John and his wife and three-year-old son moved to Hollywood in 1968 (where their daughter was born) and led the life of a smart Hollywood couple by trying to remain relatively normal in a community whose whole raison d'être is to eradicate this very concept. As Bonnie Hartford recalled, they weren't entirely successful:

> Our life together was incredible from the time we married until we moved to Hollywood. It was fun and exciting even then, but things were definitely changing . . . John was thirty-one at the time and had such a level head, I really thought he could handle all the attention. We had always been true soul mates, so it was devastating when I felt him slipping away. He became totally caught up in the 60's Hollywood scene until I barely recognized him . . . John also fired Chuck [Glaser] as his manager (and friend) and signed with Ken Kragen and the William Morris Agency. He was encouraged to cut all previous ties, including music mentors, friends and family for the sake of his new career. To his credit, John later saw the folly of his decisions and worked hard to rebuild old friendships.

Soon, John was writing for the Smothers Brothers Comedy Hour and appearing as a regular musical guest on the Glen Campbell Goodtime Hour as well as the Johnny Cash Show. John wasn't a prototypical song-writer/picker—he was a prodigious reader, for one thing (books about steamboats, especially), so working in another, entirely different art form was stimulating for a boy from Missouri, at least in the beginning. He also found time to lend his instrumental skills to several other people's records, including the Byrds' *Sweetheart of the Rodeo*, where, among other contributions, he added the yearning fiddle part to Gram Parsons' "Hickory Wind" (although the Byrds' back-to-basics country sound wouldn't affect the direction of his own music for awhile).

Musician Ronnie McCoury has testified to John's unremitting restlessness: "I don't think he ever had an idle moment. He was doing something or thinking about some-thing constantly. Playing music at his house, or going out to eat, he would order and then he'd sit there and sketch you." Another musician friend, Wes Lachot, marvelled at John's ceaseless musical curiosity: "One day we were rid-ing along and I happened to have in the cassette player some Charlie Parker stuff, and he knew immediately what it was. He said, 'I love Bird, I love trying to play that stuff. Can't really play it on a fiddle but I try anyway.'"

Bebop fiddle tunes weren't next on John's musical agenda, but because of his sudden commercial viability, RCA just as suddenly became a benign patron of the arts and let him go in whatever musical direction he wished to travel. (Neil Young producer Elliot Mazer: "After you deliver [a hit record] to the record company, they'll let you come in their mouth.") Utilizing the freedom granted by RCA to go beyond the skewed country music he'd become known for was admirable, even if the result, unfortunately, wasn't. If we're compelled to applaud artistic experimen-tation, we reserve the right to judge the results.

Housing Project and *The Love Album* (both 1968) tes-
tify to John's laudable desire to do something more significant than make agreeable radio fodder, but both fail
at their task. That by the weight of their ambition they
fail miserably is some consolation, but not enough. The
songs themselves hadn't changed much—in fact, several,
such as "The 6 O'Clock Train & a Girl with Green Eyes"
and "Natural to be Gone," were re-recorded from previous albums, something John did regularly throughout his RCA tenure—but their instrumental treatment
had certainly changed, the rudiments of the banjo-based
sound of before barely detectable beneath the morass of
violins, horns, and other inappropriately ornate instrumentation. It's as if he thought he only had to add a dash
of this and a sprinkle of that from the great pot of available orchestration and he'd instantly confer serious "art"
status to his songs. (Post-*Sgt. Pepper*, there was a lot of
this kind of thinking going on.) Because pre-determined
artiness is antithetical to organically grown, authentic
art, however, a wonderful song like "I'm Still Here" got
smothered under a mass of superfluous production, a
compact testament to everyday stoicism redolent of that
worst of aesthetic sins: pretentiousness. Anyone hoping that 1969's eponymous album would signal a retreat
from this tendency would have been disappointed by the
title of its opening cut alone: "Dusty Miller Hornpipe
and Fugue in A Major for Strings, Brass and 5-String
Banjo." Even the lyrics and song titles began to bloat:
the album's second song, for example, is called "I've
Heard That Tearstained Monologue You Do There By
the Door Before You Go."

Realizing he'd gone as far as he could go in this direction and he still hadn't achieved creative contentment,
1970's *Iron Mountain Depot* is thankfully scaled down,

orchestra-free, and comprised of several typically witty, tuneful songs in his previous banjo-adorned, country-pop mode. Nothing overwrought or overwritten, for sure, but nothing special, either. Except that the album's last song, an instrumental treatment of the Beatles' "Hey Jude," hints at another musical path entirely. Not quite bluegrass, it nonetheless features the first serious *picking* (including John letting go on banjo) on any of his six albums. It's also wonderfully loopy—is a recent hit song most notable for its passionate vocal performance done up entirely instrumentally and which at one point includes the sound of the song breaking down, the players briefly discussing how they want it to come out, and their happy resumption of playing. Odd, one can't help but think, but honestly odd, the sound of some open-minded (and likely slightly stoned) bluegrass musicians playing for themselves, looking to get off by going in a new direction in an old-fashioned way. They clearly haven't found it yet, but they sure sound as if they're having a hell of a lot of fun trying.

Personally, 1970 couldn't have been much fun, as John and Bonnie divorced. (Bonnie Hartford: "He did not want the divorce, but he did want to keep up his lifestyle. This became untenable for the children and me, so we separated. I took the children and moved back to Nashville.") In retrospect, Bonnie Hartford saw the seeds of John's next musical move being planted with the change in his domestic state of affairs:

[T]he end of a traditional marriage, giving up old friends and business associates, all this allowed him an exhilarating freedom he had never known. It would be the perfect time to, as John would say, "Let it all hang out"—get completely out of the box and blow some minds. He was beyond caring what everyone thought; he could [also now] afford to pursue any musical direction he liked.

Although *Iron Mountain Depot* would be John's last album for RCA—his string of commercial misses not so gentle on their bottom-line minds—he did record another LP for the company in 1971 that wouldn't be released for another thirty-one years. *Radio John* takes the pared-down, bluegrass-based sound of "Hey Jude" a step further, the picking even more prominent, the songs less poppy (although still deeply melodic), the lyrics less loquacious. Having already reconnected with bluegrass, his first musical love, in writing "Skippin' in the Mississippi Dew" he returns to his other early obsession: steamboats and the rivers they travel. As if to illustrate how pleased he is to be playing this kind of music again, there's even a cover of that most standard of bluegrass standards, "Orange Blossom Special." RCA didn't think much of the cumulative results, though, and John was allowed to leave and sign with Warner Brothers.

Falling in love after the age of forty is rare. You've known what thrills you for a long time, and you've been thrilled—or not—the same way for almost as long. The natural excitement of discovery has naturally given way to the melancholic fulfillment of finding what you were looking for. Fresh fervours yield to autumnal satisfactions and *c'est la vie*, every dog has its day, and all the barking in the world isn't going to change that.

But sometimes we're surprised—jolted, actually—out of our sober contentment by something new-found, something unexpected, something extraordinary. Like when I discovered a battered but still playable copy of John Hartford's album *Aereo-Plain* in a second-hand Toronto record store in 2005. I'd heard of Hartford, but

257

never—except for Glen Campbell's saccharine performance of "Gentle on My Mind"—heard him. The cover
of the record is what made me pick it up—an extreme
close-up of a man's face (Hartford's, it turned out) sporting a bushy beard and long hair and topped off with bug-
eyed aviator goggles—but it was the rudimentary instrumentation listed on the back of the album (banjo, fiddle,
acoustic guitar, dobro, and occasional bass) and the price
($5) that convinced me to give it a try. The cover shot
said zonked-out hippie; the musician credits said minimal
mountain music. I wasn't thinking of Heraclitus' claim
that "Out of discord comes the fairest harmony," but that's
what I was feeling. Besides, you couldn't even buy a pint
of beer for five bucks anymore; what did I have to lose?

My preconceptions about bluegrass music, for one
thing. *Aereo-Plain* sounds like smoking hash out of an old
corncob pipe; or, if you prefer, Paul McCartney being
molested by Flatt and Scruggs. More important than
helping to serenade elevators and dentist offices around
the world, Campbell's lucrative version of "Gentle On My
Mind" allowed John the financial freedom to quit his various day jobs and leave LA behind (and a brief second
marriage and divorce) and move back to Nashville and
hire the best pickers around—Vassar Clements on fiddle, Tut Taylor on dobro, Norman Blake on guitar—and
create *Aereo-Plain*, an album that his new label certainly
wasn't expecting but which he'd been preparing for his
entire life.

The record begins (and ends) with a faithful version of
its only cover tune—"Turn Your Radio On," an old gospel
call-to-angelic-arms—before sneaking into "Steamboat
Whistle Blues" (the first of two songs featuring boats
and rivers), a verse-verse-chorus corker delivered pickin'
and strummin' style but which, if you stop humming long

enough to really listen, isn't just some old-timey sing-a-long but is actually about how the food we eat is processed and the news we're allowed to hear is processed and the buildings we live in all look the same and that the only thing you can trust these days is an antebellum steamboat minding its own business chugging down the river. This is post-Manson-murder music—wilted-flower-power music—made by a hippie with a head on his shoulders, somebody who knows that to forget the past is just as foolish as being afraid of the future. It's then that you clue into what "Turn Your Radio On" is really about in the context of *Aereo-Plain* and why it's the album's lead-off (and—for emphasis—concluding) track: Albert Brumley's 1938 lyrics enjoin their listeners to tune into a gospel radio station and hear God's word electronically transmitted as far as there are souls who need saving, modern technology in aid of the old, true message. Hartford's version is faithful—not a word is altered and the music remains the purest of gospel-grass—but he nevertheless still manages to flip the song on its head, using an old, true form (bluegrass, his boyhood passion) to proselytize a new but true(r) message (hayseed humanism). To "turn on" in hippie parlance is to get high and become enlightened; "turn on" your musical taste, Hartford seems to be singing, and become hip to a much-needed, revitalizing worldview.

And because it didn't matter anymore if *Billboard* magazine liked his latest album or whether or not he got invited to perform on *Hee Haw*, *Aereo-Plain* could comfortably be what it wanted to be: full of songs about falling in love with first cousins ("First Girl I Loved") and being too pot-paranoid to talk on the telephone ("Holding") and the insanity of dehumanizing, modern urban planning ("Tear Down the Grand Ole Opry") and the enduring value of friendship ("Back in the Goodle Days") and the necessity of wide open spaces (mental even more than physical) and even acapella odes to the wonderful word "boogie." "Steam Powered Aero Plain" is *Aereo-Plain* in essence, Hartford recounting a dream of enjoying the speed and freedom of flying high through the air on a 747 while being simultaneously disappointed that he's unable to see much of anything from such an alienating distance and through the obfuscating clouds. His solution? A flying, stream-powered riverboat, of course, the best of the new combined with the best of the old resulting in the best that existence has to offer. In an era when to be young meant to be at least distrustful and usually antagonistic toward anything not officially deemed "counterculture," John's enlightened conservatism was, both musically and lyrically, stunningly radical. (The closet comparison in pop is the Kinks' *Village Green Preservation Society*, except that even though the message was similar, the medium was rock and roll, the sounds of the moment.)

Although grounded in old-timey bluegrass, even the music was founded on the sort of delightful tension that permeates the entire *Aereo-Plain* attitude. Yes, all of the band members were bluegrass veterans (Vassar Clements had served time with bluegrass godhead Bill Monroe, for instance; part-time bass player Randy Scruggs was the son of John's first bluegrass hero, Earl Scruggs), but Hartford's approach to how they'd be employed in performing his new set of songs was anything but traditional. Unlike Monroe, for example, who, like most bluegrass bandleaders, could be dictatorial, "John," Tut Taylor recalled, "let us play what we wanted to play. 'Cause that was one of the beautiful parts about it—he just let us get in there and pick." Not literally, of course—*Aereo-Plain* is no free-form jam session; the majority of John's latest material was as tight and instantly melodic as the most radio-friendly pop song—but John's goal had been to combine the compactness and accessibility of the songs he'd been writing for RCA with all of the acoustical purity and instrumental pliability of his favourite musical form, bluegrass. Which is what "newgrass" is, fundamentally—a new genre of music that Hartford is rightfully seen as having helped to originate. *Aereo-Plain* producer David Bromberg remembered how he and John initially worked up the album's unique sound:

> [W]e'd sit around and smoke pot and play "Sally Goodin" for an hour and a half. That approach kind of became, after a while, newgrass. John wanted some of the wild playing that we did in New York [to make it onto the album]. After about 30 choruses of "Sally Goodin," it begins to get strange. And that's what he liked.

Lyrically, the *Aereo-Plain* material is no less of a departure, the long, conspicuously "poetic" lines of before giving place to crisp, image-rich writing suffused with plenty of distinctly Hartfordian wit. Gone are the hallmarks of someone straining to sound poetic—big words, lots of adjectives, generalized expressions—and in their place specific objects, people, and events described with careful, shrewd verve. (And in keeping with his old-is-new, new-is-old aesthetic, "Steamboat Whistle Blues" and "Back in the Goodle Days," songs that reference, among other things, pot smoking, waterbeds, garbage dumps, *Rolling Stone* magazine, and the inner-city poor, also contain sly allusions to antique country and bluegrass musicians—specifically, Roy Acuff and the Skillet Lickers.) The best writers sound as if they're speaking only to you, and the voice that John discovered during the *Aereo-Plain* sessions would be the one he used to musically express his worldly wonder, befuddlement, and exasperation for the rest of his career.

Even the picture of the Aereo-Plain band, as they came to be known, on the back of the album, was genre-smashing. Standing in the middle of the shot is John—still goggled and vastly shaggy and cradling a banjo—flanked by Blake and Taylor, the former looking like a hip college professor at the end of a three-day toot, the latter like a firm-but-fair balding machine-shop foreman. Standing just behind John is Clements, his short hair greased back and ready to sell you some real fine feed for your chickens. Radicals or reactionaries? Hipsters or hicks? Does it really matter?

John later described the short time that the Aereo-Plain band was together (around a year) as one long jam session, and as soon as work on the album wrapped up in the summer of 1971 the group hit the road, playing small clubs, outdoor festivals, and every college radio station that asked them to perform. And even when they weren't on stage performing or promoting their album somewhere, they were almost always playing. Canadian multi-instrumentalist David Essig has fond memories of encountering the roving band of jamming junkies in Toronto:

> I was trudging through the snow down Jarvis St. to do a guest set, with my mandolin-shaped case in hand. A taxi pulled up next to me, the back window rolled down and a guy yelled out, "Is that an F-5 or an F-12?" I yelled back "F-12," and the guy in the cab said, "Okay, come on and get in." It was John and the entire Aereo-Plain band: Tut Taylor, Vassar Clements and Norman Blake. They were playing at the Riverboat and took me there with them. It was the first time I'd ever been in the place. I hung out for the afternoon and evening, talking, jamming a little with Norman and

staying for the show. Once my career was established and I was performing regularly at the Riverboat as a headliner myself, I could never go up those narrow back stairs without remembering John and the band. And years later, when I was performing at festivals with John I'd remind him of that day and how important it had been to me. He'd shrug and ask me if I still had that mandolin.

Such had been his disinclination to fashion anything resembling his overproduced RCA albums, that one of John's mandates when he'd hired Bromberg to produce *Aereo-Plain* was that the band wouldn't listen to playbacks, would only hear the result of their labours once the songs were assembled on a master tape. Warner Brothers decided to make a virtue of what was obviously some overtly non-top-40 material, and in the press release for John's next (and last) WB album, *Morning Bugle*, extolled John as "a pioneer of sorts; never afraid to point his music in a new direction to see what happens. He is too, though, aware of the foundations of his music in a way that few other contemporary singer-songwriter types are." The glass isn't half empty of hits, in other words, it's half full. Instead of retreating from the eventual commercial failure of *Aereo-Plain*, John plunged into the organic sounds he and the Aereo-Plain band had created even further, employing only himself on banjo, fiddle, and occasional guitar, Norman Blake on guitar, dobro, and mandolin, and bass player Dave Holland to record the songs that make up 1972's *Morning Bugle*. Musically, *Aereo-Plain* was startling because it was world-class bluegrass fused with a pop (in the best sense of the word) sensibility; *Morning Bugle* is all of that plus the additional amazement created by its being pared down to just two players and a bassist. *Morning Bugle* sounds as emotionally intimate as a solo-folk LP yet as musically rich as the busiest full band recording.

"Streetcar" sets the pace, John's simmering banjo and Holland's slippery bass a deceptively simple underpinning for what was becoming a typical Hartford technique: new music made old, modern-life concerns made old-timey familiar. Here and elsewhere Holland is no plodding time-keeper, his bass blanketing the bottom but also acting as another snaky lead instrument, befitting his time playing with such jazz giants as Chick Corea and Miles Davis. "Nobody Eats at Linebaugh's Anymore" is high-lonesome because of a different kind of heartache, the urban-sprawl blues and the deserted downtown glooms; "Howard Hughes' Blues" is a nimble tale of what happens when there isn't anything left to buy but somehow something's still missing; "All Fall Down" is apocalyptic pickin' and grimacin'; "On the Road" is about the touring life and what you really get paid for—the twenty-two hours a day you're *not* on stage; "Old Joe Clark" is a song as old as the hills where bluegrass began (but in which John manages to include references to, among other things, concerns about his current management and a direct appeal to the listener to drop him a line if he or she just happens to have a Orpheum five-string banjo with a twelve-inch open-back pot); and the title tune is a two-minute-and-twen-ty-three second masterpiece, a plaintive ode to accepting who you are (and aren't) as painful but necessary prepa-ration for constructing the self you *can* be, and how it will be all worth it when you're sitting in your broken rowboat in the middle of the dirty pond by the railroad yard with your good old banjo and a lid of good, mellow-making weed by your side. Although expertly assisted by Blake and Holland, the sole black-and-white photo on the back of *Morning Bugle* shows a fiddle-playing John standing in front of an old building, shorn of his *Aereo-Plain*-era beard, but, with his shoulder-length hair and two-tone shoes, still looking like no one's idea of a bluegrass musician. No one's but his own.

Touring *Morning Bugle*—there wasn't any other way to flog it, since Warner Brothers had seen the error of their artistic-freedom-granting ways and pulled the plug on any post-release promotion—the paring-down process continued, only John and Norman Blake left to replicate the songs from the new album as well as select *Aereo-Plain* material and the odd bluegrass chestnut done up as oddly as the spirit struck them. A bootleg exists of John and Blake performing at the 1972 Philadelphia Folk Festival that gives a tasty taste of what the pair got up to on the road. High-quality pickers—only jazz players are jazzier than A1 bluegrass musicians—with a sackful of soulful acoustic-pop bombs programmed to—Boom!—deprogram unsuspecting audiences, the duo spread their twangy wise words wherever they went. (In the picking pocket? Introducing "Old Joe Clark" at the aforementioned festival, John declares that the only thing he knows for sure is that he and Norman aren't Jesus freaks, at which point the two of them then proceed to burn the old song right down to the ground, Jesus freaks or not, Jesus happily weeping by tune's end and with no option but to rush right out and buy the new album.)

Having released eight albums over the previous six years, it's not surprising that there wasn't a new one until 1976. Playing live in various configurations (by himself, with Norman, with the Nitty Gritty Dirt Band); lending his instrumental talents to scads of other people's records (even receiving co-billing on *Tennessee Jubilee: Benny Martin with His Guests John Hartford and Lester Flatt*); falling in love with Marie Barrett, the woman who would eventually become his third wife; gaining his riverboat license and spending hours on the water piloting the Julia Belle Swain; giving up on the major record companies (after they'd given up on him) and joining up with the newly formed, independent acoustic-music label Flying Fish; and writing new songs, of course, lots and lots of new songs. For his return to the recording studio, however, 1976's *Mark Twang*, John had something even more different in mind.

Mark Twang is just like its title sounds—Twain-like wit wedded to inventively twangy timbres—plus the aural oddity of Hartford accompanying himself alone on banjo or fiddle or whatever other instrument the tune at hand required (on one song it's just him and his cheek—that's right, his *cheek*); plus, for rhythmical accompaniment, periodic clogging. Rock critics are prone to going on and on about another album recorded around this time, the Sex Pistols' *Never Mind the Bollocks*, as being a punk-music watershed, about how its aesthetic is so raw and primitive and DIY. But Pistols' guitarist Steve Jones laid down *weeks* of electric guitar overdubs on every track on that album and its budget came in at well over $100,000. Compared to *Mark Twang*, *Never Mind the Bollocks* sounds like LA session hacks backed up by the London Philharmonic.

"Skippin' in the Mississippi Dew" was originally recorded for the back-to-basics but ultimately shelved *Radio John*, but the version that kicks off *Mark Twang* —literally—goes back still further, the sounds of John's busy fiddle and even busier feet the ideal accompaniment to this ode to the mystery of rivers, which, as he reminds us, will still be here being mysterious long after our fleetingly skipping selves are gone. There'd been one-man-band records before—Paul McCartney's first post-Beatles offering, Skip Spence's *Oar*, Emitt Rhodes' self-titled debut—but those records were built to greater or lesser degrees via diligent overdubbing; *Mark Twang* is the sound of one man playing, clogging, and singing live, frequently all at the same time.

"Long Hot Summer Days," "Let Him Go On Mamma" and "The Julia Belle Swain" are three more river songs, all of them narrated from the viewpoint of some of the people who live and work on the river (and—because *Mark Twang* isn't affable nostalgia—some who no longer work). "Don't Leave Your Records in the Sun" is a falsetto-assisted public service announcement, with John helpfully demonstrating with his voice what it will sound like when, for example, your LP becomes warped or scratched. And then things begin to get really weird. "Tater Tate and Allen Mundy" is a sung recitation of the names of forty or so of John's favourite bluegrass musicians; "The Lowest Pair" is a spoken-word deconstruction of The Lord's Prayer which is audibly prefaced by a deep pull from a joint (just in case you didn't know by now that bluegrass music should be a living art form utilized to express the players' actual lived joys, sorrows, and beliefs, and not for slavishly duplicating stale formulas and non-observed doctrines); "Little Cabin on the Hill Waugh Waugh" is a Bill Monroe/Lester Flatt song that it's safe to say its co-authors never imagined sssssss-sounding likelikelikelikelikelikelikelike thththththththth-this; and "Tryin' to Do Something to Get Your Attention" is five-and-a-half minutes of just that, John too smart to call himself postmodern, but admitting in song that love songs are great but sure are hard to write so he'll just have to amuse the listener anyway he can—by making funny noises with his mouth, by slapping different parts of his body, et cetera—and that, as a result, he should probably give the listener a co-compositional credit for compelling him to write what's written. And there you go: The Death of the Author and the Birth of the Reader and without any of that boring theory and with a pleasant tune to whistle while you skip in and out of the frame.

Realizing he couldn't travel much further in this minimalist direction without becoming the John Cage of country music, *Nobody Knows What You Do*, John's second release of 1976, is bluegrass with a rhythm section and a steel guitar. Typically, when it's most seemingly traditional—as on the scorching instrumentals "Didn't Want to Be Forgotton," "John Mclauglin," "Down," and "Sly Feel" (Sam Bush on mandolin, Benny Martin on fiddle, and Buddy Emmons on pedal steel guitar all blazingly outstanding), the bass and drums are prominent in the mix, John helping to give birth to yet another musical genre: R&BG (Rhythm and Bluegrass). The non-instrumentals vary widely in quality, from the pleasantly daft ("Granny Won't You Smoke Some Marijuana") to the simply sublime ("In Tall Buildings," a touchingly melancholic goodbye to the idylls of youth told from the perspective of a recently hair-shorn, besuited young man disappearing into the subway on his way to the tall building where he now spends his days). The only other song that's up to John's own high standards is the title track, a rollicking manifesto of individualism that not only makes its point lyrically, but—in the extended fade, where John sings the chorus in a voice that alternates between absurdly high and absurdly low—formally as well. Gleefully droning away in as many delightfully off-key ways as he can, *Yes*, his voice seems to be saying, *D.I.Y. is definitely the way to do it, and remember to do it for yourself in the only way you can—your own.*

Like its predecessor, the cover of 1977's *All in the Name of Love* features John on a steamboat, but that's about all that's the same, the qualitative fall from *Nobody Knows What You Do* to his latest offering even more noticeable than that from *Mark Twang* to its successor. *Nobody Knows What You Do* may have lacked an entire LP's worth of first-rate songs, but among its filler are the classic "In Tall Buildings" and the invigorating title track. And what filler there is is of the funky, freaky variety, the ferocious picking found throughout never less than exhilarating. *All in the Name of Love* maintains the basic bluegrass-plus-bass-and-drums set-up, but features, in place of the fervent ensemble playing of before, a flaccid-if-pleasant sound that's admittedly easy to listen to (except for the occasionally intrusive electric piano and stiff drumming), if just as easy to ignore. The originals, such as the title tune, "In Sara's Eyes," and "Don't Try to Hide Your Tears From Me," are lyrically commonplace and musically lackluster, the whole record sounding like a bunch of good friends having a nice time spending a few lazy days in the studio. Significantly, John chooses to cover three of his own songs to pad out the album—"Gentle on My Mind," "Boogie," and "The Six O'Clock Train and a Girl with Green Eyes"—all agreeable, all unnecessary.

Slightly revitalized by teaming up with old friends Doug and Rodney Dillard for that same year's *Glitter Grass From The Nashwood Hollyville Strings* collaboration— the playing more committed (what else would you expect from the Dillard brothers?) and the songwriting burden shared, so the good-humored but slight material not so conspicuously below-par—John released *Headin' Down Into the Mystery Below* in 1978, and it set the template for the next two decades' worth of recordings: enjoyable but underwhelming, the undeniable pleasure of John's always warm, never less than quirkily clever efforts undercut by the nagging feeling that he could be doing more, much more. Don't misunderstand: once you've fallen under John's *joie-de-vivre*-with-a-banjo-jolt spell, you *have* to own it all. And whether it's further collaborations like 1979's *Slumberin' on the Cumberland* (John joined by Benny Martin and Pat Burton) or solo LPs such as *You and Me at Home* (1980), *Gum Tree Canoe* (1984), or *Down on the River* (1989), it's always bracing to be in the company of someone so obviously happy to be doing what they're doing.

Maybe that was one of the problems — John and Marie married in 1980 and, by all accounts, were a mutually supportive, contented couple, remaining together until his death twenty-one years later. (Marie Hartford died approximately six months after John — on what would have been his sixty-fourth birthday.) "Happiness writes white," Henry de Montherlant maintained. Maybe every artist has only so many things he or she *needs* to say, the fiery desire necessary to undertake the difficult task of making the world over gradually giving way to the cooling acceptance of what simply is. Maybe the non-Hodgkin lymphoma he was diagnosed with in the early eighties was a factor: when your own mortality is a daily concern, struggling to make immortal music takes an understandable drop in your list of life's priorities. Maybe the instant gratification of playing live — which he did more and more of as he grew older, to larger and increasingly more sympathetic audiences — began to satisfy some of his creative urges, John and Marie and a driver, who doubled as the sound man, touring all over North America on a bus with just John's banjo and fiddle and guitar and a four-by-eight-foot piece of A-grade plywood that he'd use for clogging (later, John would assemble the seven-piece Hartford String Band for a fuller sound and a change-of-circuit pace). Maybe I'm under-appreciative of the turn John's creativity took in the last ten years of his

life toward recording (and hence preserving and propa-
gating) old fiddle tunes on albums like *Wild Hog in the Red
Bush*, *Speed of the Old Longbow*, and his final album, *Hamilton
Ironworks*. Invariably attired in bowler hat and vest, John
in later life seemed like a slightly seedy musical scholar,
and maybe one has to be an old-timey music historian or a
serious player oneself to recognize the appeal of an entire
album's worth of antique fiddle music.

But he kept on being alive—and not only physically,
which is oftentimes not the most difficult part—until the
disease he battled to a draw in the last two decades of his
life eventually won the war. Even near the end, though,
when he was unable to play an instrument or even speak
loud enough to be heard across a room, he was more alive
than most people are in the physical prime of their lives.
Friend and fellow musician Mike Seeger:

> He lived on the Cumberland River, and he was on the porch
> there. And it was a point where he was barely able to talk,
> and had no use of his hands, or very little use of his hands,
> he could walk a hundred feet. Whatever he said, you could
> barely understand the whisper, (so) everything was to the
> point. Gillian Welch and David Rawlings were there, and his
> agent, Keith Case at some point was there, and Bruce Molsky
> came in for a while. And what he did, was to ask each person
> to play a little bit. And he asked Bruce to play about five
> or ten tunes, by name, in a certain way, and then discussed
> them a little bit, or had a comment about each one. And then
> he asked me to play particular pieces, which showed that
> he knew my repertoire. Gillian and David played for a little
> while, and there was some discussion there. He beckoned to
> a neighbor or somebody to bring his newest, yet unreleased
> CD out, and we listened to it. My sense of all this was that
> he was having an afternoon's entertainment, just as it would

have been, but the only way that he could play was to play the CD. He was entertaining us in yet another way.

The story goes that, after John died on June 4, 2001, Marie gave the mortician the bag containing the suit she wanted him buried in, but somehow his prized Batman cape got mixed up inside. The mortician was obviously a little surprised when he opened up the bag at the funeral home, but figured that since the deceased was an artist, it was probably what his widow wanted. People showed up for the viewing the next day and were understandably taken aback, but Marie took one look and laughed. "Leave it," she said. "John would have loved it."

NOTES

INTRODUCTION

Music washes away from, Herb Galewitz, *Music: A Book of Quotations* (Courier Dover Publications, 2001), iii.

Of all noises, I, Nat Shapiro, *An Encyclopedia of Quotations About Music* (Da Capo Press, 1981), 134.

Difficult do you call, Oxford Dictionary of Quotations ed. Elizabeth M. Knowles (Oxford University Press, 1999), 418.

If it rained knowledge, John Wain, *Samuel Johnson* (Macmillan, 1974), 345.

Lives of the Poets, Wain, *Samuel Johnson,* 345.

if at times his, Conrad Aiken, *Collected Criticism* (Oxford University Press, 1968), 358.

greater or lesser heat, Karl Shapiro, *In Defence of Ignorance* (Random House, 1960), 275.

For it is your, Ford Madox Ford, *The March of Literature* (Allen & Unwin, 1947), 6.

GENE CLARK

Deprivation is for me, Philip Larkin, *Required Writing* (Faber and Faber, 1983), 47.

didn't know the rules, John Einarson, *Mr. Tambourine Man: The Life and Legacy of Gene Clark* (Backbeat Books, 2005), 51.

as for Gene, he'd, Johnny Rogan, *Timeless Flight: The Definitive Biography of The Byrds* (Square One Books, 1990), 68.

273

When I got there, Johnny Rogan, *Byrds: Requiem For the Byrds, Volume 1* (Random House, 2011), 393–94.

When Gene got with, Einarson, 134.

Remarkably, the best stuff, Rogan, 599.

Pretty soon he started, Einarson, 197.

I think if someone, Ibid, 196.

Gene was one of, Ibid, 207.

Gene was into [heroin], Ibid, 225.

Near the end Gene, Ibid, 229.

barely had management . . . barely, Ibid, 245–46.

RONNIE LANE

Outside our house the, Andy Neill, *The Faces: Had Me a Real Good Time* (Omnibus Press, 2011), 5.

We [the Muleskinners]had, Ibid, 15–16.

I remember this commotion, *The Passing Show* (DVD), 2006.

They didn't seem to, CD Boxset: *Faces: Five Guys Walk Into a Bar* (Warner Brothers/Rhino, 2004), 39.

Faces—that's my band, Ibid, 42–43.

I was a very serious, Uli Twelker and Roland Schmitt, *The Small Faces & Other Stories* (Sanctuary Publishing, 2002), 123–24.

They always used to, Neill, 302.

Ronnie Lane always used, Ibid, 288–89.

When The Faces toured, David Cavanagh, "One for the Road," *Uncut*, July 2010.

It was a bloody mess, Neill, 299.

So, there I was, http://www.slim-chance.co.uk/pages/stories.html

It was in 1974, http://www.slim-chance.co.uk/pages/stories.html

One morning we woke, Neill, *The Faces*, 350.

Kate would be washing, Cavanagh, "One for the Road," *Uncut* (July, 2010).

[W]e were driving along, Neill, 363.

I hated to see, Ibid, 347.

We got pawned off, Ibid, 348–49.

Ronnie was often right, Pete Townshend, *Who I Am* (Harper Collins, 2012), 297.

Ronnie would wake up, Neill, 389–90.

Ian Stewart called Ronnie, Ibid, 379–80.

Ronnie was still drinking, Ibid, 390.

had a brilliant innate, e-mail to author.

RAMONES

Once we all went, Everett True, *Hey Ho Let's Go: The Story of the Ramones* (Omnibus Press, 2002), 13.

I passed my guitar, Clinton Heylin, *Babylon's Burning: From Punk to Grunge* (Viking, 2007), 126.

Tommy was able to, True, 18.

All their songs were, Legs McNeil and Gillian McCain, *Please Kill Me: The Uncensored Oral History of Punk* (Penguin, 1996), 212.

It looked like the, End of the Century: The Story of the Ramones, DVD, 2005.

Until I saw the, True, 31.

The Ramones had everything, Monte A. Melnick and Frank Meyer, *On the Road with the Ramones* (Sanctuary, 2003), 60.

I watched them and, End of the Century: The Story of the Ramones.

When I first saw, True, 31.

When the great innovation, Mark A. Runco, *Problem Finding, Problem Solving, and Creativity* (Greenwood Publishing Group, 1994), 56.

Hell, I thought they, Clinton Heylin, *From the Velvets to the Voidoids* (Chicago Review Press, 2005), 252.

The Ramones didn't stand, True, 66.

The first indication to me, Mickey Leigh and Legs McNeil, *I Slept with Joey Ramone* (Simon and Schuster, 2009), 174.

as a gesture of, Ibid, 169.

[w]e got known as, Ben Edmonds, " . . . Tomorrow the World," *Mojo* (November, 2005), 78.

He was Mr. Negative, Melnick and Meyer, 43.

We used to call, Ibid.

first wife Vera Davie, Ibid.

I had no idea, Vera Ramone King, *Poisoned Heart* (Phoenix Books, 2009), 72.

He used to walk around, Melnick and Meyer, 46.

We had a central, Ibid, 155.

He'd get in and, Ibid, 153.

of the biggest things, *Rocket to Russia*, CD reissue (Warner Archines/Rhino, 2001).

[T]he Ramones mowed down, True, 87.

The metal fans were, Ibid, 85.

in Manchester, in some school, Ibid, 88.

the Ramones didn't socialize, Leigh and McNeil, 178.

Marky is the character, True, 114.

We [the band] came, Ibid, 117.

Phil just loved their, Mick Brown, *Tearing Down The Wall of Sound: The Rise and Fall of Phil Spector* (Bloomsbury, 2007), 323.

Phil never came to, King, 40.

The sessions were grueling, Melnick and Meyer, 207.

Too many people around, Leigh and McNeil, 218.

Monte [Melnick] was a, Melnick and Meyer, 175.

The friendship died after, Ibid, 174–75.

SISTER ROSETTA THARPE

It was just her, Gayle F. Wald, *Shout, Sister, Shout! The Untold Story of Rock-and-Roll Trailblazer Sister Rosetta Tharpe* (Beacon Press, 2007), 20.

She would sing a, Wald, 31.

There is no such, Oscar Wilde, *The Portable Oscar Wilde* (The Viking Portable Library, 1971), 138.

I said, 'Say, man, Wald, 70.

[M]y favorite singer, Sister, Charles White, *The Life and Times of Little Richard* (Pan Books, 1984), 29.

One day when Sister, Ibid.

The first morning in the, Robert Gordon, *Can't Be Satisfied: The Life and Times of Muddy Waters* (Back Bay Books, 2002), 187.

When I saw Rosetta, Anthony Heilbut, *The Gospel Sound: Good News and Bad Times* (Limelight Editions, 1975), 316.

TOWNES VAN ZANDT

For sweetest things turn, G. Blakemore Evans, *The Riverside Shakespeare* (Houghton Mifflin, 1974), 1766.

We had been drinkin', John Kruth, *To Live's to Fly: The Ballad of the Late, Great Townes Van Zandt* (Da Capo, 2007), 28.

None of us were, Ibid, 48.

[i]n the first apartment, Robert Earl Hardy, *A Deeper Blue: The Life and Music of Townes Van Zandt* (University of North Texas Press, 2008), 64.

In the back room, Kruth, 49.

It breaks my heart, Ibid, 83.

[a]fter J.T. [their son], Hardy, 81–2.

It was one of, Brian T. Atkinson, *I'll Be Here in the Morning: The Songwriting Legacy of Townes Van Zandt* (Texas A&M University Press, 2012), 126.

[O]ut comes this guy, Ibid, 181.

Townes bet me $100, Ibid, 21.

Townes would call up, Hardy, 98.

The years are tragic, Wilifrid Sheed, *Essays in Disguise* (Knopf, 1990), xi.

When J.T. would swing, Hardy, 108.

[H]e would fuck with, Kruth, 125.

I don't even remember, Lauren St John, *Hardcore Troubadour: The Life and Near Death of Steve Earle* (Fourth Estate, 2003), 81.

Goddamn you, you motherfucker! Kruth, 124.

Whenever Townes would show, Ibid, 144.

pretty much drank all, Hardy, 126–27.

—such a price/The, Matthew Arnold, *Poems* (Macmillan, 1928), 194.

The last show I did, Atkinson, 30.

LITTLE RICHARD

was the most trouble, Charles White, *The Life and Times of Little Richard: The Quasar of Rock* (Pan Books, 1984), 18.

I was having lunch, Ibid, 47.

I want to do, Charles Shaar Murray, *Crosstown Traffic: Jimi Hendrix and the Post-War Rock 'n' Roll* (St. Martin's Press, 1989), 39.

There had been no, White, 59.

You couldn't get a, Ibid, 45.

He'd just burst on, Ibid, 74.

the races together. When, Ibid, 75.

I was so naïve, Arnold Shaw, *Honkers and Shouters: The Golden Years of Rhythm and Blues* (Macmillan, 1986), 209.

It is through the, Logan Pearsall Smith, *All Trivia: Trivia, More Trivia, Afterthoughts, Last Words* (Constable, 1947), 135.

Malt does more than, A.E. Housman, *The Collected Poems of A.E. Housman* (Jonathan Cape, 1948), 88.

We were recording one, White, 104.

We were late because, Ibid, 111–12.

ALAN WILSON

The blues is a, Bruce Cook, *Listen to the Blues* (Da Capo Press, 1995), 241.

When he'd wake up, Rebecca Davis Winters, *Blind Owl Blues: The Mysterious Life and Death of Blues Legend Alan Wilson* (2007), 14–5.

Anything harmony-based, with, Ibid, 66.

His apartment was pretty, Ibid, 33.

used to pull at, Ibid, 24.

He could not be, Daniel Beaumont, *Preachin' The Blues: The Life and Times of Son House* (Oxford University Press, 2011), 144.

Al Wilson taught Son, Ibid, 22.

What really happened was, Ibid, 23.

Wilson refused to take, Winters, 64.

Why don't you take, Stephen Calt, *I'd Rather Be the Devil: Skip James and the Blues* (Chicago Review Press, 2008), 269.

Alan was just a, Winters, 102.

If it wasn't for, Charles Shaar Murray, *Boogie Man: The Adventures of John Lee Hooker in the Twentieth Century* (St. Martin's, 2002), 328.

He thought that he, Winters, 99–100.

He just looked kind, Ibid, 23–4.

We'd check into a, Ibid, 147.

you could almost see, Ibid, 84.

He would be extremely, Ibid, 153.

His whole outlook on, Ibid.

stopped rappin' and laughin', Bob Greenfield, *Rolling Stone*, Issue #68 (October 29, 1970).

I say that man, Murray, 384.

[W]e were all in, Fito de la Parra with T.W. and Marianne McGarry, *Living the Blues: Canned Heat's Story of Music, Drugs, Death, Sex and Survival*, 165.

WILLIE P. BENNETT

lived initially for a, e-mail to author.

first heard Willie sing, e-mail to author.

Willie and his band, e-mail to author.

It was a tough, e-mail to author.

I first heard about, Chris Vautour, "Willie P. Bennett: Squirrel of the Rodeo," *No Depression*, Issue #13 (January/February, 1998).

I first played with, e-mail to author.

Poetry is the spontaneous, William Wordsworth, *Selected Poems and Prefaces* (Houghton Mifflin, 1965), 460.

We were at a, Werner Bergen, "Peterborough musicians remember Willie P. Bennett," *The Peterborough Examiner* (July 10, 2007).

Willie was bored with, e-mail to author.

was always mystified about, e-mail to author.
Playing with Willie was, e-mail to author.

GRAM PARSONS

Gram was a sweet, David D. Meyer, *Twenty Thousand Roads: The Ballad of Gram Parsons and His Cosmic American Music* (Villard Books, 2007), 32.

Gram would get anywhere, Ibid, 33.

his mother stayed at, Ibid, 65.

I played this version, Ibid, 73.

Gram's mother was dying, Ibid, 141.

I started right away, Ibid, 161.

met . . . in a bank, John Einarson, *Desperados: The Roots of Country Rock* (Cooper Square Books, 2001), 84.

We just hired a, Ben Fong-Torres, *Hickory Wind: The Life and Times of Gram Parsons* (St. Martins Griffin, 1998), 87.

Chris Hillman never got, Meyer, 335.

Unfortunately it's all, 'Gram, John Einarson with Chris Hillman, *Hot Burritos: The True Story of the Flying Burrito Brothers* (Jawbone Books, 2008), 23.

How can you compete, Ibid, 22.

I felt like I was, Bob Kealing, *Calling Me Home: Gram Parsons and the Roots of Country Rock* (University Press of Florida, 2012), 182.

a wild beast — tamed, Brian McGuinness, *Approaches to Wittgenstein* (Routledge, 2002), 22.

I was into experimentation, Meyer, 221.

We got into the, Ibid, 223.

Gram was the boss, Ibid, 238.

With Gram's energy, Ibid, 223.

Gram used the ISB, Ibid.

spiritual greed, V.S. Pritchett, *The Complete Essays*, (Chatto & Windus, 1991), 784.

As far as Nancy, Meyer, 248.

I had a sniffer, Ibid, 241.

Gram came over and, Johnny Rogan, *Byrds: Requiem For the Byrds, Volume 1* (Random House, 2011), 445.

People to this day, Ibid, 449.

Gram wasn't going on, Ibid.

He probably got me, Einarson/Hillman, 87.

There was a brotherly, Einarson/Hillman, 101.

After he left The Byrds, Ibid, 85.

It was unbelievable. He, Ibid, 114.

There was no way, Ibid, 115.

[A]ll of the other, Ibid, 130.

they greeted us with, Pamela Des Barres, *Rock Bottom: Dark Moments in Music Babylon*, (Macmillan, 1996), 233.

We were more than, Sid Griffin, *Gram Parsons: A Music Biography* (Sierra Books, 1985), 87.

[t]wo models we wanted, Ibid, 95.

The volume, which was, John Einarson with Ian Tyson and Sylvia Tyson *Four Strong Winds* (McClelland & Stewart, 2011), 217.

Our first showcase after, Einarson/Hillman, 141.

One night Hank Thompson, Ibid, 174.

Gram was hanging out, Einarson, 167.

It was like, 'Here's, Fong-Torres, 134.

Chris [Hillman] used to, Meyer, 323.

He [Gram] would sometimes, Einarson/Hillman, 192.

He showed up late, Einarson/Hillman, 224.

About four thirty in, Meyer, 341.

So I got a, Griffin, 153.

There is a quality, Ibid, 164.

The first night Gram, Meyer, 368.

By singing with Gram, Ibid, 370.

They went crazy *for*, Ibid, 388.

Gram was blasted out, Ibid, 387.

You were silly like, Gary Geddes, *20th-Century Poetry & Poetics* (Oxford University Press, 1969),134.

He was a good, Meyer, 439.

HOUND DOG TAYLOR

[T]heir equipment [was], Jason Gross, "Hound Dod Taylor," *Perfect Sound Forever* (online music magazine) (June, 1998), http://www.furious.com/perfect/hounddogtaylor.html, and email to author.

[O]ur goal . . . was to, email to author.

After I began to, Gross, http://www.furious.com/perfect/hound dogtaylor.html, and email to author.

Hound Dog was very, email to author.

When my friends and, email to author.

Only mediocrities develop, Philip Larkin, *Further Requirements: Interviews, Broadcasts, Statements and Boom Reviews 1952–1985* (Faber, 2001), 26.

poetry begins to atrophy, Ezra Pound, *ABC of Reading* (New Directions, 1960), 14.

usually the guys got, email to author.

Brewer Phillips was over, email to author.

On the weekend of, email to author.

WILLIS ALAN RAMSEY/PAUL SIEBEL

Proper words in proper places, Deborah Baker Wyrick, *Jonathan Swift and the Vested Word* (UNC Press Books, 1998), 46.

I remember [singer-songwriter], Kathleen Hudson, *Women in Texas Music: Stories and Songs* (University of Texas Press, 2007), 205.

We make out of, Vassiliki Kolocotroni, Jane Goldman, Olga Taxidou, *Modernism: An Anthology of Sources and Documents* (University of Chicago Press, 1999), 492.

a little unsure as, Petter Doggert, http://ca.myspace.com/paulsiebel

I learned every song, Lyle Lovett, http://www.willisalanramsey.com/biography/

I'll never forget my, Jan Reid, *The Improbable Rise of Redneck Rock* (University of Texas Press, 2004), 325.

JOHN HARTFORD

Our life together was, email to author.

I don't think he, The Old-Time Herald: A Magazine Dedicated to Old-Time Music, Volume Eight, Number One, http://www. oldtimeherald.org/archive/back_issues/volume-8/8-1/full-hartford_remin.html

One day we were, Ibid.

After you deliver, Jimmy McDonough, *Shakey: Neil Young's Biography* (Random House, 2002), 381.

He did not want, email to author.

[T]he end of a, email to author.

Out of discord comes, Philip Wheelwright, *The PreSocratics* (The Odyssey Press, 1983), 77.

John let us play, Steam Powered Aereo-Takes CD booklet.

[W]e'd sit around and, http://johnhartford.com/pdf/bromberg.pdf

I was trudging through, email to author.

Happiness writes white, Claude Rawson, *The Cambridge Companion to English Poets* (Cambridge University Press, 2011), 531.

He lived on the, The Old-Time Herald: A Magazine Dedicated to Old-Time Music, Volume Eight, Number One, http://www. oldtimeherald.org/archive/back_issues/volume-8/8-1/full-hartford_remin.html//www.oldtimeherald.org/archive/back_issues/volume-8/8-1/full-hartford_remin.html

ABOUT THE AUTHOR

PHOTO BY MARK RAYNES ROBERTS

Ray Robertson is the author of the novels *Home Movies, Heroes, Moody Food, Gently Down the Stream, What Happened Later, David,* and *I Was There the Night He Died*, as well as the non-fiction collections *Mental Hygiene: Essays on Writers and Writing* and *Why Not? Fifteen Reasons to Live*. Born and raised in Southwestern Ontario, he lives in Toronto.